China and Globalization

Series Editors

Huiyao Wang, Founder and President of Center for China and Globalization (CCG), Dean of the Institute of Development Studies of Southwestern University of Finance and Economics of China, Beijing, China

Lu Miao, Secretary-General of CCG, Young Leader for Munich Security Conference (MSC), and the Deputy Director General of the International Writing Center of Beijing Normal University, Beijing, China

This series is designed to address the evolution of China's global orientation, challenges of globalization and global governance facing China and the rest of the world, actions and proposals for the future of sustainable development, prospects of China's further capital and market liberalization, and China's globalizing trajectories as experienced by the world.

This book series seeks to create a balanced global perspective by gathering the views of highly influential policy scholars, practitioners, and opinion leaders from China and around the world.

Henry Huiyao Wang · Mabel Lu Miao
Editors

The Future of China's Development and Globalization

Views from Ambassadors to China

Editors
Henry Huiyao Wang
Center for China and Globalization
Beijing, China

Mabel Lu Miao
Center for China and Globalization
Beijing, China

ISSN 2730-9983   ISSN 2730-9991 (electronic)
China and Globalization
ISBN 978-981-99-7511-2   ISBN 978-981-99-7512-9 (eBook)
https://doi.org/10.1007/978-981-99-7512-9

© The Editor(s) (if applicable) and The Author(s) 2024. This book is an open access publication.

Open Access This book is licensed under the terms of the Creative Commons Attribution-NonCommercial-NoDerivatives 4.0 International License (http://creativecommons.org/licenses/by-nc-nd/4.0/), which permits any noncommercial use, sharing, distribution and reproduction in any medium or format, as long as you give appropriate credit to the original author(s) and the source, provide a link to the Creative Commons license and indicate if you modified the licensed material. You do not have permission under this license to share adapted material derived from this book or parts of it.

The images or other third party material in this book are included in the book's Creative Commons license, unless indicated otherwise in a credit line to the material. If material is not included in the book's Creative Commons license and your intended use is not permitted by statutory regulation or exceeds the permitted use, you will need to obtain permission directly from the copyright holder.

This work is subject to copyright. All commercial rights are reserved by the author(s), whether the whole or part of the material is concerned, specifically the rights of translation, reprinting, reuse of illustrations, recitation, broadcasting, reproduction on microfilms or in any other physical way, and transmission or information storage and retrieval, electronic adaptation, computer software, or by similar or dissimilar methodology now known or hereafter developed. Regarding these commercial rights a non-exclusive license has been granted to the publisher.

The use of general descriptive names, registered names, trademarks, service marks, etc. in this publication does not imply, even in the absence of a specific statement, that such names are exempt from the relevant protective laws and regulations and therefore free for general use.

The publisher, the authors, and the editors are safe to assume that the advice and information in this book are believed to be true and accurate at the date of publication. Neither the publisher nor the authors or the editors give a warranty, expressed or implied, with respect to the material contained herein or for any errors or omissions that may have been made. The publisher remains neutral with regard to jurisdictional claims in published maps and institutional affiliations.

This Springer imprint is published by the registered company Springer Nature Singapore Pte Ltd.
The registered company address is: 152 Beach Road, #21-01/04 Gateway East, Singapore 189721, Singapore

Paper in this product is recyclable.

Preface

As the world began to emerge from the fear and uncertainty of the COVID-19 pandemic and enter a period of recovery, a new set of challenges appeared. The origins of these challenges began long before the pandemic and have repercussions that will reach far into the future. Changes in globalization and global influence, continued tensions stemming from regional conflicts, and the rise in influence of an economically and politically more capable and confident Global South are just a few of the trends that began long before 2020.

In this context of constant flux, it is the job of ambassadors to keep the lines of communication open and ensure that the policies and positions of their own countries are conveyed clearly and correctly, while also working to understand the workings and true state of the countries to which they are posted. These diplomatic envoys from countries around the world serve as pivotal contact points between nations across a wide range of fields, from economics and culture to health and the environment. Their perspectives, representing both developing and industrialized countries, are both invaluable and illuminating—not only in conveying the views and experiences of their own country, but also for their insights into global affairs and China's development.

The Center for China and Globalization (CCG) is proud and honored to have maintained good, long-term relationships with embassies and individual ambassadors to China from many countries around the world. Since it was founded, CCG has recognized and highlighted the unique role and expertise of ambassadors and worked hard to establish and forge close relations with ambassadors representing both developing and industrialized countries from every corner of the globe. Our work is manifold and includes regular engagement with foreign embassies in Beijing through invitations to events at CCG's offices in Beijing as well as participation in external meetings that focus on topics ranging from trade and economic relations to geopolitics and global governance. Some foreign diplomats have also worked with CCG to pass on their views and suggestions to the Chinese government.

In addition to these ongoing ad hoc meetings, CCG also hosts regular events that bring Beijing-based ambassadors together and has created platforms through its flagship forums to facilitate dialogue and bridge gaps between China and the rest of the world. The Ambassadors Roundtable is a regular and eagerly anticipated part of

CCG's annual China and Globalization Forum. Marking its ninth year in 2023, the China and Globalization Forum has grown in size and influence, but a key element of the Forum has always been candid discussions featuring ambassadors from a dozen countries on a range of topics from geopolitics and multilateralism to the Belt and Road Initiative and regional trade integration.

At the Sixth China and Globalization Forum in November 2020, the Ambassadors Roundtable welcomed twelve ambassadors at a crucial moment in international affairs, amidst the ongoing global crisis caused by COVID-19 and shortly following the US presidential election. Participants discussed trends in multilateral cooperation, climate change, and how to reform multilateral institutions such as the WTO and G20. The following year, at the Seventh China and Globalization Forum, the Ambassadors Roundtable focused on the theme of "Global Trade and Mobility in Post-Pandemic Times," discussing how different countries can work together to support the cross-border movement of people, goods, and capital amidst the ongoing challenges of the COVID-19 pandemic, while in 2022 ambassadors continued the discussion on the challenges, trends, and responses each of their countries were facing in a world working to recover economically and social from the pandemic, as well as how China is contributing to those efforts. In 2023, the Ambassadors Roundtable focused on a world facing increased geopolitical tension and instability, as well as the need for major powers such as the United States, Europe, and China to work together to lead the world in combating major issues that we face as global community including global governance, technology, and climate change.

The perspectives that official envoys from countries around the world share are both invaluable and illuminating—not only in conveying the views and experiences of their own country, but also for their insights into global affairs and China's development. The impact and importance of sharing these valuable insights was proven in the first iteration of this book, *China and the World in a Changing Context—Perspectives from Ambassadors to China*, which collected contributions from twenty-seven ambassadors representing five continents. It was the success of this initial publication that gave us the confidence to continue with a second iteration, reaching out again to ambassadors to share their insights into a continually changing world plagued by uncertainty, conflict, and risk.

The book is divided into three main parts, covering the history and current state of China's diplomatic relations, perspectives on major issues and how various countries are working with China to face those, as well as the future of development in a world in which China is increasingly an essential part of the overall equation.[1]

The first part titled "*The Ebb and Flow of Relations with China*", provides an overview of several key countries' relations with the People's Republic of China from a historical perspective up to the modern day, examining both what links us and makes us different. It starts off with one of China's oldest friends, the Islamic Republic of Pakistan, with Ambassador Moin Ul Haque sharing his personal experiences with

---

[1] The essays in this book have been arranged thematically and each piece has been reviewed and approved by the author. Prior to publication, speakers on CCG events and dialogues were given the chance to review and edit their transcripts for clarification and accuracy.

China and its people, as well as what it means to be a "*batie*".[2] The next chapter, from Ambassador Mihelin of Croatia, focuses on the great potential for cooperation with China in a "Dario Diamond Era" of relations between the two countries. Looking to the future, the Ambassador of Switzerland, Mr. Jürg Burri, shares the many areas in which his country is working with China, ranging from trade and green technology to education and travel, highlighting his country's willingness to engage even more deeply with China.

Ambassador Dr. Palitha Kohona of Sri Lanka paints a historical narrative of relations with China as friendly neighbors that have contributed to each other's development for centuries and continued this tradition through to the present day. In the next chapter, noting that Spain and China will celebrate 50 years of diplomatic relations next year, Ambassador Rafael Dezcallar de Mazarredo emphasizes the importance of maintaining links with China, despite the presence of issues on which both countries have very different views. The Ambassador of the European Union to China, Jorge Toledo Albiñana, also emphasizes the importance of maintaining channels of communication in a world that has fundamentally changed and needs both the EU and China working together to move forward.

The second part of this book is titled "*On the Issues—The Immense Potential in Cooperation with China*" and focuses on specific issues that China and countries around the world are working together on, leveraging their respective advantages to make constructive contributions to development and global recovery. The Ambassador of Norway, Ms. Signe Brudeset, begins this part with an overview of Norway's impressive system of economic governance that benefits all and how Norway and China can share experiences to face issues like demographic changes and how digitalization can help in the management of welfare programs. In the next chapter, the Ambassador of Mexico, Mr. Jesús Seade, looks at the various areas in which China and Mexico can benefit each other as developing countries working to recover economically in a post pandemic world. Mr. Hussam A. G. Al Husseini, Ambassador of Jordan to China, continues this theme by looking at China's resilience in terms of the fight against COVID-19 and efforts to eradicate global poverty, also emphasizing that Jordan has the potential to work with China to bring stability and progress to the Middle East.

Returning to Europe, the Ambassador of Finland, Ms. Leena-Kaisa Mikkola, focuses on the importance of education and how Finland has used access to and equality in education to foster a sense of trust and support that has created a solid foundation for the future. She also recognizes China's rapid development and key contributions in poverty alleviation and the fight against climate change. Next, the Belgian Ambassador, Dr. Jan Hoogmartens, focuses on the issue of the current "tech war" brewing between major powers, examining trends in multilateralism and how best to govern technology on a global level, emphasizing the advantage of the EU in effective multilateralism.

---

[2] A conjunction of the Chinese words for Pakistan ("*bajisitan*") and "iron brothers" ("*tiegemen*"), demonstrating the iron-clad friendship between the two countries.

Perhaps one of the most important issues the world faces today is the environment, and the next three ambassadors in this part focus on their unique contributions to limiting the impact of climate change while also adapting to changes that are already underway. Representing Oceania, one of the potentially most affected areas of the world in terms of climate change, Mr. Graham Fletcher, the Ambassador of Australia offers recommendations how his country and China can work together to promote decarbonization and green economic growth. Next, Mr. Thórir Ibsen, the Ambassador of Iceland, a country that has led the world in developing of alternative energy sources, focuses on how his country and China are working on reducing CO_2 emissions to improve public health and quality of life. Moving south to the equatorial African country of Gabon, Ambassador Baudelaire Ndong Ella describes how his country has worked hard to keep is forests green, but is still feeling the effects of climate change, highlighting the importance of Gabon's efforts to work with China on green development.

Another issue that is on the minds of many global leaders in today's unstable and unpredictable world is security. The last two contributors to this part share their views in terms of both the geopolitical aspect of national and global security as well as security for individuals and groups society-wide. The Ambassador of Sweden to China, Ms. Helena Sångeland, focuses on the geopolitical factors that caused Sweden to join NATO and how this reflects and contributes to Swedish and regional security in response to instability in Europe due to Russian aggression in Ukraine. The last contributor in this part, the Ambassador of Ireland, Dr. Ann Derwin, chooses to focus on the Women, Peace and Security (WPS) Agenda at the UN as she reflects on Ireland's presidency of the UN Security Council, and its efforts in building peace, preventing conflict, and ensuring accountability.

The final part of this book is titled *"Global Development and a Future with China"*, and focuses on continued development and roads forward as the world continues to change. This part begins with a perspective from South America in a contribution from the Ambassador of Brazil, Mr. Marcos Galvão, who presents a sensible, practical vision for the future of globalization through the lens of his own personal experience as a career diplomat. Moving back across the Atlantic to the African nation of Mozambique, Ambassador Maria Gustava, presents several future scenarios in which China and her nation can cooperate in the current global environment and the promising state of growth in Africa. As we continue to move east, the Ambassador of Thailand, Mr. Arthayudh Srisamoot focuses on the continued shift of global power and influence to Asia and the role of ASEAN nations, including China, in shaping the future of an "Asian Century".

The last three countries in this part, and this book, focus on continued change and a global future. The Ambassador of Algeria, Mr. Hassane Rabehi, emphasizes the need for multilateralism in to avoid the pitfalls of historical inequality, focusing on China's efforts in multilateral institutions as well as bilateral interactions with China in creating better future in a changing world. Mr. Akram Zeynalli, ambassador from the central Asian nation of Azerbaijan, focuses on three major areas as key to the future of development in his nation and the wider world—infrastructure, digitization, and green energy. The final contribution in this book is from the Ambassador of

Poland, Mr. Wojciech Zajączkowski, who provides a balanced critique of the future of China and globalization from the perspective of a vibrant European country with a unique outlook.

We are once again indebted to all of the ambassadors that have contributed to this book. Their wealth of knowledge and experience is a rich source of perspective and insight that can benefit not only academics and policymakers, but also the private sector and individuals. The ambassadors that have shared their views in this book have dedicated their careers to promoting international dialogue and cooperation, a mission which the Center for China and Globalization also holds dear to its heart. We firmly believe that candid, open discussion is the key to building mutual trust and resolving many, if not all, of the issues that we currently face today. We look forward to deeper cooperation with Beijing's diplomatic community in this endeavor.

As the world engages and adapts to an increasingly uncertain world, it is more important than ever that we keep the channels of communication open to find common solutions to problems that affect us all, not least climate change. It is cooperation, especially among great powers like China, the United States, and the EU, that will be necessary to effect change that will create a stable, prosperous world. It is our hope that the views expressed in this volume will inspire even more conversation and discussion on the next best steps to take in finding solutions to the problems we face and in particular how China can better contribute and engage with the world to find solutions based on its own experience and wisdom.

Beijing, China
December 2023

Henry Huiyao Wang, Ph.D.
Mabel Lu Miao, Ph.D.

Acknowledgements

A work such as this requires the contributions of many individuals. The greatest contribution is, of course, that of the ambassadors, who have lent their knowledge, experience, and candid views on a range of issues that are both timely and relevant to today's world. Naturally, we are also grateful for the continued support the ambassadorial community has given CCG over the years.

We would also like to recognize the immense contribution from our commissioning editors at Springer Nature Group and their team, particularly Yingying Zhang and Leana Li. We thank them for once again supporting a work that brings together so many perspectives. As we work to recover from COVID-19 and adapt to a new and uncertain world, the insights contained in this book, which provide invaluable food for thought, could not have come to fruition if not for the support of Springer Nature.

The continued engagement with the ambassadorial community and the dedication with which they approached this task continues to impress and motivate us. The team at the CCG Publishing Centre worked with each author to ensure their contributions were treated respectfully and incorporated in a way that was both relevant and in keeping with their wishes. We are proud of this latest iteration of the book, and we would like to express our warmest thanks and appreciation to Yueyuan Ren, Joshua Dominick, Yan Li, Hong Liu, Beijie Tang, and Ge Ou.

This second book of contributions by Beijing-based ambassadors is further proof of the importance we attach to our relationship with the diplomatic community, which we hope will only grow deeper and closer. Our final message goes to our readers—without you our work would be in vain. Thank you for your ongoing support and constructive feedback. Your continued readership gives us the confidence and drive to continue to produce innovative and insightful publications like this one.

Henry Huiyao Wang, Ph.D.
Mabel Lu Miao, Ph.D.
Center for China and Globalization (CCG)

Contents

The Ebb and Flow of Relations with China

Convergences in Pakistan–China Development: Perspectives of the Pakistani Ambassador 3
Moin Ul Haque

Croatia and China in the Diamond Era of Bilateral Relations 11
Dario Mihelin

Future Milestones in Switzerland–China Relations 19
Jürg Burri

China and Sri Lanka: Neighborly Relations in a Rapidly Evolving World 27
Palitha Kohona

For a Useful Dialogue Between Spain and China 37
Rafael Dezcallar de Mazarredo

Status and Prospects of EU–China Relations 43
Jorge Toledo Albiñana

On the Issues—The Immense Potential in Cooperation with China

Norway: Creating a System of Economic Governance Tailored to Benefit All 55
Signe Brudeset

Mexico–China Bilateral Relationship in the Context of Changing Globalization 65
Jesús Seade

China's Economic Resilience, and Jordan's Potential 75
Hussam A. G. Al Husseini

Education, Equality and Resilience—Finnish Recipe for Success 79
Leena-Kaisa Mikkola

Multilateralism Versus Unilateralism in International Economic Governance: How to Deal with the "Tech War"? 83
Jan Hoogmartens

Strengthening Australian–Chinese Collaboration in Decarbonisation and Green Economic Growth 95
Graham Fletcher

Iceland and China: Cooperating to Reduce CO_2 Emissions, Improve Public Health and Better Quality of Life 101
Thórir Ibsen

Gabon's Green Forests Whisper to a Major Carbon Emitter 109
Baudelaire Ndong Ella

Swedish Security Policy in a New Security Environment 115
Helena Sångeland

Ireland on the UN Security Council—Our Work on Women, Peace and Security and Women's Participation in Decision-Making 123
Ann Derwin

Global Development and a Future with China

Working for Change: Brief Observations by a Brazilian Diplomat 133
Marcos Galvão

Prospects for Mozambique-China Partnership in the Context of the Current Global Environment 139
Maria Gustava

Thailand and China Amid a Changing Global Landscape 149
Arthayudh Srisamoot

The Future of Algeria-China Relations in a Changing World 159
Hassane Rabehi

The Next Phase of Development in Azerbaijan-China Relations: From Infrastructure and Digitalization Toward Green Energy 163
Akram Zeynalli

The Future of China's Development and Globalization: A View from Poland 171
Wojciech Zajączkowski

Appendix 177

About the Center for China and Globalization 209

Index 215

About the Editors

Dr. Henry Huiyao Wang is Founder and President of Center for China and Globalization (CCG), a think tank ranked among top 100 think tanks in the world. He is also Dean of the Institute of Development Studies of Southwestern University of Finance and Economics of China, Vice Chairman of China Association for International Economic Cooperation, and Director of Chinese People's Institute of Foreign Affairs. He is currently a steering committee member of Paris Peace Forum and an advisory board member of Duke Kunshan University. He has served as an expert for the World Bank, IOM, and ILO. He pursued his Ph.D. studies at the University of Western Ontario and the University of Manchester. He is the Chief Editor of the Springer Nature book series China and Globalization series, Chinese Enterprise Globalization Series and the International Talent Development in China Series. He was Senior Fellow at Harvard Kennedy School and Visiting Fellow at Brookings Institute. His books in English include *Globalizing China* (2012); *China Goes Global* (2016); *Handbook on China and Globalization* (2019); *Globalization of Chinese Enterprises* (2020); *Consensus or Conflict?: China and Globalization in the 21st Century* (2021); *China and the World in a Changing Context: Perspectives from Ambassadors to China* (2022); *The Ebb and Flow of Globalization: Chinese Perspectives on China's Development and Role in the World* (2022); *Understanding Globalization, Global Gaps, and Power Shifts in the 21st Century: CCG Global Dialogues* (2022); and *Escaping Thucydides's Trap: Dialogue with Graham Allison on China–US Relations* (2023).

Dr. Mabel Lu Miao is Co-founder and Secretary-General of CCG, a Munich Security Conference (MSC) Young Leader, and the Founder of Global Young Leader Dialogue (GYLD). She is also Deputy Director General of the International Writing Center at Beijing Normal University. She received her Ph.D. in Contemporary Chinese Studies from Beijing Normal University and has been a visiting scholar at New York University's China House and the Fairbank Center at Harvard University. She is a co-author of many Chinese Social Science Academy blue books and Chinese Social Science Foundation's research project reports. She has published a number of books in Chinese, which detail China's outbound business and global talent. Her latest publications in English are: *International Migration of China: Status, Policy and Social Responses to the Globalization of Migration* (2017); *Transition and Opportunity: Strategies from Business Leaders on Making the Most of China's Future* (2022); *Strategies for Chinese Enterprises Going Global* (2023); and *The Challenge of "Going Out": Chinese Experiences in Outbound Investment* (2023).

The Ebb and Flow of Relations with China

Convergences in Pakistan–China Development: Perspectives of the Pakistani Ambassador

Moin Ul Haque

I vividly recall the day in 2020 when I received the news of my appointment as Pakistan's Ambassador to China, which was indeed an honour and a privilege. At that point, while I truly understood the significance of my assignment in a country with which Pakistan undoubtedly has her most consequential bilateral relationship, I could barely fathom the enormity of the task or the extent of the special experience awaiting me in China.

On arrival, I was set on a journey that was both rewarding and fulfilling in terms of my humble contributions to strengthening our bilateral relationship; it was also a great learning experience not only gaining insight into world's greatest and oldest civilization, but also providing me an opportunity to witness the modern miracle of China's economic rise.

On a personal level, I could feel the intensity of our close friendship and the special love and affection the people of Pakistan enjoy in China. Everywhere, I was greeted with the nickname 'Batie', an expression reserved for Pakistanis alone. It was so touching and heart-warming.

The China-Pakistan friendship is a historic reality and a conscious choice that our two peoples have made, while also being underpinned by political support, strategic partnership and practical cooperation. It transcends the traditional precepts of inter-state relations; it is unaffected by vicissitudes of time, and this time-tested relationship is the pride of our two nations and the envy of others.

During my almost three years in China, I have made an effort to study and learn from China's experiences and achievements as it continues to develop. To this end, I have travelled to different provinces, cities, villages, projects, factories, and cultural sites across the country. I met political leaders, entrepreneurs, scholars, researchers, and farmers, and I have given over 200 interviews. Over this period, during my visits

---

Ambassador of the Islamic Republic of Pakistan to the People's Republic of China.

M. U. Haque (✉)
Beijing, China

to over 40 cities and countless interactions, I was privileged to have received such an outpouring of respect and affection. I also consider myself fortunate to be in China at this momentous time in its history and learn from the 'China Miracle', Here I would like to share some key lessons learnt and how they can be applied to China-Pakistan bilateral cooperation now and in future.

The Road to 'Win–Win Cooperation' Can Be Paved by Building a Shared Community of Mankind

As China marches ahead towards a brighter future, ancient Chinese philosophy continues to play a vital role in the country's development strategy. The application of the concept of *tiānxià,* which translates as "land under heaven" and refers to the whole world, promoting diversity, while emphasizing harmonious and mutual interdependence as means for enduring peace, can be seen in domestic socio-economic policies, China's inclusive growth, and the quest for common prosperity.

Externally it is manifested through President Xi Jinping's vision for building a Shared Community of Mankind through the landmark Belt and Road Initiative (BRI), which he unveiled ten years ago. Subsequently, the launch of the Global Development Initiative (GDI), Global Security Initiative (GSI) and Global Civilization Initiative (GCI) have further crystallized the concept of a 'Shared Community'.

Being China's strategic partner, Pakistan has naturally endorsed all President Xi Jinping's key initiatives. The China–Pakistan Economic Corridor (CPEC) is a shining example of the BRI's promise of economic prosperity and connectivity. It has transformed the economic landscape of Pakistan, upgrading physical infrastructure, ensuring energy security, creating jobs, and uplifting the lives of the masses.

Pakistan is also a pioneering member of the GDI Group of Friends and has played an active role in giving it a more concrete shape. China has committed US$ 4 billion and, in partnership with UN, will carry out projects in areas of education, health, climate change, and poverty reduction, thus making meaningful contributions to achieving the SDGs in a timely manner. As the first priority partner under GDI, Pakistan stands ready to benefit from this cooperation.

Pakistan has also supported the GSI and its adherence to the UN Charter and principles of multilateralism and non-interference in internal affairs. Having suffered for a long time due to unresolved disputes, conflicts, and terrorism, we also advocate dialogue and constructive engagement based on mutual respect for ensuring regional peace in South Asia.

The GCI is another landmark and timely initiative, promoting respect for diversity, peaceful co-existence, mutual learning, and inclusiveness. In a world marred with discord and divisiveness, a dialogue between civilizations can be a means to peace and reconciliation. Pakistan and China are united through centuries of cultural exchange and people-to-people contacts. Ancient Chinese monks who traversed the Silk Road brought back with them not only wisdom of ancient civilizations, but also a sense of togetherness and friendship that has endured to this day.

Constant Evaluation and Rethinking to Further Strengthen the Basics

There is a famous Chinese idiom that "the wise adapt themselves to circumstances, as water moulds itself to the pitcher".[1] This adage very aptly reflects the resilience and adaptability of the Chinese governing model and developmental philosophy. Each of China's leaders, while retaining the spirit of the Communist Party of China and the key messages of their predecessors, have brought with them a fresh perspective to China's development philosophy. From "Mao Zedong Thought" to Deng Xiaoping's "Reform and Opening Up", Jiang Zemin's "Three Represents", Hu Jintao's "Scientific Outlook on Development" to now President Xi Jinping's "Thoughts on Governance" and "Great Rejuvenation of the Chinese Nation", the call for a "Chinese path to modernization" and the journey to build a "Shared Community of Mankind"—Chinese theory and practice has always adjusted and adapted to changing times, the prevalent regional and global landscape and China's own developmental realities.

Soon after the proclamation of the People's Republic of China, Pakistan and China established formal diplomatic relations. The foundation of our friendship was laid down under the leadership of Chairman Mao Zedong and Premier Zhou Enlai and nurtured by successive generations of leaders in both countries. We remain undeterred by the vicissitudes of time and geopolitical upheavals, maintaining a steady and sure upward momentum. Most recently our relationship was elevated to an 'All-Weather Strategic Cooperative Partnership' during President Xi Jinping's historic visit to China in April 2015.

Having the privilege of serving as Chief of State Protocol during the historic visit of President Xi, it was heartening to see our time-tested ties transformed into a more comprehensive, concrete and practical partnership. With the launch of CPEC, economic cooperation has now taken the centre stage, and there is a growing focus in areas of infrastructure, energy, industry, agriculture, health, and IT.

Later when I came to China to serve as Ambassador, I was proud to contribute to CPEC's evolution into a high-quality development project. Recently, we added a new element to the CPEC with the launch of sector-specific corridors: China-Pakistan Digital, Green, Industrial and Health Corridors. While we have kept the fundamental spirit of our bilateral friendship intact, we have also strived to keep evolving and upgrading our relationship based on our shared interests and the needs of our people.

---

[1] 上善若水 (shàng shàn ruò shuǐ), which appears in the Dao De Jing by Laozi.

Security Is an All-Encompassing Concept

In today's world, national security is not just about having a strong military, rather it is a holistic concept transcending traditional security paradigms and encompassing essential elements of economic, human, energy, and food security.

This approach to national security is manifested in China's long-term vision and people-centric policies focusing primarily on socio-economic development. Through carefully crafted development plans, China has upgraded its infrastructure, expanded its manufacturing base, modernized agriculture, promoted research and innovation, developed new technologies, and prioritized capacity-building. A series of Special Economic Zones and industrial parks were built where local and foreign companies produced goods that were then supplied to the entire world.

This made China the world's leading manufacturer, enabling it to sustain an economic growth rate of nearly 9% over a period of four decades. Never before in human history has a nation achieved such high growth and in such a short period of time. Many Chinese friends have shared their pride with me in seeing this transformation in their lifetime.

Given the strategic nature of China's relationship with Pakistan, economic security has also taken centre stage in our bilateral relations. Learning from Chinese experiences, Pakistan is also setting up new industries, building special economic zones, modernizing agriculture, enhancing its export base, and focusing on skills development among its youth. Under the framework of the CPEC, cooperation in these areas is being intensified, which will surely bring economic dividends, create new jobs, improve livelihoods, and promote regional trade and connectivity.

Success Will Be Achieved Through a Knowledge-Based Economy

A key aspect of the Chinese developmental model is the steady evolution from a primarily labour-intensive industrial/manufacturing economy serving as world's factory to a knowledge-based economy, with a focus on research, innovation, smart technologies, and high-quality developmental strategies.

This shift did not take place overnight, but was a result of a long-term vision under the "Four Modernizations"[2] where science and technology were identified as one of the core areas for high-quality development. China has now overtaken the U.S. as the world's leading researcher with the largest number of patents. Its total expenditure for R&D was a whopping US$ 456 billion in 2022. It has also become a key player in cutting-edge technologies like AI, robotics, cloud computing, and big data.

---

[2] 四个现代化 (sìgè xiàndàihuà), originally proposed by Zhou Enlai.

In Pakistan, we too are focusing on science and technology, and digital governance. We also have a demographic advantage, with 60% of our population consisting of youth who are tech-savvy, enterprising and drawn towards innovative fields.

Science and technology and IT exchanges now also form a key component of our bilateral relationship with China. Two specialized joint working groups have been established under CPEC, focusing on ICT and science and technology cooperation. Last year, we launched the China–Pakistan Digital Corridor to focus on deepening bilateral cooperation in emerging technologies as well as the joint development of high-quality digital infrastructure and hi-tech industrial zones and parks.

There is also an increasing interest from the private sector and academia in both countries to strengthen institutional linkages. During my recent visit to Guangdong Province, I was pleased to learn about the ongoing collaboration between Pakistan's National University of Science and Technology (NUST) and the Guangzhou Institute of Software Application Technology (GZIS) for the development of an AI lab in Pakistan. Last year, a dedicated science and technology cooperation centre was also established in collaboration with the Special Technology Zones Authority (STZA) of Pakistan and the Zhongguancun Belt and Road Industrial Promotion Association (ZBRA) of China for Chinese technology companies interested in investing in Pakistan.

We are also focusing on enhancing linkages in education and skill development among Pakistani youth, with China being the largest overseas destination for Pakistani students. Cooperation in Technical and Vocational Education and Training (TVET) is being emphasized to train Pakistani youth and the existing workforce to upgrade their skills in new and emerging technologies. The recently launched China–Pakistan International Industry Education Alliance Initiative in Beijing and our growing partnership with Chinese TVET institutions will further harness the potential of youth to contribute towards national development of our two countries.

Harmony Between Man and Nature

The age-old Chinese concept of "harmonious co-existence of man and nature"[3] has become the guiding principle for achieving balance. President Xi once said "man and nature need to coexist in harmony - when we protect nature carefully, it rewards us generously; when we exploit nature ruthlessly, it punishes us without mercy."

In my visits to various Chinese regions, I was fascinated to see the focus of local governments on environmental protection, ecological conservation, and biodiversity management. Everywhere, I saw President Xi's iconic words "lucid waters and lush mountains are invaluable assets" put into real practice. This has also become a key component of China's new development strategy, resulting in nationwide projects, focusing on restoring forests, combating desertification, pollution control, preserving

---

[3] 人与自然和谐共生 (rén yǔ zìrán héxié gòngshēng).

wetlands, and protecting wildlife. This has resulted in a marked increase in the quality of air, water, and overall living conditions.

In addition, there is a conscious effort to reduce China's carbon footprint by adopting green technologies and solutions and transitioning to clean energy. China is slowly but surely inching towards achieving its targets of carbon peaking before 2030 and carbon neutrality by 2060.

In Pakistan, environmental protection has assumed added importance given our vulnerability to climate change. It is ironic that despite having one of the smallest carbon footprints, Pakistan is one of the most affected countries, as evidenced by the devastating floods of last year.

Together, China and Pakistan are working bilaterally and multilaterally to combat the scourge of climate change. In our developmental partnership, we are also encouraging use of clean energy and green technologies. The solarization initiative of Former Prime Minister Shehbaz Sharif aims to produce 10,000 MW of solar energy in the next 5–10 years.

As part of our cooperation in agriculture, we are also promoting cooperation to increase efficiency of land and water resources, develop new seeds, and increase forest cover. The CPEC and our partnership under the GDI covers cooperation in these key areas.

Further building upon our mutual interest in proactive actions to prevent climate change and related multi-sectoral impacts, particularly on agriculture, our two countries recently launched the China–Pakistan Green Corridor, which covers cooperation in areas such as corporate farming, enhancing crop yields, new seed development, food conservation, cold chains, smart irrigation, pollution, tree plantation, and as well as climate-induced emergencies and disasters.

Concluding Remarks

Many people outside China lack a true appreciation of China's rich history, traditions, diverse culture, governing structure, and stellar economic growth. Many may have developed misconceived notions and perhaps also formed a misguided understandings due to biased and politicized media reports.

Seeing is believing. It is only be being in China that you can get first-hand knowledge of China's development story. The extent and magnitude of development is on a different scale, one which you cannot help but marvel at and admire. From maintaining an average 9% growth rate over the last forty years to bringing 800 million people out of absolute poverty, from being the top trading partner of over 120 countries to being home to over one million foreign companies, from building the world's largest high-speed network of 38,000 km to becoming a global leader in electric vehicles, from boasting 24 cities with a GDP over one trillion yuan to being home to 56 UNESCO world heritage sites, from building the world's largest e-commerce platform to constructing the largest number of skyscrapers, China's mind-boggling journey of development leaves some people in awe, some places in envy or while there are others who remain in disbelief, but it is indeed inspiring, especially for us in the developing world.

Firmly intertwined by historical and geographical linkages, Pakistan and China not only have mutual interests and shared aspirations but also a shared outlook for global peace and development. Over time, the depth, scope and spectrum of China–Pakistan cooperation has become so comprehensive that it cannot be summarized in only a few pages.

Ever since my arrival in Beijing, I have steered and spearheaded this relationship as Ambassador, which has only reinforced my faith in the timeless and time-tested nature of our relationship. Now I can say with conviction that ours is truly 'all-weather' and 'strategic' partnership, which I am confident will grow stronger with time and achieve even greater heights. We owe this to the sweat and toil of our forefathers as well as the efforts of successive generations of leaders and people. We pledge to pass on the spirit of friendship and goodwill to our youth and forge a relationship, which in Chinese is truly 独一无二 (dúyī-wú'èr)—unparalleled and one of a kind.

H.E. Moin Ul Haque Ambassador Extraordinary and Plenipotentiary of the Islamic Republic of Pakistan to the People's Republic of China, has had a distinguished career in Pakistan's Foreign Service since 1987. Mr. Haque has filled important roles within the Ministry of Foreign Affairs and served at various diplomatic postings in Ankara, Brussels, Colombo, New York, Paris, and Vancouver. Most notably, served as Ambassador of Pakistan to France from July 2016 to July 2020, with an additional accreditation to the Principality of Monaco and as Permanent Delegate to UNESCO. Mr. Haque has also received specialized training in management and national security.

Open Access This chapter is licensed under the terms of the Creative Commons Attribution-NonCommercial-NoDerivatives 4.0 International License (http://creativecommons.org/licenses/by-nc-nd/4.0/), which permits any noncommercial use, sharing, distribution and reproduction in any medium or format, as long as you give appropriate credit to the original author(s) and the source, provide a link to the Creative Commons license and indicate if you modified the licensed material. You do not have permission under this license to share adapted material derived from this chapter or parts of it.

The images or other third party material in this chapter are included in the chapter's Creative Commons license, unless indicated otherwise in a credit line to the material. If material is not included in the chapter's Creative Commons license and your intended use is not permitted by statutory regulation or exceeds the permitted use, you will need to obtain permission directly from the copyright holder.

Croatia and China in the Diamond Era of Bilateral Relations

Dario Mihelin

Introduction

On 13 May 2022, Croatia and China marked the 30th anniversary of the establishment of diplomatic relations and of the development of our partnership, which was strengthened and broadened by Croatia's membership and activities within the European Union. As the President of the State Council Li Keqiang so illustriously described during his official visit to Croatia in April 2019, Croatia and China are in a "diamond" era of bilateral relations. We confirmed this at the beginning of the pandemic through solidarity and mutual support. While people-to-people contacts have been rare since early 2020 and the anniversary itself was not marked properly in China due to severe pandemic restrictions, there is an underlying confidence that cooperation will take flight with the restart of contacts we have already witnessed in 2023. We are also looking forward to a resumption of high-level bilateral meetings, as these provide strong impetus to further strengthen better mutual understanding and cooperation.

Cooperation between Croatia and China, formally elevated to a comprehensive cooperative partnership since 2005, actually consists of four tracks, with a foundation in bilateral and EU–China relations, complemented by Croatia's participation in the Belt and Road Initiative and China-Central and Eastern Europe Cooperation. Regardless of their differences in size, economic power, international influence, and geographical distance, our countries share a lot of common points of connection and interests. Apart from our mutual respect and understanding, our cooperation has been growing at an increasing rate, especially in the areas of economy, tourism, science, culture, sports, and people-to-people contacts. The "European Great Wall" is in southern Croatia, around the old city and sea salt works of Ston. There is also

---

Ambassador of the Republic of Croatia to the People's Republic of China.

D. Mihelin (✉)
Beijing, China

evidence that Marco Polo, who travelled the old Silk Road and brought Europe and Asia closer together, was born in the Croatian city and island of the same name, Korčula, which was then a part of the Venetian Republic.

When celebrating important anniversaries, it is customary to reflect on some of the achievements that symbolize the efforts and successes of years past. In this regard, the first and foremost of these is appropriately the Pelješac Bridge, a strategically important project uniting Croatian territory, the completion of which coinciding with the year in which we celebrated 30th anniversary of the establishment of our diplomatic relations, will remain a symbol of the practical cooperation between Croatia, EU and China.

Cooperation: Achievements, Opportunities, and Expectations

Croatia awarded the tender for the construction of its symbolically most important infrastructure project, the Pelješac Bridge, which links two parts of Croatia, and thus two parts of the European Union, to the China Road and Bridge Corporation (CRBC). This project has become not only a testimony of the high level of trust between our countries, but also a way to showcase Chinese building expertise within the EU. The Pelješac Bridge was a pilot project for CRBC in the EU, and it had to adopt EU standards throughout implementation and competition of the project, including those regarding public procurement and use of EU funds. This landmark bridge was officially opened on 26 July 2022, creating a lasting bridge of Croatian–Chinese friendship and a symbol of Croatia-EU–China cooperation. The importance of EU–China cooperation in today's world was underlined by the message Premier Li Keqiang had delivered on that occasion.

Another flagship project that must be highlighted here, as it is the biggest Chinese investment in Croatia to date, is the construction of Croatia's largest wind farm near the city of Senj by the Chinese company Norinco International, which was finalized at the end of 2021. The 156-MW wind farm, consisting of thirty-nine 4-MW turbines, stretches over 45 square kilometres and is estimated to be in operation for 23 years, with an annual output of 530 million kWh. This project, which is worth EUR 230 million, is an excellent example of investment and green cooperation between Croatia and China.

I am particularly pleased that some Croatian flagship companies are finding their way into doing business in China, yet I would like to see even more Croatian companies here. By creating a more level playing field and giving Croatian companies similar opportunities to those given to CRBC and Norinco International in Croatia, I believe this can be accomplished to our mutual benefit within the scope of economic cooperation. The global champion in cloud communications platforms, Infobip, and special vehicles producer DOK-ING are developing partnerships with renowned Chinese companies.

Infobip is a global cloud communications platform that enables businesses to build connections across all stages of the customer journey. With over fifteen years of industry experience, Infobip has expanded to 70+ offices across six continents offering natively built technology with the capacity to reach over seven billion mobile devices and "things" in 190+ countries, connected directly to over 700 telecom networks. This includes established operations in Shenzhen, Beijing, Shanghai, and Hangzhou serving the local tech scene, start-ups, and online firms seeking to expand outside mainland China.

DOK-ING and its partner XCMG established a joint venture in 2020, with the intention of entering the humanitarian demining and crisis management market in China using DOK-ING's mature technology. With DOK-ING's 30 years of R&D and sales experience in the field and XCMG's production capabilities and market position in China, the cooperation between two parties was a logical step. Since it was founded, this new company has branched out beyond core markets and is currently involved in development of special purpose robots used for rescue, which will further expand both companies' product portfolios.

There are also two more Croatian-Chinese joint ventures in China that should be highlighted here. The first is the Croatian electrical equipment flagship company Končar, whose subsidiary, Mjerni transformatori d.d. (KMT), established cooperation with TBEA (Shenyang) Transformer Group Co., Ltd. The second is the Croatian electric automobile company Rimac Automobili, which cooperates with the Chinese Camel Group in production of electric batteries. In mentioning visionary electric car developer Mate Rimac, we hope to see Rimac Automobili's stunning hyper electric car Nevera, which is a force like no other, like the mighty Adriatic summer storm from which it takes its name, designed, engineered, and handcrafted in Croatia, on Chinese roads soon. Mate Rimac established partnership with the Kingsway Group as Rimac Automobili's official partner in Greater China, with a spectacular showroom in Shanghai.

I would also like to mention the renowned Croatian architectural design studio 3LHD, which is behind the unique philosophy of the LN Garden Hotel located in southern China's Guangdong Province, on the banks of the Pearl River in the Nansha Seaside Park. The architectural concept is based on the idea of four wings oriented towards the main environmental features of the site: the sea, the river, the mountains, and the park. Croatian design, in architecture and furniture, as captured by another Croation firm called Prostoria, is being recognized around the world, and I am pleased to see it entering China.

Croatia also works with Chinese partners to attract more investors from China and diversify their investments. It should be noted that Croatia offers many opportunities for Chinese investors and equal rights equal to those of domestic investors, including various incentives in both public and private projects ranging from infrastructure projects to smaller production-based projects. Being a member of the European Union and NATO, and on the way to the OECD membership, Croatia guarantees stability and the safety of business activities. Croatian legislation, harmonized with European Union law, ensures business activities of the highest standard and offers the possibility of using EU funds. Agreements that avoid double taxation signed with over 50 countries provide investors in Croatia with additional benefits. The Croatian Chamber of Economy has an office in Shanghai, and together with the Embassy in Beijing, it serves as an initial gateway for Chinese companies looking to do business, trade, and investment in Croatia.

According to the Croatian National Bank, total FDI investment from China in the last thirty years was less than EUR 160 million. However, actual numbers are higher, as the investments from Chinese companies have been mostly carried out through European companies, subsidiaries, or branches.

Croatia's unique geostrategic location makes it a valuable part of the Belt and Road Initiative, as Croatia's ports shorten shipping from the Far East to Europe by up to seven days compared to northern routes. Furthermore, as part of the EU, Croatia is an entry point to a market of over 500 million people. The Sea port of Rijeka is the largest port in Croatia and accounts for more than 50% of total turnover of all Croatian ports. It is also one of the most important ports linking the Far East and Central Europe with the shortest transit time. Most prominent Chinese companies choose Croatian ports as their entry points or hub centres for Central and Eastern Europe. The modern infrastructure of these ports and their good connections with European countries create numerous opportunities for the development and implementation of investment projects in logistics industry, especially in intermodal transportation, logistics, and distribution centres.

Croatia also has a highly developed road network in addition to its network of key international seaports (Rijeka, Ploče, Šibenik, Zadar, Split, Dubrovnik), river ports (Vukovar, Osijek, Slavonski Brod, and Sisak) and airports (seven international airports include Zagreb, Split, Dubrovnik, Zadar, Rijeka, Pula, and Osijek), as well as inland waterways and intermodal terminals. Its network of modern motorways put Croatia on par with top European countries. Croatia also aims to revitalize its entire railway network, meeting the highest European standards by increasing the capacity of the railway lines as well as the speed of travel and safety, with plans to upgrade as many as 750 km of railway lines between 2020 and 2030, providing opportunities for renowned Chinese companies to participate in public tenders.

Renewables and green transition are certainly one of Croatia's priorities. The Russian aggression against Ukraine has confirmed that green and digital transition is even more important to increase our overall resilience, which has been a valuable lesson not only for Europe. By further accelerating development of renewables and increasing green investments, diversifying energy sources, putting more emphasis on savings and green transition, we believe we can turn the current situation into a new opportunity for our economies. Croatia is expected to reduce CO_2 emissions by 45% by 2030 and stop using coal by 2033, perhaps even sooner. Another goal is to reach 39% of renewables in end consumption by 2030, using the country's own potential in the process; we aim to have more than 65% of renewables and 100% low-carbon in final production. Croatia's energy development strategy must be based on new and clean technologies, innovation, and research to improve the quality of life and ensure the necessary transformation of the economy. Croatia met 29% of its energy needs through hydropower facilities and wind and solar parks, surpassing the renewable energy targets in the Europe 2020 strategy. Although Croatia has made progress in using its potential for wind energy, solar and solar thermal are still underused compared to the obvious potential in our very sunny country. The estimated technical potential of solar power plants in Croatia is 5303 MW, with an estimated production of 6364 GWh of electrical energy annually. As we can see, incentives for further development of renewable energy resources are abundant, and Chinese companies recognize this investment opportunity.

Trade between Croatia and China has grown steadily (USD 1.54 billion in 2022, according to Croatian statistics), but this is characterized by a significant trade deficit on the Croatian side. Recognizing the potential of China as one of the world's leading economies and markets, Croatia is continuously working to bring more Croatian food and agricultural products to the Chinese market. More and more high-quality Croatian products are succeeding in entering the vast Chinese market, with wine being the most prominent, which can be paired with cheese. However, we would like other products such as tuna, fish, honey, and meat products to follow soon. Chinese citizens already have their Croatian favourites—Podravka's Vegeta and Linolada—and we hope to present more Croatian food products in the future. From China, Croatia mostly imports special purpose vessels, automatic data processing machines, electric generators and converters, and iron and steel products. Croatia exports mostly processed wood, presses for rubber or plastic product moulding, special purpose motor vehicles, cut marble and travertine, and food preparations for animal feed to China.

Croatia puts great value on the opportunities provided by the framework of the Cooperation between the Central and Eastern European Countries and China, the 10th anniversary of which was marked in 2022. For Croatia, the EU's values, principles, and rules are a paramount framework for operating within this Cooperation. We hope the platform will realize the goals it set out a decade ago and achieve tangible results, particularly in its focal areas of balanced trade and investment, which were highlighted at the last in-person summit held in the crown jewel of Croatian tourism, Dubrovnik, in April 2019. The Croatian Prime Minister publicly praised this Cooperation for the opportunities for high-level political dialogue with Chinese leadership it provides.

The pre-pandemic year of 2019 was particularly significant for our two countries in the tourism sector. Not only it was proclaimed as the Croatian-Chinese Year of Culture and Tourism, but in 2019 Croatia recorded the highest number of Chinese tourists (including mainland China, Hong Kong, Macao, Taiwan). With almost 500,000 arrivals and more than 650,000 overnight stays, this was strong evidence of the enviable trend of positive change in economic relations between two countries. This steady growth created a solid foundation for ultimate introduction of direct flights between China and Croatia, but unfortunately, the arrival of the pandemic postponed this project. Croatia is a popular vacation destination in Europe and the most visited tourist market in the Central and Eastern European region. In terms of its size, Croatia may not be a big country, particularly when compared to China, but it has an attractive location in Europe. Likewise, Croatia boasts a very high quality of life. It is a safe country, with a welcoming population, delicious food, well-preserved natural areas, a mild climate, and abundant historical and tourist attractions.

As the newest European Union member state, Croatia marked the 10th anniversary of its accession on 1 July 2023 and entered 2023 by anchoring itself firmly in the European mainstream, joining the Schengen travel area and the Euro currency zone, which should bring more opportunities for cooperation with China as well as it will make travel and doing business much easier.

The thriving sports cooperation between our two countries should not come as a surprise—Croatian athletes, particularly footballers, are widely known in China, as are Croatia's trademark red-and-white checkerboard jerseys. Many Chinese people mention the brilliant Luka Modrić wherever I travel around the country. The same goes for the famous pianist Maksim Mrvica, who received wide praise here when he played *Croatian Rhapsody*. Our cooperation in sports covers not only football, but also basketball, handball, and tennis. Before the pandemic, over a hundred talented young Chinese athletes trained in Croatia annually with their peers. Here, I would like to particularly highlight the longstanding cooperation between the Beijing Sports University and the University of Zagreb, as well as the fact that Croatia is in charge of coordinating mechanism for summer sports within CEEC-China Cooperation.

We have also increased the frequency of bilateral relations at the local level—contacts and exchange between our provinces and cities flourish. Relations at the local level have been long term: the Croatian capital city Zagreb marked the 40th anniversary of its sister city relationship with Shanghai and the 25th anniversary of partner relations with Beijing in 2020. Other cities and provinces that have developed partnerships include Rijeka, Split, Dubrovnik, Opatija, Varaždin, Primorje-Gorski Kotar County, Osijek-Baranja County, Zadar County, Lika-Senj County, and Vukovar-Srijem County, which are linked to Chinese partner cities including Dalian, Qingdao, Ningbo, Xi'an, Hangzhou, Harbin, Liaoning, Hainan, Sichuan, Qinghai, Hebei, and Henan, just to name a few.

I would like to emphasize the continuous and fruitful cooperation between Croatia and China in protecting fragile biodiversity within our flagship national parks (Plitvice Lakes and Jiuzhaigou, Krka and Huanglong). Thanks to the longstanding cooperation between the Faculty of Science of the University of Zagreb and the Chengdu Institute of Biology of the Chinese Academy of Science, a joint laboratory on biodiversity and ecosystem services was awarded within the Belt and Road Initiative.

Conclusion

Anniversaries of diplomatic relations offer a symbolic opportunity to express gratitude to all those who have contributed to the deepening of friendly relations between our two countries as well as to reflect on future prospects. While building on our successes in the first 30 years of our diplomatic relations, it is with optimistic anticipation that we look forward to expanding the spectrum of our bilateral interests and using opportunities to unify our efforts in addressing global challenges, Croatia, EU, and China together.

With the strong partnership relations, increasing investment and enviable advances in increasing Chinese tourist arrivals, which we have begun to witness again after the pandemic, we can truly say that the future is bright for further development of our mutual relations in all aspects. Croatia attaches great importance to furthering cooperation with China in all spheres of mutual interest. As I often say, we owe it to the legacy of Marco Polo, whose family is believed to have come from the Croatian island of Korčula, to strengthen our cooperation and bonds. To once again return to Premier Li's assessment, diamonds are not only sparkling and valuable, but also strong, just like the Croatian-Chinese friendship and partnership.

For Croatia as an EU member state, enhanced cooperation between the European Union and China on global issues, such as global peace and security, climate change, development assistance, and energy issues are of the utmost importance. Our world has changed dramatically, and in these new circumstances, there is no alternative but to increase international cooperation based in the established tenets of the rules-based international order, buttressed by the global institutions centred in the United Nations system and the corpus of international law. Unjustified Russian aggression against Ukraine reminds us of the importance of preserving this order and demands a responsible response from everyone in the international community, particularly from the permanent members of the Security Council of the United Nations, calling for the respect of sovereignty and territorial integrity of Ukraine, and bringing about a just peace, with all the atrocities condemned and perpetrators brought to justice— might cannot be allowed to be right and obsolete concepts of spheres of influence should be banished to history.

H.E. Dario Mihelin obtained his Master's degree in European studies in 1999 at the London School of Economics and Political Science, having graduated with a degree in law from the University of Zagreb. He also graduated from the Diplomatic Academy of the Ministry of Foreign and European Affairs of the Republic of Croatia. He started his career in 1999 in the then Office for European Integration of the Government of the Republic of Croatia, subsequently the Ministry of European Integration, working on a process of drawing Croatia closer to the EU and serving as an adviser to several ministers. After a number of years working on Croatia-EU, he became Head of the Department for Latin America, Australia and Oceania. His next post was in the Croatian Embassy to the USA where he was in charge of political affairs and bilateral relations between the two states from mid-2008 to late-2012. Following his successful term in Washington, he moved to Ankara where he was actively involved in economic and energy diplomacy as deputy head of mission. He was appointed as Foreign and European Policy Advisor to the President of the Republic of Croatia Kolinda Grabar-Kitarović in February 2015, a position he held until January 2019 when he was appointed as Croatia's Ambassador to the People's Republic of China and Mongolia.

Open Access This chapter is licensed under the terms of the Creative Commons Attribution-NonCommercial-NoDerivatives 4.0 International License (http://creativecommons.org/licenses/by-nc-nd/4.0/), which permits any noncommercial use, sharing, distribution and reproduction in any medium or format, as long as you give appropriate credit to the original author(s) and the source, provide a link to the Creative Commons license and indicate if you modified the licensed material. You do not have permission under this license to share adapted material derived from this chapter or parts of it.

The images or other third party material in this chapter are included in the chapter's Creative Commons license, unless indicated otherwise in a credit line to the material. If material is not included in the chapter's Creative Commons license and your intended use is not permitted by statutory regulation or exceeds the permitted use, you will need to obtain permission directly from the copyright holder.

Future Milestones in Switzerland–China Relations

Jürg Burri

A History of Engagement

Switzerland was among the first western states to recognize the People's Republic of China (PRC) in 1950. Since then, bilateral relations have deepened in all areas, especially after the PRC introduced policies that facilitated the opening up of the country for foreign investment during the early 1980s. The relations and engagements of our two countries now cover numerous fields including politics, human rights, trade and investment, finance, the labor market and employment, science and technology, education, the environment, and culture.

When the Swiss Federal Council decided to recognize the PRC in 1950, the decision was guided by a desire to enhance relations between Swiss businesses and citizens and their pre-existing contacts and engagements in trade, society, and diplomacy—relations that were first formed during the Qing Dynasty.

Switzerland and China are different in many ways: from the sizes of their population and territory to their political, societal, and economic systems. But on a person-to-person level, there has always been mutual interest in many issues. The Swiss and the Chinese have continuously contributed to each other's development; learned each other's languages, made friends, founded families, and traded and worked together. This is nicely illustrated in a new book published in 2023 by the Consulate General of Switzerland in Guangzhou, which paints a picture of the activities of Swiss citizens and companies residing in the Pearl River Delta over the past 100 years.

Throughout the last 40 years, as China has undergone a tremendous transformation, there has been a boost in interest from both Switzerland and Swiss companies, and they have actively taken part in this development. Some milestones that deserve particular mention include:

Ambassador of the Swiss Confederation to the People's Republic of China.

J. Burri (✉)
Beijing, China

© The Author(s) 2024
H. Wang and M. L. Miao (eds.), *The Future of China's Development and Globalization*, China and Globalization, https://doi.org/10.1007/978-981-99-7512-9_3

- Establishing the first Joint Venture of a Chinese and Swiss company in 1980 (Schindler elevators)
- The first western recognition of China as a market economy in 2007
- The first European state to bring into force a Free Trade Agreement with China in 2014

As a next step, in 2016 Switzerland and China chose to categorize their relationship as an "innovative strategic partnership". Finding additional ways to develop bilateral ties is at the core of the Sino-Swiss relationship. As such, the two countries decided to establish more than two dozen intergovernmental dialogues where strategic and technical discussions could take place. For the main Strategic Innovation Dialogue, exchange is coordinated on a ministerial level, which allows for all topics to be included. Two highlights of this renewed relationship with China worth mentioning were Chinese President Xi Jinping's official visit to Switzerland in January 2017 and Swiss President Ueli Maurer's official visit to Beijing in April 2019.

The Swiss government adopted its "China Strategy 2021–2024" in March 2021, which outlines Switzerland's Foreign Policy Strategy with respect to the PRC. China is the only country where bilateral engagement constitutes such a high level of priority that it requires the attention of a specialized policy strategy by the Swiss government. It shows just how much importance the Swiss government attaches to its country's relations with China.

Switzerland has continuously built up its diplomatic presence in China and today has an Embassy in Beijing, as well as Consulates in Shanghai, Hong Kong, Guangzhou, and Chengdu. The Consulate in Shanghai has been upgraded with a science office, known as "Swissnex", to promote cooperation in science and education. Switzerland Global Enterprise is also present in China with a Swiss Business Hub integrated into the diplomatic network. Swiss companies are connected through a Swiss Chamber with Chapters in Beijing, Shanghai, Hong Kong, and Guangzhou. Furthermore, Switzerland Tourism is in China promoting Switzerland as an attractive travel destination in yet another network. And also Pro Helvetia runs a culture office in Shanghai.

In 2020, shortly before the global pandemic began, we celebrated the 70th anniversary of diplomatic relations. The Speaker of Swiss Parliament visited the PRC on January 17, the same day as the official recognition back in 1950. Today, we face the challenge of reactivating the positive relations we have built over the past 70 years following three years of very limited interaction. Almost 3000 Swiss citizens live in China today, a number that has considerably reduced as a result of the strict Covid policies. We hope to see a reconsolidation soon now.

Shared Commitment to Sustainable Growth

Trade and Investment

In 2010, China became Switzerland's most important trading partner in Asia. And it has further consolidated this position as Switzerland's third biggest trading partner after the USA and Germany—and higher than other large neighboring countries such as France or Italy.

Over the last 10 years, the value of goods that have found their way from Chinese manufacturers to Swiss homes and businesses has nearly doubled. At the same time, Swiss products exported to China have risen from a total value of roughly 7.4 billion Swiss francs in 2012 to a value of nearly 15.9 billion Swiss francs in 2022. It is evident that the Free Trade Agreement of 2014 has contributed substantially to this rise.

At the same time, it is important to keep in mind that goods are just one part of the equation. Since the establishment of the Free Trade Agreement, trade in services between Switzerland and China has risen by more than 47%. Swiss foreign direct investment has continued its positive trajectory, gaining an additional five billion Swiss francs over the same period. Swiss companies have integrated China into their value chains and established hundreds of subsidiaries to manufacture goods for local consumption and export, as well as to conduct research and development and to offer maintenance, training, and other services. For Switzerland, openness to trade and access to international markets is the basis for economic growth and general welfare. This has been demonstrated by the growing number of Swiss companies trading in and with China. Today, practically every international company in Switzerland has important stakes in the Chinese market.

One recent development is the launch of the China–Switzerland Stock Connect program, which includes listings of the Global Depository Receipts of Chinese companies on the Zurich Stock Exchange. This may become an important form of cooperation with a view to also placing GDRs of Swiss companies on the stock markets in Shanghai and Shenzhen.

Sustainable Development

The United Nations' 2030 Agenda for Sustainable Development states: "International trade is an engine for inclusive economic growth and poverty reduction and contributes to the promotion of sustainable development." To fully harness its potential, international trade has to positively contribute toward sustainable development and enhanced policy coherence at a national and international level are key requirements. To help achieve this objective, Switzerland is committed to including provisions governing the social and environmental aspects of trade in all its free trade agreements, including the existing one it has with China. As part of this process, we believe Sino-Swiss economic relations can offer interesting perspectives and become even more relevant.

The past years have brought about many developments that impact not only the Sino-Swiss relationship, but the global community as a whole. China and Switzerland have both begun to see more clearly the effects of pollution, climate change, and other environmental risks, as well as rising tensions in international politics, accelerated digitization, and global health crises including the most recent COVID-19 pandemic.

Sustainability of business is an important topic that is already being addressed through Sino-Swiss relations. Switzerland was an early mover promoting projects that support China's green transformation. Today, these projects focus on sustainable energy, zero emissions, and other topics that are managed by the International Cooperation Office at the Swiss Embassy.

Addressing developments in the markets toward more sustainable products requires corresponding changes in the world of business too. Many Swiss companies have made this step and today operate at the forefront, making product sustainability a key asset equal to quality, innovation, and price. They are responding to the greater interest of consumers in the conditions under which goods and services are produced, and governments strongly support this trend of responsible and sustainable business conduct.

Travel and Exchange

Switzerland is a beautiful country that prides itself on its natural environment and welcomes a large number of visitors as a result. Much like China, Switzerland believes that clear rivers, lush green hills, and snowy mountains are deserving of the utmost attention. We therefore use our high standards of environmental protection as a selling point for people to visit Switzerland, and we have received positive responses for this approach among the Chinese travel industry and the public.

Cooperation Through Science and Education

In 2003, the Sino-Swiss Science and Technology Cooperation program was established and today over 250 agreements between Chinese and Swiss public universities form the backbone of our scientific cooperation. One of many interesting projects is the research conducted by scientists from the Federal Institute of Technology in Lausanne (EPFL) and the Huazhong University of Science and Technology (HUST) on Perovskite solar cells. These high-performing solar cells have the potential to make solar energy more accessible and affordable, contributing to the future of cleaner energy.

Many Chinese students choose to study at internationally renowned Swiss universities. There are approximately 3000 Swiss university alumni in China who have actively organized themselves into a network of large chapters all across China, maintaining regular contact with Swiss institutions and companies. And many more have chosen to study in Switzerland, with around 3000 Chinese students entering the lecture halls of Swiss institutions every year.

Swiss students, albeit fewer, are likewise keen to discover China and have sought to do so even when pandemic measures made such endeavors almost impossible. Student contacts are crucial for creating a better understanding between countries and are essential for lively relations. It is therefore important that we can begin to grow the Swiss student population again in China now that travel restrictions are being lifted.

Switzerland is also happy to cooperate with China on vocational and professional education and training (VPET). Common projects in this area can help address current and future challenges, such as youth unemployment and talent development. Like in Switzerland, Swiss companies in China are in the driver's seat when it comes to implementing VPET. Companies such as ABB, George Fischer, Schindler, and many more have been cooperating with Chinese vocational schools on a variety of projects over the past years. In the area of teacher training, the Swiss Federal University for Vocational Education and Training holds regular training sessions together with Chinese stakeholders on the national and provincial level. A special achievement thanks to cooperation in this area was the recent "White Book on VPET" issued by the Sino-Swiss Chambers of Commerce.

Neutrality as a Core Swiss Value

China is playing an increasingly important role in international diplomacy, and so regular, high-level exchanges are very important to Switzerland. Since the establishment of bilateral relations in 1950, Switzerland and China have built a number of mechanisms to support exchange. We cultivate high-level contacts with China, not only in the dialogues described above, but also through consultations in international forums, including the sidelines of the World Economic Forum, multilateral contexts, or other informal settings organized in cooperation with think tanks. It is a Swiss principle to address all our issues of concern with our Chinese partners, such as trade policies or human rights, in multilateral and bilateral contexts.

Especially in times of geopolitical tension and polarization, Switzerland believes in the rule of law, international law, multilateral mechanisms, and promoting dialogue on all levels. The Swiss have a proud tradition of bringing different sides together in peaceful dialogue and acting as a bridge in seemly impossible situations. Fostering international dialogue remains a central and highly visible part of Swiss foreign policy. Based on its neutral position, Switzerland takes no sides in any geopolitical bloc, but always advocates respect for international law and universal rights. On the one hand, adhering to the law of neutrality means that we do not take part in military conflicts. On the other hand, the policy of neutrality means Switzerland is actively engaged in promoting peace and stability. Fully in line with the slogan of our current UN Security Council membership, we stand behind the notion that our country constitutes "A PLUS for Peace". Being a member of the Security Council also opens new space for discussion and cooperation with the Chinese delegation representing the PRC during the two years of our term.

Neutrality does not mean that we do not stand up for what we believe in. Quite the opposite: Switzerland advocates a strong rules-based international order and an effective multilateral system committed to international law, human rights, the rule of law, and the promotion of democracy. In a conflict, and if requested by the parties, Switzerland is always ready to offer good offices. As a host state for many UN organizations, Switzerland also has a great interest in strengthening Geneva as a platform for equitable multilateral diplomacy.

To better understand this nuance between the law of neutrality and a policy of neutrality, one may look at the international armed conflict between Russia and Ukraine. Russia's military aggression against Ukraine is a serious violation of several of the most fundamental norms of international law. To credibly stand by our promise to be a force for peace and stability, actions had to be taken, such as following the EU's approach of imposing sanctions against Russia. The Swiss government used its political room to maneuver within the bounds that the law of neutrality allowed and adopted sanctions that were already levied by the EU. Yet, Switzerland has not allowed any exports of Swiss-made armaments to any of the warring parties—either directly or by third countries.

The Future of Sino-Swiss Relations

The ties between Switzerland and China have proven to be very fruitful and stable, guided by a pioneering spirit and pragmatism. Switzerland also has a strong stance in defending its interests and values. We strongly believe in open dialogue as a tool and offer cooperation on bilateral and multilateral issues. These dialogues have been negatively impacted in recent years due to limited travel, but we hope they will now fully resume and gain further substance.

Switzerland and China have better trade and engagement with each other today than ever before. These strong relations go back for decades and are now complimented with promising new prospects, such as cooperation in finance and a focus on sustainability.

On political issues, Switzerland will always strive to remain a credible advocate for multilateralism, peace, stability, and respect for universal rights. Given these factors, China will continue to find a partner in Switzerland that will respectfully, sincerely, and openly work toward mutual understanding and strive to lay the groundwork toward better cooperation. China and Switzerland have a lot to offer each other in the coming years of international cooperation. Trust and mutual understanding are key. Therefore, we need to keep fostering exchanges, whether at a political level including on topics such as human rights or an economic, academic or cultural one.

This exchange creates an advantageous environment for the Sino-Swiss relationship to reach new milestones.

The coming years will bring landmark events, such as the 10th anniversary of the Free Trade Agreement coming into force (2024), the 75th anniversary of Diplomatic Relations (2025), and the 10th anniversary of the Founding of the Innovative Strategic Partnership (2026). These will be opportune moments to reflect on what we have achieved and to consider the milestones that lie ahead.

H.E. Mr. Jürg Burri was born in 1965. A historian and former journalist, he joined the Swiss Foreign Service in 1996. He completed his diplomatic training with the Swiss Mission to the United Nations in New York, followed by postings in Berne and Brussels EU. From 2006 through 2009, he served as the Minister/Deputy Head of Mission at the Embassy of Switzerland in Beijing before being appointed Deputy to the State Secretary for Education, Research and Innovation and later DG for Consular Affairs. In 2018, he was appointed Ambassador of Switzerland to Poland. Mr. Burri was appointed Ambassador of Switzerland to the People's Republic of China, Mongolia and the Democratic People's Republic of Korea in September 2022.

Open Access This chapter is licensed under the terms of the Creative Commons Attribution-NonCommercial-NoDerivatives 4.0 International License (http://creativecommons.org/licenses/by-nc-nd/4.0/), which permits any noncommercial use, sharing, distribution and reproduction in any medium or format, as long as you give appropriate credit to the original author(s) and the source, provide a link to the Creative Commons license and indicate if you modified the licensed material. You do not have permission under this license to share adapted material derived from this chapter or parts of it.

The images or other third party material in this chapter are included in the chapter's Creative Commons license, unless indicated otherwise in a credit line to the material. If material is not included in the chapter's Creative Commons license and your intended use is not permitted by statutory regulation or exceeds the permitted use, you will need to obtain permission directly from the copyright holder.

China and Sri Lanka: Neighborly Relations in a Rapidly Evolving World

Palitha Kohona

Sri Lanka has enjoyed a wonderfully close relationship with China that has spanned over two millennia, despite the forbidding mountain ranges and threatening oceans that separate the two countries. These distances and the physical obstacles have not, however, prevented the two states from developing close bonds based on mutual interest. Despite constant contacts over this long period, there is no record of China ever attempting to establish a permanent presence in the country or colonize it despite Sri Lanka's attractive strategic location, natural wealth and comfortable living conditions.

Waves of traders seeking Sri Lanka's fabled spices, gems, pearls, elephant tusks and other luxury products, and holy monks searching for the sublime teachings of the Buddha (Siddhamuni to the Chinese), sailed to its shores over the centuries from China. Those who came not only left detailed observations, which corroborate our own historical records, they also contributed significant elements of their own languages, cuisine, dress, cultural traits and even some DNA, in certain cases large infusions of it, enriching our own. The contacts with Buddhist visitors from China constitute the earliest cultural exchanges between the two countries.

A History of Mutually Comfortable Neighborly Relations

Our common religion, Buddhism, was the main platform on which the cultural relationship between China and Sri Lanka flourished over the centuries and linked the two kingdoms. The earliest records indicate that the exchanges along the Maritime Silk Road began to flourish from around 207 BC during China's Han Dynasty. Cultural

---

Ambassador of the Democratic Socialist Republic of Sri Lanka to the People's Republic of China.

P. Kohona (✉)
Beijing, China

and religious exchanges blossomed. Technologies, cuisine, agricultural practices and even diseases, like the plague crossed borders along the Silk Road but did not disturb the way of life of the Lankans.

The fourth-century scholar monk Fa Xian from Shanxi, China, who spent two years at the famous Abhayagiriya Monastery in the ancient capital Anuradhapura, left records of complex international diplomatic and trading relations. After spending almost ten years in Northern India, he boarded a trading vessel and headed for Lanka in 410 AD. After two years in Lanka, during which he visited the famous Sri Pada Mountain (Mountain of the Holy Foot Print venerated by Buddhists), he decided to return to his homeland, having watched a Chinese merchant donate a valuable silk fan to the Abhayagiriya dagoba (pagoda). He wrote of the intense homesickness he felt after witnessing this act of devotion by his compatriot. He carried a ship load of religious texts, written mostly in Sinhala, from Lanka to China, which he later translated into Chinese. Later, Amoghavajra, a powerful Buddhist monk, traveled to Sri Lanka and translated the *Karandamudra Sutra* into Chinese, which he took back to his homeland in the eighth century.

Over the centuries, social, cultural and religious interactions between Sri Lanka and China have thrived and both countries benefited. China was, at the time, a major civilization and, judging by historical evidence, supremely confident in itself, but relatively less known to the other flourishing civilizations further to the West. Distance kept China relatively isolated, both physically and in awareness of other peoples, but the unique natural wealth of Sri Lanka and its Buddhist religious heritage gave it a reputation that far exceeded its geographical size and attracted waves of Chinese traders and Buddhist monks. It is interesting that some emperors themselves were aware of the combination of treasures that Sri Lanka possessed. The enviable geographical location of Sri Lanka, in the very center of the Indian Ocean and at the confluence of the two monsoons, made it the logical meeting place for traders sailing East from the kingdoms of the West (Rome, Greece, Egypt, Persia, etc.) and those sailing West from the kingdoms of the East, (China, Sumatra, Khmer, etc.). The interactions that took place on the island included a myriad of nationalities and traders and conferred on it a larger-than-life reputation. This also brought wealth, making it possible for the Lankans to construct large cities and marvels that were impressive even by modern standards, such as the palace in the sky, Sigiriya and the 130 meter-high brick pagoda, Jethavanaramaya. Tales brought back of the island of Lanka by sailors and traders may have resulted in an exaggerated image in the listeners' mind, as could be imagined from the Claudius Ptolemy's first century map of the island of Taprobane. Eratosthenes (276–196 BC) first mentioned Taprobane and the name was later adopted by Claudius Ptolemy (139 AD) in his geographical treatise, referring to a relatively large island south of continental Asia. The Greek geographer Strabo also makes reference to the island, noting that "Taprobane sends great amounts of ivory, tortoise-shell and other merchandise to the markets of India." Eratosthenes' map of the known world, c. 194 BC, also shows an island south of India called Taprobane.

The religio-cultural link that was established then and the people-to-people contacts developed have also been the foundation for nurturing future brotherly bonds. As will be discussed later in this paper, today Sri Lanka, serving as a hub for the BRI in the middle of the Indian Ocean, has more to offer than the luxury goods of yesteryear and the sublime doctrine of the Buddha.

The Influence of Two Friendly Neighbors on Each Other

Although it is natural that China would have had a significant impact on a small kingdom like Lanka, as a small country with something vital to give to the world, Sri Lanka has also played a valued role as a cultural partner for China. Chinese traders and Shaolin monks probably introduced Chinese martial arts to Lanka, as did the same monks who bravely ventured across the Gobi desert in search of true Buddhism, armed only with self-defense techniques to ward off waylaying robbers. One of the terms in Sinhala for martial arts is Cheena–Adi, far too close to be a coincidence. Needless to say, *kung fu* is very popular among young people in Sri Lanka and there is considerable potential for the further development of the sport. Even today, Shaolin Temple in China's Henan Province maintains close links with key Sri Lankan temples. During a recent visit, the Chief Abbot, Venerable Master Shi Yongxin, the 30th abbot of the Shaolin Temple, which has close links with the state, invited me for tea and spoke fondly of his recent visit to Sri Lanka and of the potential for further expanding temple-to-temple and people-to-people links and exchanges.

The role played by Sri Lanka in China, especially through Buddhism, is illustrated by a number of Chinese records. The Chinese account, *The Biography of Bhikkunis,* written in the sixth century, details a visit by Sinhala nuns to the imperial capital, Nanjing, to inaugurate the Order of Nuns in China, which still survives in China despite having ceased to exist in Sri Lanka.

Thirteen embassies were sent by the Kings of Lanka between 131 AD and 989 AD to the Chinese imperial court. In 428 AD, King Mahanama sent a model of the shrine of the Sacred Tooth Relic to the Chinese Emperor. The Lankan King also sent an embassy with a valuable statue of the Buddha to the court of Emperor Xiaowu. A piece of the parietal (skull) bone of the Buddha, which apparently was brought over from Lanka in the tenth century, is displayed at the stunning Usnisa Palace Temple at Niushou Mountain in Nanjing. (Interestingly, this was during a period when Lanka was being invaded constantly by South Indian Chola forces).

The Arab geographer Edrisi details the extent of Lanka's international trade during the time of King Parakramabahu the Great, who also sent a royal princess to the court of the Chinese Emperor. The great Kublai Khan dispatched Marco Polo as an envoy in 1284, seeking the alms bowl of the Buddha, which was venerated by the Sinhala people, but the Lankan King politely refused this request. Marco Polo visited the island twice and proclaimed Sri Lanka to be the finest island of its size in the entire world. The lion statues at Yapauwa, the capital of Lanka in the thirteenth century, were very much Chinese influenced. King Parakramabahu VI (1412–1467) alone dispatched six missions to China, the largest number by a single Sinhala King. The troves of Chinese coins and porcelain that have been recovered from various parts of the country suggest a thriving trade between China and Sri Lanka. A large number of Chinese vessels also lie beneath our waters not too far from the shore, having sunk in rough weather. The largest known wreck is at Godawaya off the Southern coast of Sri Lanka. According to tradition, the White Horse Temple in Luoyang was the first Buddhist temple built in China and has now allocated land within its confines for the construction of a Sri Lankan-style temple. Buddhist temples in the styles of other Asian countries have already been built and plans are already being developed for the construction of a Sri Lankan temple.

Admiral Zheng He visited Lanka six times between 1405 and 1433 during his voyages to the West in the name of the Ming Emperor. During his second visit to Sri Lanka in 1411, Zheng He visited the Upulwan Shrine in Devundara and donated the following: "1000 pieces of gold; 5000 pieces of silver; 50 rolls of embroidered silk in many colors; 50 rolls of silk taffeta in many colors; four pairs of jeweled banners, gold embroidered and of variegated silk, two pairs of the same picked in red, one pair of the same in yellow, one pair in black; five antique brass incense burners; five pairs of antique brass flower vases picked in gold on lacquer, with gold stands; five yellow brass lamps picked in gold on lacquer with gold stands; five incense vessels in vermilion red, gold picked on lacquer, with gold stands; six pairs of golden lotus flowers; 2500 catties of scented oil; 10 pairs of wax candles; 10 sticks of fragrant incense." (A century and a half later, in contrast, the Upulwan Shrine was looted and burnt down by Portuguese colonists). The Admiral's visits and his involvement in the replacement of the Lankan king, Alakeshwara, are well-recorded. Parakramabahu VI sent six missions to the Ming court. Zheng He left a carved stone pillar in Galle in 1411 which is now in a local museum. A Lankan prince and his retinue accompanied Zheng He on his return, and the prince ultimately chose to stay in China. The family of Xu-Shi Yin'e living in Quanzhou, Fujian, traces its roots to this royal Lankan prince.

It is clear that Sri Lanka, despite its small physical size, had developed considerable relations through religion, trade and social links, with the Middle Kingdom. The writings of scholars, soldiers, monks, travelers and traders suggest a strong Chinese cultural interest in Lanka from very early times.

Recent Developments

More recently, particularly during the period of domination of Asia by Western powers, many Chinese migrated to other countries in search of a better life. China, which had boasted the biggest economy in the world for centuries, was reduced to a poverty-stricken shadow of its former self to be looted and exploited by a gaggle of Western colonial powers. China was forced to open its borders and coerced to accept opium under the guise of free trade. It is ironic that the concept of free trade had its origins in the Western effort to sell opium to China. In a historical twist of fate, the West is now asking China to block the export of fentanyl and its precursors in the West. (Since 1999, drug overdoses have killed approximately one million Americans). From May 1, 2019, China officially banned all forms of fentanyl and other drugs in the same category, fulfilling the commitment President Xi made during the G-20 Summit.

During this period, Chinese also came to Ceylon (Sri Lanka), then a British colony, assimilated well and settled down to become part of the Sri Lankan Chinese community. Some have since migrated to places such as Australia where Sri Lankan-born Jimmy Shu is now a celebrated chef.

Sri Lanka Gains Independence in 1948 and Renews its Links

After winning our independence from the colonial yoke of Britain in 1948, Sri Lanka was quick to adjust to the changed realities of the world and assert itself. China had also stood up and many other countries in the region had also shaken off their colonial shackles. In 2022, we celebrated the 70th anniversary of the ground breaking Rubber-Rice Pact with China and the 65th anniversary of the founding of diplomatic relations. In 1950, an independent Ceylon became the 13th country to recognize the young People's Republic of China and, since then, has unconditionally endorsed the One China Policy, a position that no Sri Lankan government has even remotely considered compromising. Subsequently, in 1952 as the Korean War raged, Ceylon breached a Western embargo on the export of strategic materials to China and concluded the Rubber-Rice Pact to trade rubber (listed as a strategic material) for rice. Ceylon agreed to export 50,000 tons of rubber to China at a higher than market price and import 270,000 tons of rice at the normal market price. This agreement remained in effect until 1982.

In the ensuing years, the relationship between our two countries continued to warm. Premier Zhou Enlai, who played a critical role in restoring the relationship, visited Ceylon in 1957 on the formal establishment of diplomatic relations and laid the foundation for lasting and solid ties, which flourished particularly during the stewardship of Prime Minister Mrs. Sirimao Bandaranayaka. Many middle-aged people in Beijing still recall fondly the rapturous reception accorded to Prime Minister Mrs. Bandaranayaka during her visits to China in 1961 and again in 1972, almost a spontaneous external manifestation of the inner warmth that had developed between our two peoples. China, for its part, highlighted the traditional Buddhist connection by sending the sacred tooth relic of the Buddha from Lingguang Temple in Beijing for a short visit to Ceylon in 1961. (Ceylon became a republic in 1972 and restored the ancient name of Lanka). To demonstrate the close ties between Sir Lanka and China, when Chairman Mao died in 1976, Sri Lanka declared eight days of mourning. The Bandaranayaka Memorial Conference Center gifted by China, which serves as the major convention venue in Colombo, stands proudly as a symbol of the bonds developed during this period. The Chinese Cultural Center, an aid project initiated by China, is located in the Bandaranaike Memorial International Conference Hall, and was inaugurated during the visit of President Xi Jinping in 2014. It is seen as a major initiative to foster cultural exchange as part of the strategic plan of the Maritime Silk Road. As in the past, cultural connections continue to play an important role under the reimagined Maritime Silk Road. The Chinese Cultural Center in Sri Lanka is not only the first of its kind built in South Asia, but also the first to be inaugurated by a Chinese head of state. In keeping with the tradition established over the centuries, close links are also being maintained between Sri Lankan Buddhist temples and leading Chinese Buddhist temples such as the White Horse Temple, the Shaolin Temple and the Guanyin Temple in Henan and the Lingguang Temple and the Yonghe Temple in Beijing. In 2021, our Embassy hosted a well-attended annual Wesak ceremony with high-level representatives from these temples in attendance.

Economic and Political Links Strengthened

It is said that Chairman Deng Xiaoping, who led China from December 1978 to November 1989, sent a delegation to Sri Lanka to study the Greater Colombo Economic Commission before creating the spectacularly successful Shenzhen Special Economic Zone, which set the tone for China's opening up and economic development. China embraced globalization and foreign investments poured in. In 2021, China received USD 168.34 billion in FDI, while China also invested USD 145.69 billion in other countries.

It was not only in assisting Sri Lanka in its economic development that China played a vital role. During Sri Lanka's conflict with the terrorist organization LTTE, China unconditionally provided arms and other assistance to bolster the country's military while Western countries withheld armaments as a means of exerting pressure on the government to stop the military advance on LTTE positions. China's steadfast support contributed in no small measure to the eventual defeat of the LTTE in May 2009 and the elimination of the terrorist threat to its territorial integrity. China also provided unconditional support to Sri Lanka at global fora, including at the UN Human Rights Council and the UN in New York. Subsequently, as the country sought desperately to recover from the devastation caused by terrorist attacks, Western assistance continued to be deliberately withheld, an economically resurgent China contributed magnificently to Sri Lanka's recovery efforts.

The Belt and Road Initiative

The Belt and Road Initiative (BRI), launched by President Xi Jinping in 2014, is intended to herald a new shared future for humanity. Today, it's a mammoth undertaking stretching across Asia, Africa and Europe with plans to construct roads, railways, ports, and, more recently, health, digital and space projects, creating physical and economic links, and enhancing trade and interconnectivity. However, it is not just a Chinese government initiative, but a collection of many different projects in multiple countries, financed through multiple avenues, including both Chinese and international banks and investment funds. According to a 2019 paper published by the Center for Economics and Business Research (CEBR), the BRI is likely to boost world GDP by USD 7.1 trillion annually within the next two decades. The Information Office of the Chinese government also reports that BRI has created more than 244,000 jobs for locals abroad.

In Sri Lanka, investment made through the BRI has made possible construction of Hambantota Harbor, Mattala Airport, multiple highways, Colombo Port City, the Performing Arts Center in Colombo and Lotus Tower. The Chinese government provided one billion Sri Lankan rupees (USD 5.1 million) for the construction of the Lotus Pond Performing Arts Center in Colombo, which was designed by the Beijing Institute of Architectural Designs (BIAD). The design was inspired by the twelfth-century lotus pond in Polonnaruwa, commissioned by King Parakramabahu. The 350 meter-high Colombo Lotus Tower, which is said to have been inspired by the Lotus Sutra, was built by a Chinese company and is the tallest self-supported structure in South Asia.

China's own stunning race toward development has been an inspiration for many developing countries, including Sri Lanka. Growing from a poor third world country, having opened up its economy, China has become the second biggest economy in the world, second only to the United States, and has modestly claimed to have reached a moderate level of prosperity. (The real GDP of China in 2020 was USD 14.72 trillion). China's trade to GDP ratio for 2021 was 37.43%, a 2.84% increase from 2020. In 2018, China exported USD 2.49 trillion in goods, while it imported USD 2.13 trillion. Beautiful highways crisscross the country, catering to an increasing number of privately owned vehicles. China is also the largest producer of electric vehicles and batteries in the world (having produced 3.4 million units in 2021, 57.4% of global EV production), and is home to the world's largest Tesla plant. China has developed advanced manufacturing capabilities and today it is the world's main exporter of manufactured goods.

Despite still relying on imported fossil fuels, it is also a leader in solar and wind power technology as well as a pioneer in nuclear and hydrogen power development. (China produces 70% of the world's solar panels). AI is also becoming a major part of everyday life in China. Sri Lankan students stand to gain much from pursuing studies in Chinese educational institutions, which cost much less than Western institutions. Almost 40,000 km of high speed railway tracks link the cities of this massive country. Cities vie with each other for architectural eminence and sheer glitz. China is surging ahead with cutting-edge technology that reaches into outer space and the depths of the ocean. Far from being the country that could barely feed millions in the 1970s, high-tech modern agriculture has also enabled China to produce an abundance of food for itself and even for export.

Part of cultural exchange through the BRI, the Association for Sri Lanka-China Social and Cultural Cooperation was established in 1997. Among its objectives, consistent with the cultural objectives of the Maritime Silk Road, are promoting people-to-people friendship and mutual understanding between Sri Lanka and China, studying the social and cultural development of China, conducting cooperation with other associations which have the same goals, implementing exchange programs in the social and cultural fields, preparing a plan for promoting Sri Lanka-China sister city programs, widening exchanges and cooperation between the performing and visual arts fields of Sri Lanka and China, developing relations in the fields of education and sports relations and working to build up the friendship and cooperation between Sri Lanka and China women and youth circles. Links have already been established between Colombo and Chengdu and Kandy and Qingdao with other intercity and interprovincial links being explored as we speak.

A Confucius Institute has been established at the University of Colombo with the objective of increasing knowledge and proficiency in the Chinese language and promoting Chinese culture. Hundreds of students have benefited from its services, but the institute also provides opportunities to scholars who seek to engage in research into relations between Sri Lanka and China.

The National Administration of Press and Publication of China has proposed a MoU with the Ministry of Buddhasasana, Religious and Cultural Affairs of Sri Lanka for the translation and publication of the classics of both countries into Chinese and Sinhala, having already chosen 50 Sinhala books and one English book for translation. In addition, the Chinese Culture Translation and Studies Support Network (CCTSS), with the assistance of the Martin Wickramasinghe Trust Fund and the Embassy of Sri Lanka, has already translated "Gamperaliya" into Chinese. Currently, an initiative has been undertaken to shoot a feature film highlighting the bilateral relationship.

In health and disease prevention, the manner in which China responded to the unprecedented threat posed by the COVID-19 pandemic has been a lesson for all. The world witnessed in amazement, as China mobilized governmental resources, medical facilities and its technological capabilities, along with its population to counter the threat. As we watched nervously, China brought the dreaded virus under control, starting with Wuhan. Thousands volunteered to help as the state mobilized its massive resource base. While COVID-19 may have been effectively brought under control, new viruses have already begun to raise their ugly heads and how China copes with these threats will be watched with eagerness.

China also contributed massive resources to counter the pandemic in other countries. It provided approximately two billion vaccine doses to the world, 200 million of which as gifts. It has also proposed that vaccines be made a "public good" without the constraints of proprietary rights. Sri Lanka benefited immensely as China provided 26 million doses, 3 million of which were free. Sri Lanka has been able to manage the epidemic effectively and has even opened the country to vaccinated tourists, largely due to the generosity of China, which also dispatched teams of medical personnel to assist other developing countries. At a time when traditional suppliers of drugs to Sri Lanka were attending to the needs of their own people with some even hoarding vaccine supplies, China came to Sri Lanka's aid. Our people will remember the significant gifts made by China and the vaccines supplied by Sinopharm for a long time to come as a remarkable act of solidarity and cooperation by China and the Chinese people.

In education, over 2000 Sri Lankan students are pursuing university degrees in China. Consistent with the goals of the BRI, they will take their new skills and knowledge home to benefit their own country. Many provinces of China have expressed interest in permitting more Sri Lankans to study in their cutting-edge institutions of higher learning, which is an excellent opportunity to further develop people-to-people contacts and mutual understanding. China has developed so rapidly in the last four decades that many outside have little understanding of China today and student exchanges are a useful way to increase awareness.

Much speculation has been generated about a Chinese debt trap that has ensnared Sri Lanka and of which other countries have been warned. Simply put, China owns less than 10% of Sri Lanka's external debt and it was Sri Lanka that sought funding from China for its infrastructure projects after it was denied by traditional sources. Sri Lanka needed the funding and China responded to its needs. Recently, Sri Lanka was also placed in a difficult situation as some expressed concerns about the port call of a Chinese scientific vessel. Consistent with its longstanding practice relating to port visits and its sovereign rights, Sri Lanka permitted the vessel to dock at Hambanthota Port.

Sri Lanka will also rely heavily on Chinese travelers to extricate itself from its financial crisis. 169 million Chinese traveled in 2019. If a fraction of this number traveling to Sri Lanka once the Chinese travel restrictions are relaxed, it even will assist Sri Lanka, long considered a tourist mecca, to generate a targeted $10 billion income annually from tourism. Sri Lanka boasts nine UNESCO-listed world heritage sites, including some of the world's oldest and most revered Buddhist religious sites, which is a big number for a small country. The most visited tourist and religious site in the country is the Temple of the Sacred Tooth Relic of the Buddha in Kandy, the last capital of the Sinhala kings. The only other known tooth relic of the Buddha is in Lingguang Temple in Beijing.

Ancient Anuradhapura, which was our capital from fourth-century BCE until the eleventh-century CE, with its enormous dagobas (pagodas) enshrining relics of the Buddha, built two millennia ago, and the sacred Bo Tree (pipal tree) that is believed to have been propagated from a branch of the Bo tree at Bodh Gaya under which the Buddha attained enlightenment are key attractions. The fifth-century Sigiriya citadel, with its amazing water and rock gardens and the palace on top of the Sigiriya rock, built by a pleasure-loving king, and its evocative frescoes of comely maidens, continues to be a major attraction.

Over 24% of the country is covered in forest and Sri Lanka has the largest concentration of Asian elephants in the wild (around 7000), which are strictly protected, as well as a large population of whales. It is possible to go whale watching in the morning and drive along dusty tracks in a nature reserve on an elephant safari in the afternoon. The country boasts of some of the cleanest golden beaches in the world and produces a range of mouth-watering sea food dishes. Traditional medicine plays a significant role in the health care of the country.

Reflections

As the BRI matures and more funding is channeled into projects in member countries, criticism may increase. However, the BRI has already addressed some of the early criticisms, including the need to be sensitive to environmental issues, protecting community interests (particularly those of indigenous people), and being sensitive to the political arena. To this end, China has publicly stated that it will no longer fund fossil fuel-based power generation. The expected investment of USD 4–8 trillion will undoubtedly make a massive difference and even those that have little interest in the needs of the developing world are now being forced to join the fray. It is a pity that that they waited until China launched its BRI to find funds instead of acting on their own. In an ideal world, one would expect countries with the ability to work together to help those who, after decades of independence, still cannot help themselves.

H.E. Dr. Palitha Kohona has been Sri Lanka's ambassador to China since 2021. Prior to this, Dr. Kohona served as the Permanent Representative of Sri Lanka to the United Nations from 2009 to 2015, before which he was the Permanent Secretary to the Ministry of Foreign Affairs of Sri Lanka and was the Head of the UN Treaty Section at the UN Office of Legal Affairs in New York. While in New York, he was also Chair of the UN GA Sixth Committee and Co-Chair of the UN Working Group on Biological Diversity Beyond National Jurisdiction. Dr. Kohona is an Honorary Professor at Utah Valley University and delivered lectures at Harvard, Yale, Columbia, NYU and Fordham. He has published extensively on environmental issues, including climate change financing and on the law of the sea. Hailing from Matale in Sri Lanka, he obtained an LLB from the University of Sri Lanka, an LLM from Australian National University in International Trade Law and his doctorate from Cambridge University in the UK. He has also been awarded a D. Litt (honoris causa) by the University of Peradeniya, Sri Lanka.

Open Access This chapter is licensed under the terms of the Creative Commons Attribution-NonCommercial-NoDerivatives 4.0 International License (http://creativecommons.org/licenses/by-nc-nd/4.0/), which permits any noncommercial use, sharing, distribution and reproduction in any medium or format, as long as you give appropriate credit to the original author(s) and the source, provide a link to the Creative Commons license and indicate if you modified the licensed material. You do not have permission under this license to share adapted material derived from this chapter or parts of it.

The images or other third party material in this chapter are included in the chapter's Creative Commons license, unless indicated otherwise in a credit line to the material. If material is not included in the chapter's Creative Commons license and your intended use is not permitted by statutory regulation or exceeds the permitted use, you will need to obtain permission directly from the copyright holder.

For a Useful Dialogue Between Spain and China

Rafael Dezcallar de Mazarredo

Spain and China have had diplomatic contacts for hundreds of years. Despite being interrupted in the mid-twentieth century, they formally resumed in 1973. This year we celebrate our 50th anniversary of diplomatic relations with a "Year of Culture and Tourism of Spain in China". We will organize exhibitions in China of artworks from major Spanish museums, concerts, and events highlighting the history of our friendly relations. We are working on all these projects together with the Chinese authorities.

The pandemic has drastically reduced contacts between China and the rest of the world. We hope that the elimination of the restrictions on mobility imposed by the Chinese authorities will allow the quick resumption of those contacts in many different fields, from the political, to the economic, educational, cultural, scientific, and touristic. It is important that our societies get in touch again. Delinking is not an option. Delinking would not be good for us, and it would not be good for the rest of the world. Not only in terms of trade and the economy, but from many other points of view too. There are many global issues on which China, Spain, and the EU need to work together: global health, the fight against climate change, food security, debt restructuring, the UN Sustainable Development Goals, as well as solutions to crises around the world.

We are not in favour of delinking. We are in favour of better managing existing links. For instance, the chronic imbalance in our trade relations could be in part corrected if Spanish firms enjoyed better access to the Chinese market. We need to establish a level playing field, in which the Spanish companies in China can operate in the same way as the Chinese companies operate in Spain. The current "Special Administrative Measures for Access of Foreign Investments" continue to impose barriers on foreign investment, while national security concerns also impose tight

---

Ambassador of the Kingdom of Spain to the People's Republic of China.

R. D. de Mazarredo (✉)
Beijing, China

© The Author(s) 2024
H. Wang and M. L. Miao (eds.), *The Future of China's Development and Globalization*, China and Globalization, https://doi.org/10.1007/978-981-99-7512-9_5

limits. As a result, Chinese firms have made investments in Spain in areas such as software, IT, communications, ports, and energy, which are areas in which Spanish firms are not able to invest in China.

Agricultural exports from Spain are also constrained by the requirement to sign specific agreements for each particular product, while the access of industrial goods is limited by the need to obtain a China Compulsory Certification (CCC). China is not part of the WTO Agreement on Government Procurement, which puts foreign firms at a disadvantage in public tenders. There are also problems with public subsidies and intellectual property, although there has been some progress in the latter.

A stronger presence of Spanish companies in the Chinese market could also benefit China. They could be of great help in the development of the service sector and the expansion of consumption in China. Both are important goals of the Chinese authorities. Spanish firms are very strong in sectors like fashion, design, cosmetics, financial services, or high quality food products.

In the industrial sector, we could intensify our cooperation in renewable energies, where China is a world leader and Spain also excels. In 2021, 47% of Spain's electric power was generated using renewable sources. The automobile sector, particularly electric mobility, or biotechnology are other areas in which we already have an important bilateral cooperation.

In this spirit of managing our links better, we would also like to open a practical dialogue on issues in which we do not necessarily agree. In fact, dialogue is particularly important when there are issues in which partners see things differently.

The Ukraine Conflict

One of these issues is Ukraine. The Russian invasion of Ukraine is a flagrant breach of the fundamental principles of the United Nations Charter, specifically sovereignty and territorial integrity. These principles are also at the core of China's foreign policy. Tolerating this aggression would mean tolerating the use of raw power.

Respecting a State's sovereignty implies respecting its peaceful decisions when conducting its foreign policy. Those decisions can never serve as an excuse for one State to invade another. The alleged "denazification" of Ukraine's democratically elected government is an insult to our collective intelligence, as well as an affront to the collective memory of the Ukrainian people and their unspeakable suffering under Nazism during World War II.

Russia's invasion is also a violation of the European security architecture, which is the result of relentless efforts spanning over generations, which were in the past actively supported by the Russian Federation. Moreover, Ukraine made a voluntary decision to undergo denuclearization and subsequently received guarantees from the Russian Federation. While only three nuclear powers—the Russian Federation, the United Kingdom and the United States—originally signed in 1994 the Budapest Memorandum on Security Assurances, China and France soon joined with individual assurances in separate documents.

Faced with this aggression, the European Union had to react. This is clearly not a "business as usual" moment for us. Remaining passive was not an option. It would have only invited further aggression in the future.

The EU has made a series of difficult decisions in order to face this menace. One of them has been to reinforce our defensive capabilities. NATO has also strengthened its deterrence measures and defence posture. Russia's attack on Ukraine is proof that countries that chose to join the Alliance after the collapse of the Soviet Union made the right choice. Even countries with a long history of neutrality like Finland and Sweden feel now threatened by the Russian invasion and have also decided to join NATO. All these changes send a strong message about what is happening today in Europe. It is a message which, alas, the Chinese media does not seem to have understood yet. But if China cares about its relations with Europe, which I believe it does, it is important that China understands it properly.

It is evident that NATO has never attacked Russia—such scenario is utterly unthinkable. NATO never considered the possibility of an invasion in Ukraine, nor has it set up a no-fly zone. Neither has NATO considered to extend their Article 5 to Ukraine.

China is not just any country. It is a permanent member of the United Nations Security Council and has a special relationship with Russia. This closeness can now be used to a positive end. It is essential that we put an end to Russia's invasion as soon as possible, stopping civilian deaths and ending a war that is threatening the security of us all, including China. Thanks to its relations with Russia, China is in a privileged position to help achieve this goal.

China has clearly expressed its wish for a swift end to the conflict. There are political, economic, and security reasons for that. Chinese leaders have recently declared that the use of nuclear weapons would be utterly unacceptable. The consequences of Russia's action against Ukraine are far from being constrained to Europe.

China's attitude towards the war in Ukraine will affect its image in Europe, but also in the rest of the world. China has a chance to send a powerful message to the rest of the international community, as a nation committed to maintaining peace and security. This is also a unique opportunity for China in its relations with Europe.

Human Rights

Another issue on which we should improve our dialogue is the protection of human rights.

Human rights are important, because they defend human dignity.

In 1948, just after the end of World War II, the United Nations General Assembly adopted the Universal Declaration of Human Rights. Its purpose was to prevent the widespread violations of human rights that had forever tainted the first half of the twentieth century from happening again.

Human dignity is at the very core of human rights. Every single person's freedom to decide about his or her destiny is precious in its own right. Nobody can be forced against his or her will to be an instrument to achieve other goals.

Human rights are universal because human dignity is an universal value. It must be protected in all places, in all climates, and in all cultures. All major civilizations and religions place human dignity at the core of their doctrines.

Human rights are also indivisible. Social, economic, and cultural rights should never be valued to the detriment of civil and political rights, nor vice versa. This is why the international community has approved two International Covenants, one on social, economic, and cultural rights, and the other on civil and political rights. Both have been signed by the People's Republic of China.

It is, of course, necessary to consider the socio-political and cultural realities of different countries where fundamental human rights and freedoms must be defended. However, those differences must not become a pretext not to defend them. Neither should they relativize their value, nor render them void of meaning. That would render human dignity equally void of meaning. The different conditions existing in each country should be the starting point for a frank, constructive dialogue. The starting point, not the conclusion of the conversation. Nor should they be an insurmountable obstacle to reach common ground.

Human rights should not be considered as a tool to criticise particular countries, but as an instrument for the defence of our citizens worldwide. No country is perfect. No country is free from facing challenges in the defence of human rights in their own territory. The point is not to deny the existence of those challenges, but to join forces in order to look for honest solutions to them.

Form and context matter greatly in this field. Human rights should be discussed both privately and in public forums. Often a discreet exchange will go further than public criticism. In fact, the latter is often an expression of frustration at the lack of results of a quiet approach.

For all those reasons, human rights should be regarded as a normal element in our relations. Spain has strongly advocated on issues where our experience can give added value to the promotion of human rights. Besides civil and political rights, I would like to highlight issues such as the death penalty, the promotion of the rights of persons with disabilities, the fight for gender equality, the right of access to drinkable water and adequate sanitation, and the fight against discrimination on the grounds of sexual orientation and gender identity. With the advances made in the eradication of poverty, China has important experiences to share in this field.

We must find ways to address all human rights. This will demonstrate that international relations are useful to address not only the main political questions of our times, but also the problems that affect our citizens in their immediate, daily lives.

H.E. Mr. Rafael Dezcallar de Mazarredo has been Ambassador of Spain to the People's Republic of China since 2018. Ambassador Dezcallar joined the Foreign Service in 1983 and previously served as Ambassador of Spain to Ethiopia and the Ambassador of Spain to the Federal Republic of Germany. Ambassador Dezcallar was born in Palma de Mallorca,1955. He holds a Master's Degree in Political Sciences from Stanford University. He has also published several articles in Spanish and foreign newspapers and magazines, including *El País*, *ABC Política Exterior*, and *The Washington Quarterly*.

Open Access This chapter is licensed under the terms of the Creative Commons Attribution-NonCommercial-NoDerivatives 4.0 International License (http://creativecommons.org/licenses/by-nc-nd/4.0/), which permits any noncommercial use, sharing, distribution and reproduction in any medium or format, as long as you give appropriate credit to the original author(s) and the source, provide a link to the Creative Commons license and indicate if you modified the licensed material. You do not have permission under this license to share adapted material derived from this chapter or parts of it.

The images or other third party material in this chapter are included in the chapter's Creative Commons license, unless indicated otherwise in a credit line to the material. If material is not included in the chapter's Creative Commons license and your intended use is not permitted by statutory regulation or exceeds the permitted use, you will need to obtain permission directly from the copyright holder.

Status and Prospects of EU–China Relations

Jorge Toledo Albiñana

Introduction

From the establishment of diplomatic relations in 1975, to the 2003 commitment for a comprehensive strategic partnership, to the European Council Conclusions on China of June 2023, the balance of challenges and opportunities in the EU–China relationship has shifted over time. Recently, the EU's China policy has been experiencing a period of recalibration, of reassessment and redefinition, to reflect changes in China and on the global stage.

At the European Council meeting at the end of June 2023, the European Union Heads of State and Government reaffirmed the EU's multifaceted policy approach towards China that was first adopted in the March 2019 in the "EU-China: A strategic Outlook" document, where China is simultaneously a partner, a competitor and a systemic rival. At the Council, the EU leaders underlined that *"despite their different political and economic systems, the European Union and China have a shared interest in pursuing constructive and stable relations, anchored in respect for the rules-based international order, balanced engagement and reciprocity."*

This strategic discussion took place after an intense spring, filled with numerous high-level interactions between European and Chinese interlocutors following the post-pandemic reopening of China's borders in early 2023. After three years where China had shut itself off from the world, in-person meetings could finally take place again. For the first time in three years, it was possible to break the bubbles that the restrictions had created.

Even if flights had not returned to pre-pandemic levels, Europeans could start experiencing China again, and Chinese could now come to Europe. Returning visitors from both sides may have found that they had arrived in a different place compared to

---

Ambassador of the European Union to the People's Republic of China.

J. T. Albiñana (✉)
Beijing, China

© The Author(s) 2024
H. Wang and M. L. Miao (eds.), *The Future of China's Development and Globalization*, China and Globalization, https://doi.org/10.1007/978-981-99-7512-9_6

a few years ago. This is why the importance of resuming people-to-people exchanges cannot be emphasised enough. It is the only way for both sides to start bridging the gap between China and Europe that grew during the pandemic.

After three years, in-person high-level meetings and dialogues between EU and China resumed even before the end of the pandemic restrictions with the visit by the President of the European Council, Charles Michel, to Beijing on 1 December 2022 with European Commission President Ursula von der Leyen later visiting Beijing on 7 April 2023. As she had underlined in her speech on EU–China relations one week before her visit, how we manage our bilateral relationship with China will be a determining factor for our future economic prosperity and national security.

Official dialogues have also resumed. After a four year suspension, the EU–China Human Rights Dialogue resumed in Brussels on 27 February 2023. Executive Vice President of the European Commission, Frans Timmermans, visited Beijing from July 3rd to 5th and held the fourth High Level Dialogue on Climate and Environment. After the summer of 2023, High Level Dialogues on digital issues, on economy and trade, as well as the Strategic Dialogue between the High Representative of the European Union for Foreign Affairs/Vice President of the European Commission, Josep Borrell, with his Chinese counterpart are forthcoming. In addition, other dialogues on agriculture, circular economy, ocean affairs, energy, water, regional policy and other technical meetings and dialogues are already planned.

At the same time, we should have no illusions that these dialogues are being held in the same environment as before the pandemic. The world has changed enormously since then. For Europe, one of the most momentous changes is related to Russia's illegal and unjustified war of aggression against Ukraine. The EU has taken a number of unprecedented initiatives to support Ukraine in areas that were previously unthinkable. Ever since I began my role as European Union Ambassador to China in September 2022, one of my most urgent tasks has been to explain the profound impact Russia's illegal full-scale invasion of Ukraine has had on the EU as well as globally, but also why this war is so relevant to EU–China relations. For us in Europe, this is a fundamental, even existential, issue. When Russia launched its full-scale invasion against Ukraine in the early hours of 24 February 2022, right at the EU's borders, it reminded us Europeans of some of the worst episodes that unleashed World War II in Europe. This war goes against everything that the European Union—a peace project at its core—stands for.

Russia's illegal aggression has been condemned by over 140 UN member states, but unfortunately not by China. China has not recognised Ukraine's right under the UN Charter for self-defence in the face of such aggression. Instead, China continues to place an abstract concept of Russia's "legitimate security concerns" on par with the principles of the UN Charter. I am sometimes told that the roots of this "conflict" are complex, but the facts about the war are simple. We are faced with an aggressor that has invaded another sovereign country, and a victim whose internationally recognised borders have been assaulted and territories illegally occupied. The aggressor has even organised fake referenda in an attempt to illegally annex those territories! No "legitimate security concerns" can justify this. It is precisely this kind of aggression that the United Nations was created to prevent, and represents a flagrant violation of the most basic principles of the UN Charter. This is why the European Union is helping Ukraine to defend itself and why we demand the withdrawal of the Russian troops from Ukrainian territory to completely restore its territorial integrity and sovereign independence. There is no doubt that Russia's war against Ukraine directly affects EU–China relations. From the European Union side, we have consistently cited China's particular responsibility, as a permanent member of the United Nations Security Council, to safeguard the principles and values that lie at the heart of the UN Charter. We also ask China to play a constructive role in advancing a just peace, based on upholding the sovereignty and territorial integrity of Ukraine. We closely monitor China's relationship with Russia, in particular vis-à-vis the Russian war machine. Our measures towards Russia, including sanctions, are aimed to limit Russia's capacity to wage this illegal war, and we attach great importance at preventing their circumvention.

Also in China, things are shifting. It is striking how much focus there now is in China on security and control, in an ever-expanding range of areas. China is also changing as an international actor, and we can see how China's extraordinary economic, technological, political and military rise over the last decades has led to new geopolitical adjustments and alignments. There is a growing perception by outside observers that this rise is no longer as "peaceful" as it used to be, especially in the Indo-Pacific region and particularly in the South China Sea. We also have concerns that China is trying to use its economic power and influence to reshape, reinterpret or even rewrite the international order—the same international order, based on effective multilateralism and international law, without which we would not have had the globalisation and development that both China and the European Union have benefitted so greatly from.

As the EU and China prepare for our various dialogues, we do so against the backdrop of a changed world. It is clear that we cannot go back in time, no matter how much we would wish to do so. As High Representative/Vice President Borrell so aptly pointed out in his blog in April this year: *"…the world has changed and so has China. The time of the "mondialisation heureuse" is over. The benefits of the economic integration are being re-evaluated through the lens of national security. We have to face the climate emergency, the consequences of the pandemic, and Russia's war of aggression against Ukraine. This war has fuelled shocks on supply chains, and a food and energy crisis. In this context, we believe that China must exercise more responsibility, also for security and peace. It cannot avoid this. If we want an international order where cooperation prevails over confrontation, everyone must fully exercise their responsibilities to ensure respect for international law."*

At the same time, there is an imperative for the EU and China to work together on facing global challenges. The European Council reaffirmed that the EU will continue to engage with China to tackle global challenges and encouraged China to take more ambitious action on climate change and biodiversity, health and pandemic preparedness, food security, disaster reduction, debt relief and humanitarian assistance.

EU–China Trade and Investment Relations

From a trade and investment point of view, the challenges facing China and its economic model have continued to grow, whilst problems related to market access/a level playing field remain and, in some sectors, have even worsened. Against increasing geopolitical tensions, there are growing concerns related to critical dependencies and economic coercion.

At the same time, the EU's economic relationship with China continues to be consequential. In 2022, trade in goods reached EUR 856 billion, or EUR 2.3 billion in two way trade every day. EU Foreign Direct Investment into China amounted to EUR 8.1 billion in 2022, the lowest since 2018 (however, not far from the average of the last four years of EUR 8.5 billion). Most of the investments came from large companies that already have significant operations in China.

Globally, the "Open Strategic Autonomy," announced in the EU Trade Policy review of 2021, drives EU's trade and investment approach. It means that whilst we remain open to trade and investment, we need to be able to defend our interests in case other partners do not respect the multilateral rules. Being able to defend ourselves against illegal behaviour is necessary in order to maintain the openness of our economy, instead of resorting to protectionist policies. In a nutshell, we work with others whenever we can, and autonomously whenever we must.

With this background, we have been adopting several instruments that will help us defend our interests when we face trade distortions or unfair competition, such as the International Procurement Instrument (IPI) and the Foreign Subsidies Regulation, or the Anti-Coercion Instrument, on which a political agreement has recently been found. Our existing and new autonomous instruments, which are not country-specific, are to protect the EU's interests when faced with economic coercion, trade distortions or unfair competition. In addition, the EU has advanced its diversification strategy by diversifying imports and by enhancing the resilience of supply chains.

Whilst we were busy working on our toolbox, two things happened that changed the situation dramatically: COVID and Russia's aggression against Ukraine.

The pandemic caused disruptions in global supply chains, and the EU discovered that for a handful of critically important products, we depend too heavily on too few suppliers. Furthermore, Russia's brutal invasion of Ukraine and its consequences also revealed the pitfalls of our energy dependency from Russia. China's ambiguity about the war and the "no-limits partnership" with Russia also had a profound impact on the way Europe sees China.

Communication and meaningful bilateral engagement remain a necessary and important part of the EU–China relationship. Importantly, engagement works in parallel with our autonomous instruments. We wish to continue to develop our relations in areas where we have a mutual benefit, such as handling global challenges such as WTO reform and climate change. But we equally want to engage China to reset our relationship on the basis of transparency and predictability, setting fair terms and removing irritants to bilateral trade in areas in which there are no security considerations; in certain cases, there is simply no alternative to China for European business.

Whilst EU channels of communication with China have indeed remained open—for example, through the visit of Commission President Ursula von der Leyen in April—unfortunately, tangible results have mostly not materialised. To safeguard its credibility, it is important that China deliver on its commitments. This applies in particular to economic and trade relations, where the EU and its Member States have long pending requests related to better market access and a level playing field for European companies with investments in China.

There is a clear lack of progress on market access, as witnessed by the EU Chamber's position paper, which lists as many as 967 market access barriers in China. A growing number of barriers and measures disadvantage European companies, which are getting more cautious about bringing their money and business here because the regulatory environment lacks transparency. This is not good for China. If investment caps, unpredictable treatment and regulatory issues are pushing away investment, capital, goods, experience and skills from the Chinese economy—then businesses on both sides stand to lose.

Observers are therefore increasingly questioning whether the EU–China engagement can deliver concrete results, especially when political commitment, even at highest level, does not translate into regulatory action at technical level.

For instance, at the 2019 EU–China Summit, work on adherence to international standards and market access were highlighted as main areas of work and the parties resolved to achieve concrete results by the 2020 EU–China Summit. It was agreed to pay particular attention to recognise the animal disease regionalisation principle that would apply in case of animal disease outbreaks (for example, African Swine Fever in pigs or Highly Pathogenic Avian Influenza in poultry). Regionalisation would allow the export of pork and poultry and its products to continue without disruptions and this would lead to the expansion of mutual market access for food and agricultural products in a transparent and predictable manner. However, after the 2019 Summit, no progress was made. The 2022 High Level Economic and Trade Dialogue (HED) again agreed to prioritise progress on a regionalisation approach in particular for African Swine Fever. A technical working group on regionalisation has been set up—yet, as we prepare for the forthcoming High Level Economic Trade and Dialogue, we regret the lack of tangible results. We expect an EU–China agreement on regionalisation, nothing less, as we want our engagement to deliver.

Even in the services sector (financial services and beyond), where there have been a number of measures implemented since 2017 that have eased access on the part of international investors, markets remain firmly under the control of domestic companies in China. Almost all of them are state-owned, with international market shares being in the very low single digits. International investments are directed at small niches of the market with the explicit goal on the part of policy-makers to transfer knowledge and skills in due course and thus help develop the Chinese market and domestic companies.

China's abrupt end to its COVID-zero policy at the end of 2022 and the reopening may lead to some revival in European FDI in China, as travel by company executives is again possible. However, geopolitical tensions, China's weakened medium-term growth prospects and general politicisation of trade and economic relations have eroded business confidence. General perspectives do not look good in this respect, as witnessed by the results of the European Chamber's 2023 Business Confidence Survey.

Perhaps more importantly, the Chinese government has for a long time already put into place various measures and policies which have pushed decoupling from the rest of the world. China has used economic coercion to penalise trading partners over political disputes, as witnessed by Lithuania and Australia. The focus on national security and dual circulation, as well as the growing role of the State in the economy, are unlikely to disappear. The Chinese government can enact sudden policy changes that may disrupt supply chains, independently of whether the changes pose problems to third countries or foreign companies.

The end of the pandemic, also in China, now offers the prospect of further realising some of the potential that remained latent in recent years. For China's decision-makers, this year presents an important opportunity to show that China is serious about reform and opening up, that it is serious about addressing the concerns of foreign investors and that it is able to address the imbalances in its trade and investment relationship with its partners.

As President Ursula von der Leyen underscored, the European Union has no interest in decoupling from China. Nevertheless, it needs to de-risk. This approach clearly resonates as well with our international partners, as it was confirmed amongst the leaders of the G7 recently in Hiroshima in May this year, and later on by several others.

In order to reduce our economy's vulnerabilities to external shocks, on 20 June 2023, the European Commission and the High Representative published a Joint Communication on a European Economic Security Strategy. This Joint Communication focuses on minimising risks arising from certain economic flows in the context of increased geopolitical tensions and accelerated technological shifts, whilst preserving maximum levels of economic openness and dynamism.

The Strategy proposes to set up a framework for building a shared understanding of risks to the EU's economic security. It also aims to ensure the most effective and coordinated use of existing instruments to address those risks, be that at the EU, national or business level. In light of evolving risks, the EU also proposes to assess the effectiveness of existing tools and consider new measures that may be needed.

Our strategy rests on the following key pillars: promoting the EU's competitiveness; protecting against risks; and partnering with the broadest possible range of countries to address shared concerns and interests.

The fundamental principles of proportionality and precision continue to guide our work. Our response is to maximise the benefits of openness, whilst minimising vulnerabilities through a concerted EU approach to economic security.

The EU's Economic Security Strategy ultimately sets out a framework that could make each level and actor in the EU stronger and ensure that they can use their respective instruments more effectively. Any approach that the EU takes is rooted in the rules-based international system, and any economic security action is in line with EU's international obligations, including the WTO rules.

In the context of EU–China trade and investment relations, it is important to repeatedly underscore that the intention behind de-risking is not by any means to stop trade and investment or to limit China's technological development. The EU intends to stay open for trade and investment but is also adamant on diversifying its sources of supply. Our positioning factors in the evolution of China's own policy response to the use of autonomous tools and unilateral actions, as well as its evolving economic interests.

Climate, Biodiversity and Environment

When looking at EU–China engagement on climate, biodiversity and environment, China's contribution is key for achieving the Paris Agreement goals. With big economic power comes a great responsibility for the related emissions, too. China has seen tremendous economic growth in the past few decades. Its per capita emissions now exceed the EU's by a third. This is another reason why ambitious emission reductions in China are vital. China made remarkable progress in renewable energy already and may even surpass its own objectives. There is value in under promising and over delivering, but setting ambitious targets is important too: it inspires others to follow suit.

Throughout our dialogue with China on the environment and climate, we have been exploring avenues for collaboration in areas such as methane reduction, climate adaptation strategies, the circular economy, pollution control, biodiversity conservation, as well as combatting deforestation and wildlife trafficking. These have been the key issues that were addressed in the successful last edition, in-person for the first time in four years, of the High Level Climate and Environmental Dialogue that was held in Beijing at the beginning of July 2023 by Vice-Premier Ding and Executive European Commission Vice President Timmermans.

A major topic of EU–China discussion on climate is the Carbon Border Adjustment Mechanism (CBAM). It is important to underline that the EU's CBAM initiative is not at all a protectionist trade measure. It is exclusively a climate measure, the only aim of which is to avoid that Europe's strong efforts to reduce its own emissions do not lead to emissions being just moved ("carbon leakage") to other parts of the world. China is actually in a favourable situation as it already has in place an emissions trading system that, if extended to other important emitting economic sectors, would result in a CBAM exemption of Chinese exports to the EU.

The Need for Dialogue

De-risking not only refers to aspects of economics and trade, but also to the need for an open and frank exchange between the EU and China. This is why we have set up several high-level dialogues—such as the one on economics and trade, on digital issues, environment and climate, as well as the Strategic Dialogue. We also have consultations in other areas, such as human rights, security and defense, and a number of sectoral dialogues. The EU is committed to a summit—but a summit with concrete deliverables.

The EU will never shy away from raising issues of concern. These are typically "systemic" issues like the respect for human rights as enshrined in international law and their universality and indivisibility, which are being challenged and reinterpreted by China. The EU remains firmly committed to the promotion of respect for human rights and fundamental freedoms. We continue to be seriously concerned about the human rights situation in China and particularly in regions like Xinjiang or Tibet, as well as about the recent developments in Hong Kong. However, we welcome the resumption of the bilateral Dialogue on Human Rights earlier this year.

As we look to the future of EU–China relations, the challenge before us is to embark in a constructive and constant dialogue to make our partnerships work to solve global issues, to create a level playing field for our companies to invest and trade with China and to manage our differences, all of it using dialogue as the instrument. This will serve the interests of the EU, China and the world. It is a sign of the maturity of our relations that we can engage in dialogue even on matters where we disagree, and my assumption is that both sides are aware of the responsibility we both have to manage our relations responsibly and for the greater good.

Ambassador Jorge Toledo Albiñana is a career diplomat from Spain. After taking his Degree in Law and entering the Diplomatic School in Spain, he joined the Spanish Foreign Service in 1989. Since then, except for three years in Senegal, where he was Ambassador of Spain from 2008 to 2011, his career has been devoted mostly to European Union Affairs. Amongst others, he was Spanish Secretary of State for the EU and European Affairs. In Asia, he has been posted to India and Japan before arriving to China in September 2022 as the Ambassador of the European Union. Ambassador Toledo strongly believes in the European integration and that only together can EU Member States have a meaningful relation and dialogue with a strong world power as China. He is married and has two children.

Open Access This chapter is licensed under the terms of the Creative Commons Attribution-NonCommercial-NoDerivatives 4.0 International License (http://creativecommons.org/licenses/by-nc-nd/4.0/), which permits any noncommercial use, sharing, distribution and reproduction in any medium or format, as long as you give appropriate credit to the original author(s) and the source, provide a link to the Creative Commons license and indicate if you modified the licensed material. You do not have permission under this license to share adapted material derived from this chapter or parts of it.

The images or other third party material in this chapter are included in the chapter's Creative Commons license, unless indicated otherwise in a credit line to the material. If material is not included in the chapter's Creative Commons license and your intended use is not permitted by statutory regulation or exceeds the permitted use, you will need to obtain permission directly from the copyright holder.

On the Issues—The Immense Potential in Cooperation with China

Norway: Creating a System of Economic Governance Tailored to Benefit All

Signe Brudeset

Introduction

"*The goal of the economic policy is economic growth that contributes to work for everyone, more equitable distribution that reduces social and geographical differences, and a strong welfare state with good services regardless of people's wallets and place of residence*". This is the first paragraph of Norway's National Budget for 2023, and it shows that there is a close link between economic policy and welfare services in Norway.

It also shows the importance Norway attaches to having a strong workforce, which is seen as its most important resource. The main goal of the Norwegian employment policy is to make it possible for as many people as possible to participate in the labour market and contribute to society. This is a prerequisite for the sustainability of Norway's welfare schemes; *we must create before we can share.*

In this chapter, I would like to present certain traits of the Norwegian model of economic governance that have contributed to realization of the current Norwegian system of welfare transfers and services. This welfare system has, in interaction with the coordinated labour market model, contributed to a high level of social, economic, and gender equality throughout Norwegian society. The priorities and circumstances of different countries vary, and the features of the Norwegian model might not be feasible for or transferable to other countries. This chapter aims to show how the Norwegian model has succeeded in fostering a trajectory of economic growth and development tailored to Norway's particular situation and preconditions. Hopefully, it will carry interest also beyond Norway's borders and lay a foundation for discussions on topics such as employment policy, redistribution, gender equality, and welfare policies across cultures and boundaries. It is important to develop dialogue

---

Ambassador of the Kingdom of Norway to the People's Republic of China.

S. Brudeset (✉)
Beijing, China

and experience sharing on these issues, and at the Norwegian Embassy in Beijing, we follow China's "common prosperity" policy with great interest.

The Norwegian model has never followed a fixed blueprint and is a label given in retrospect for the way in which the organization of our society has evolved. It includes responsible economic management aimed at providing a high level of employment through monetary and fiscal policy, an organized working life with coordinated wage setting based on cooperation and negotiations between the associations of employees, employers, and the government, as well as universal welfare services. The Norwegian system and culture expect that all who are capable of participating in the labour market do so, and seek—through free training and education—to facilitate everyone's inclusion in the workforce. Norway has thus a relatively high retirement age, normally 67 for both men and women. Our high labour market participation, together with a broad tax base, generates income to the state, which in turn can be redistributed for the common good of society.

In the wake of broad class compromises in the 1930s, the Norwegian welfare system was gradually developed in the post-World War II era, at the same time that our Scandinavian neighbours were building up theirs. A universal welfare system financed by taxes is an important part of the Norwegian model, contributing to a low level of income inequality, a high degree of gender equality with high female employment rates as well as free education from primary school and accessible and affordable kindergarten before that.

Norwegians have always lived off their national resources and taken advantage of the possibilities the land and ocean have given them. The discovery of oil resources on the Norwegian continental shelf in 1969 has contributed to strong government finances. But, as several other countries have experienced, abundant petroleum resources are no guarantee of good and stable economic results. In order to maintain sustainable welfare services, it is more important to promote a high degree of employment through long-term economic policies, and sound management of human and natural resources.

Main Tools of Economic Governance

The Norwegian Tax System

A healthy tax system is key to maintaining a prosperous economy and funding universal public services and welfare schemes, which have made Norway an affluent and safe society. To achieve this, the Norwegian tax system is designed to promote fair distribution, value creation, and work incentives. As a central tool in the government's policies to foster economic growth, tax revenues are also used to reduce inequalities between people socially, economically, and geographically. To promote these goals and ensure sufficient revenue, a broad tax base and a high level of participation in the labour force are indispensable prerequisites. Making sure that those with the highest incomes and most wealth contribute most helps generate sufficient revenue and a fair tax burden, but it also fosters trust. Besides taxation of income and capital, Norway also collects a value-added tax (VAT) on goods and, since 2001, on services. The VAT amounts to 15% or 25% depending on the goods or services to be purchased. The corporate income tax is 22%.

In general, Norwegian taxpayers seem to be willing to pay taxes. Reasons for this include transparency, which the national bureau Statistics Norway contributes to, and efficiency, through the digitalization of tax declarations and the tax authorities' services. Combined with the opportunities to draw politicians to account, there is a high degree of trust in the system and that the money is well spent. Citizens seem to accept paying taxes when they see that they are used for high-quality services such as universal education, healthcare, and income security, which almost everyone benefits from over the course of their lifetime.

Income, wealth, and opportunities are often unevenly distributed geographically. To even out these disparities, successive Norwegian governments have developed policies that promote geographical redistribution. Payroll tax varies between regions from 14% in most of the country to zero in the northernmost part. Subsidies are offered to various industries located in the periphery, such as agriculture where national food security is an important aim. People living in certain rural areas are also offered free kindergarten and rapid down-payment on student loans.

In a world of sweeping transformations, Norwegian society is also changing—driven by an ageing population, the transition to green growth, digitalization, and globalization. To ensure the tax system's feasibility, reviews are carried out on a regular basis.

The Government Pension Fund and Budgetary Rule

Redistributing Revenue Across Generations

When oil and gas were discovered on the Norwegian continental shelf in 1969, it sparked discussions about how revenue should be handled in order to benefit all Norwegians, including future generations. For the initial years, investments were substantially higher than revenues. In 1990, Norway established a Sovereign Wealth Fund, today known as the Government Pension Fund Global. After the first deposits were made in 1996, surging oil and gas production brought rapid growth of the fund over the following years, mirroring the high tax rates of almost 80% on surpluses in the petroleum sector. The state's revenues from oil and gas extraction are now kept in the fund, together with the returns on the fund's investments. Saving money for the welfare of future generations, the fund's statutes and investment rules are regulated by the Parliament. The organization of the fund is supervised by the Ministry of Finance. Norges Bank[1] Investment Management (NBIM) is operationally responsible for the

---

[1] In English: Bank of Norway.

investments of the fund and operates independently and free from political interference. As the fund's capital cannot be invested in Norway, the majority of investments are made in low-risk international equities and bonds. At the time of writing, the fund stands at close to $1.4 trillion and is the second largest sovereign wealth fund in the world.

In accordance with its statutes and corporate governance objectives, NBIM makes public its expectations of how companies in its portfolio should address global challenges in their operations. The expectations are formulated in line with standards such as the UN Global Compact and the OECD's guidelines for multinational companies, and largely coincide with the UN's sustainability goals. NBIM has prepared expectation documents in the following eight areas: climate change, water management, human rights, children's rights, tax transparency, anti-corruption, ocean sustainability, and biodiversity and ecosystems.

The Budgetary Rule

To avoid the so-called resource curse, around the millennium visionary politicians developed a fiscal rule of thumb to determine how much of the petroleum wealth saved in the fund the state can use to finance its expenses every year. Effective from 2002 on and named "*the budgetary rule*", this fiscal rule says that "*transfers from the fund to the central government budget shall, over time, follow the expected real return on the fund*". This is today estimated to about 3%. As "*significant emphasis is placed on evening out economic fluctuations and contributing to sound capacity utilization and low unemployment*", the annual transfers may exceed 3% in difficult times and be well below that in normal times. The transfers are thus used in a counter-cyclical manner.

The budgetary rule has allowed a gradual in-phasing of petroleum revenues into the Norwegian economy, without risking Dutch disease and surging cost-inflation. The fiscal policy framework has thus aimed to preserve the real value of the fund for the benefit of future generations. Conversely, the fund and the fiscal rule insulate the budget from short-term fluctuations in petroleum revenues, and leave space for fiscal policy to counteract economic downturns. In the event of large oscillations in the value of the fund or in factors that affect the structural fiscal deficit of the mainland economy (excluding oil and gas), the adjustment in the use of fund revenues shall be smoothed out over several years, based on an assessment of its real rate of return in the next few years.

To sum up, the budgetary rule implies that government expenditure over time shall equal government revenues from the mainland economy plus the expected future real return from the fund. This rule has been followed under changing governments and parliamentarian majorities since its adoption around the turn of the millennium.

State Ownership

Private ownership is, as a rule, preferred in Norway's mixed market economy and direct state ownership requires a special justification. The extent of state ownership is assessed in light of what is considered the most suitable alternative for achieving societal goals in contexts where the market alone does not provide the best socio-economic outcomes. In the area of common resources, the state owns a higher share in the domains of energy and the extraction of natural resources, but private companies also participate in this sector and contribute to a competitive business environment. It is, however, worth underlining that state-owned companies in Norway operate at an arms-length distance from the government, and are subject to the same rules and objectives as privately owned companies. The state can exercise its rights as a shareholder, but the company is managed and operated independently by its management personnel and board of directors. The latter is appointed by the Minister of Trade and Industry. Typically, the government focuses on the rate of return with many state-owned companies listed on the stock exchange and include private shareholders as well.

Since the petroleum sector is particularly profitable due to high resource rent, there is an additional 56% special tax rate on top of the normal corporate income tax of 22%, resulting in a full 78% tax on profits. The government also receives revenues from its 67% majority share of the Equinor energy company, and direct ownership of petroleum fields. All in all, about 90% of the petroleum resource rent goes to the government. Given the profitability of the petroleum sector, this generates significant revenues for the state.

The high tax rate has not been an obstacle in attracting foreign companies to the industry. The Norwegian government has developed flexible and risk-friendly policies that attract safe investments from foreign investors.

In October 2022, the government released a white paper on state ownership that aims for greener and more active state ownership. The Government will also develop and strengthen the state's expectations of the companies it owns, including expectations in terms of climate, nature, risk management, transparency and reporting, working conditions, and remuneration of senior executives. By defining clear expectations of its companies, the state can take a more active role in pushing the companies it owns towards a greener, fairer, and more sustainable path.

Norway's Welfare Society

The post-World War II era in Norway was characterized by political stability and broad consensus across the (main) parties. In 1945, all political parties ran for election on the same political platform, with a distinct social democratic flavour. Across party lines, there was broad consensus about avoiding a return to the class struggle of the interwar period. The aim of the government, supported by social partners and private business, was to lay a foundation for strong economic growth and secure increased living standards and social security. Empowered by sound economic development, the government introduced a range of public welfare and education services in the ensuing decades.

The discovery of oil on the Norwegian continental shelf in the late 1960s boosted investment in the Norwegian economy and fueled expansion of the universal welfare system, which was based on equal access to social services for everyone. Whilst the level of most welfare benefits depends on how many years individuals have been working and their earnings, it is an aim that the quality of public services should be such that it is accepted by individuals with high incomes as well.

Today's public welfare schemes include, amongst others, free healthcare (beyond a small deductible) and education, generous maternity and paternity leave, retirement and disability pensions, unemployment benefits, 100% sick pay, and other welfare services and benefits. In addition to ensuring a strong social safety net, the interaction between the welfare system and a well-functioning labour market with small wage gaps, has contributed to a high employment rate, low income inequality, a high degree of transparency, equal opportunities, and social trust.

Internationally, there is a widely held perception that strong, overarching welfare services make people lazy, hindering innovation and economic growth. However, the Norwegian experience has been that welfare services such as free education and affordable and accessible healthcare, kindergarten and elderly care, enable more people—and women in particular—to work and contribute to economic growth. Thus, Norway has a high rate of employment especially amongst women. State funding is also utilized to support entrepreneurship and innovation, and some of the largest state-owned companies are at the forefront of supporting and investing in efforts that contribute to a greener future.

Welfare Services That Promote Gender Equality

From the 1970s in particular, a fundamental goal underpinning the Norwegian model has been to bring as many citizens as possible into the labour market regardless of gender and social background. The expansion of public services and higher education in the 1970s brought about a substantial increase in the number of women working outside of the home. As the population has become more heterogeneous, however, Norwegian policymakers have in recent years recognized the need to develop a more inclusive labour market that not only makes it possible for men and women, but also for immigrants, the young, the elderly, and people with disabilities to find gainful employment and continue working longer. Leveraging the potential of the entire population increases production and societal/macro productivity, and increases the state's tax revenues.

Breaking with the traditional model of the housewife enabled more women to join the workforce, and created a dual-earner family structure that has contributed greatly to Norway's economic and social progress over the past 50 years. In 1972, the employment rate of women in Norway was 44.7%; today it is 69.5%, only six percentage points lower than that of men. Although gender equality is good for the economy, enlarging the tax base, creating value, and forming the basis for a sustainable welfare state, there are more women working part-time than men and many immigrant women are outside the labour market.

The Norwegian Gender Equality Act was introduced 45 years ago, and today, the share of women in Parliament is close to 45%, whilst the share is 47% in the cabinet. There are several policies in place in Norway that promote gender equality in the workplace. One is the distribution of parental leave between men and women. Parents get 46 weeks of parental leave when a child is born. This period is divided into a maternal quota (15 weeks), a paternal quota (15 weeks), as well as a joint period of 16 weeks, in which the parents can decide who will work and who will stay home with the kids. Although this scheme treats mothers and fathers equally and allows every family to divide their parental quota in a way which is most suitable to them, the majority of men still only uses their minimum 15 weeks. However, the numbers are slowly changing as shorter time away from work increases female participation in work, advances women's careers, and increases income. There are still discussions about how this scheme can be made more efficient in promoting gender equality in the labour market.

A related regulation in Norway is that employers are not allowed to ask questions related to family planning during job interviews. This is meant to avoid discrimination against women who might want to raise kids in the near future. Additionally, in order to promote female participation in the boards of public companies, Norwegian statutory law states that there must be a certain percentage of representation from *both* genders in such boards—generally at least 40%. This also shows that gender equality goes both ways.

Despite Norway's longstanding, determined efforts to eradicate gender inequality in the workplace, there is still considerable room for improvement in terms of employment and income for women. The same pertains to ethnic minorities, people with disabilities, and youth with only a basic level education. Avoiding the creation of new forms of inequality as diversity in the workforce is growing and has become an important topic in Norwegian society today.

The Norwegian State Educational Loan Fund

Free education has been a hallmark of the Norwegian welfare state. Equal access to education is not only fundamental for developing a relevant, well-qualified workforce, and maintaining a high employment rate, it is also crucial to ensure broad participation in the democratic elements of civil society. Norway offers free compulsory and secondary education for all, and the government covers tuition costs in higher education and public universities. Furthermore, the Norwegian State Educational Loan Fund (Nw.: *Statens lånekasse for utdanning*) allocates grants and loans to all students in higher education, covering their living and other expenses whilst studying. The loan schemes are interest free until graduation, and the interest rate on loans after graduation is significantly lower than the market rate. After successfully passing exams each semester, up to 40% of the total loan can be converted into grants, essentially eliminating the loans retroactively. This financing scheme was established in 1947, and makes it possible for everyone to attend higher education institutions regardless their geographical, economic, and social circumstances, contributing to more equal opportunities irrespective of background. Of Norway's then 5.4 million people, 304,900 were enrolled in higher education in the fall of 2021. Of these, 40% were men and 60% were women. This disparity partly indicates that female occupations are often more education-intensive, but partly also that parts of the young male population find it difficult to adjust to more skill-intensive careers.

The Right to Necessary, Equitable, and Affordable Healthcare

Everyone who lives in Norway has the right to necessary healthcare. Moreover, healthcare is free, beyond a small deductible. The government's goal is to provide everyone with access to the same healthcare services. As Norway is a country with a relatively dispersed population, this goal requires a great deal of economic and human resources, especially when it comes to high-level services and readiness in rural areas. In order to secure emergency room services in all regions, the current government has increased allocations to local governments, particularly in the smallest municipalities.

An ageing population requires an increased need for attention and care. In Norway, around half of the population over 80 years old receive some form of government-funded care, and the number of people above the age of 80 is expected to increase substantially in the years to come. The services are either provided in the patient's home or at an elder care institution. Government-funded elder care aims to take into account the needs and dignity of elderly people, whilst at the same time making it possible for their next of kin to work full time. In 2020, life expectancy in Norway was 84.9 years for women and 81.5 years for men.

New Challenges Ahead

Creating a perfect system for economic (and social) governance is nearly impossible, as most variations on any system have their advantages and disadvantages. Nevertheless, economic systems need to be well adapted to the changing situation in the countries that have adopted them, and a fair balance between competing ends and considerations must be found. This also means adapting the system in line with changing times, to face new challenges and seize new opportunities. A shared challenge for Norway and China going forward is addressing the demographic changes of an ageing population. This requires an even broader, more skilled, and efficient workforce, as well as smarter utilization of technology and human resources—particularly within the healthcare sector.

How can we ensure that our welfare system can handle a growing number of older pensioners with an increasing need for care? How can we finance such a system in the future? Is the current distribution of human resources across sectors and fields appropriate? Can digitalization be better implemented? What is the potential for innovation? Which measures can be implemented to support families in having more children? How do we at the same time best respond to the growing expectations of a population that has been accustomed to economic growth and increased living standards over time?

These questions display some of the hard choices Norway will face in the future, when the growth in petroleum revenues and returns from the pension fund are likely to plateau whilst expenditure and employment needed to cater for the elderly will soar. Although the Norwegian and Chinese systems and realities differ, we believe it would be highly valuable to engage in discussions and experience sharing with our Chinese counterparts on these and other issues going forward.

H.E. Ms. Signe Brudeset has been the Ambassador of Norway to China and Mongolia since 2019, and has previously been Ambassador of Norway to Japan. Ms. Brudeset has served in several senior positions within the Norwegian Ministry of Foreign Affairs, including Director in the Section for Middle East and North Africa and Special Envoy for Syria and Iraq. Ms. Brudeset has also been Deputy Director in the Private Office of the NATO Secretary General. Ms. Brudeset holds an MSc degree in Business Administration from the Norwegian School of Economics (NHH), with additional studies in international business and marketing from University of Barcelona. She has studied Chinese language at universities in Oslo and Taipei.

Open Access This chapter is licensed under the terms of the Creative Commons Attribution-NonCommercial-NoDerivatives 4.0 International License (http://creativecommons.org/licenses/by-nc-nd/4.0/), which permits any noncommercial use, sharing, distribution and reproduction in any medium or format, as long as you give appropriate credit to the original author(s) and the source, provide a link to the Creative Commons license and indicate if you modified the licensed material. You do not have permission under this license to share adapted material derived from this chapter or parts of it.

The images or other third party material in this chapter are included in the chapter's Creative Commons license, unless indicated otherwise in a credit line to the material. If material is not included in the chapter's Creative Commons license and your intended use is not permitted by statutory regulation or exceeds the permitted use, you will need to obtain permission directly from the copyright holder.

Mexico–China Bilateral Relationship in the Context of Changing Globalization

Jesús Seade

Mexico and China are currently commemorating the 50th anniversary of the establishment of diplomatic relations, which were established on 14 February 1972.

The official relationship started a few months after the People's Republic of China resumed its seat in the United Nations, which it did with strong support from Mexico.

In this half-century, the links between our two countries have evolved rapidly. We share an aspiration to provide a better life for our societies and to strengthen international cooperation to face global challenges. For five decades, Mexico and China have worked together in order to strengthen their bilateral relations.

An important episode occurred in 2013, when a comprehensive strategic partnership was established between the two countries, with the aim of developing the potential of our exchanges in several fields. The communication between legislative bodies represents an important part of the China–Mexico comprehensive strategic partnership, and is strongly expressed in the Mexican Senate's long-held stance of upholding the one-China principle and maintaining non-interference in China's internal affairs, creating a solid foundation of the long-standing friendship between both countries.

China and Mexico have maintained close and friendly exchanges at all levels, and the development of bilateral ties has maintained a good momentum. China and Mexico are already working, under the joint guidance of our two heads of state, to further align development strategies, and cultivate new growth points for cooperation in emerging areas such as clean energy, e-commerce, smart cities, and satellite aerospace.

Mexico attaches great importance to deepening its comprehensive strategic partnership with China, which is a priority for Mexico's diplomacy.

Ambassador of the United Mexican States to the People's Republic of China

---

J. Seade (✉)
Beijing, China

Overview of the Current Relationship Between Mexico and China

50 years after the establishment of diplomatic relations between Mexico and China, and nine years after the start of our Comprehensive Strategic Association, the relationship between our countries is stronger than ever. China is Mexico's biggest trading partner in the Asia-Pacific region, its second-largest trading partner in the world, and its third-largest export market.

The Comprehensive Strategic Association between Mexico and China governs a bilateral agenda promoting investment, trade, tourism, and connectivity; ensuring a fluid political dialogue; and supporting academic exchanges and cooperation on technical and scientific development.

According to figures from the Observatory of Economic Complexity (OEC) and the Central Bank of Mexico (Banxico), bilateral trade between Mexico and China 25 years ago was close to 550 million dollars and in 2021, all-time highs were reached, exceeding 110 billion US dollars, an increase of 200 times over that period. And this upward trend continued in 2022, which saw an increase of 27% compared to 2021, marking a new historical record.

Foreign Direct Investment (FDI) by China in Mexico has been similarly very strong. Despite the COVID pandemic, Chinese FDI in Mexico almost doubled between 2020 and 2021, going from 215.3 million dollars in 2020 to 413.8 million dollars in 2021. Like trade, in 2022, investments have continued on an upward trend and many new relocation projects have been completed. And yet, according to studies carried out by the National Autonomous University of Mexico (UNAM), China's Foreign Direct Investment in Mexico represents only 0.2% of the total FDI that reaches Mexican soil. Without a doubt, there is a lot of room to strengthen business relationships between China and Mexico.

Mexico in the Digital Economy and Electronic Commerce

According to the OECD, Mexico has huge opportunities to develop computer skills and digital experience—and to increase mobile coverage—which is essential for most digital tools and creates technology-rich environments that enhance proficiency in literacy, numeracy, and problem-solving.

A quick look at Mexico's fundamentals speaks loudly of its huge potential, as an economy, and as an investment partner. Over half its population is under twenty-nine years of age, which offers a huge consumer base and driver of productivity. Second, its location. As part of North America and Latin America, with vast transportation links by land, air, and sea with our neighbours to the north as well as a natural connection with our partners to the south, we are at the centre of our great continent. And last but not least, we have free trade agreements with 50 countries throughout the Americas and around the world. Launched in 2020, the US–Mexico–Canada

Agreement (USMCA) is a unique replacement and improvement of the old North American Free Trade Act (NAFTA), which turned Mexico into the manufacturing power-house it has become today, whilst the new version of the USMCA provides greater certainty and unprecedented protection to foreign investors operating from Mexico.

SMEs in Mexico, a universe of 4.49 million micro, small and medium-sized enterprises (MSMEs), which are responsible for the majority of employment, were highly impacted by COVID. About 95% of Mexican companies are categorized as SMEs, representing over 70% of formal jobs. But microenterprises—those with fewer than ten people—are also part of the backbone of Mexico's economy. 97% of SMEs are microenterprises and employ 47% of the country's workforce, contributing 64% of GDP.

Nevertheless, running together with our new trade agreement in North America, the COVID pandemic has dramatically highlighted the need for Mexico and its SMEs to innovate in order to remain competitive, and in the twenty-first century, that means going digital. The transition towards a digital economy and society has the potential to spur innovation, enhance productivity, and improve the well-being of the people—providing SMEs with new opportunities to participate in the global economy, innovate, and grow. Demonstrating how important this transition could be, a 2020 International Data Corporation (IDC) survey estimated that accelerating digital adoption amongst Mexico's SMEs could add 65bn US dollars to the economy.

But achieving that deeper digital infrastructure is a challenge, and cooperation with China is key. For example, when we talk about the penetration of digital payments, 88% of payments in Mexico are made in cash whilst in China this number is only 6%. More generally, China has done an exceptional job in developing and using online platforms to drive significant changes and progress, a best practice that Mexico needs and wants to replicate.

We are looking at China as an example of how e-commerce and messaging platforms can lead to more digital payments. The Chinese example is more integral, permeating digital elements into every aspect of commercial activity. Large internet firms in China like Baidu, Alibaba, and Tencent (together commonly called BAT) have successfully driven broad digital adoption throughout the country. By the early 2010s, they had already made e-commerce an important channel for consumers, providing consumers with a digital experience.

Learning from China and Asia's best practices, in September 2019, Banxico launched a new payment platform, Cobro Digital (CoDi), as part of the government's "Program to Promote the Financial Sector". It uses a combination of smartphones and QR technology in a new system based on models used widely in China. Banks that join CoDi are able to offer access to their customers via their own app. This system had a complicated start for several reasons, but access is improving.

Our cooperation with China has also enabled us to connect and share knowledge in this regard, exemplified by an initiative led by the Office of Foreign Affairs of Chongqing, which organized a workshop to train local government officials in Mexico in digital skills and e-commerce. This 120-h virtual workshop was offered by the Chongqing University of Technology and Business and represents an important strategy for the development of technical capacities in Mexican state and municipal authorities.

Online platforms have the potential to drive significant change in Mexico, as has been the experience in China. They provide SMEs with local and national access to sell goods and services online and secure financing. Widespread digitalization in this regard has helped China's economy withstand the pandemic better than Mexico's. Extending the country's digital infrastructure beyond dense urban centres can also better distribute economic benefits, and what better way to achieve this than by developing strong and continued cooperation with China in this regard.

Science, Technology, and Innovation as Mechanisms to Modernize the Economy

China's remarkable efforts to maintain its economic growth, strengthen supply chains, develop strategic sectors like science, technology, and new industries, lead various cutting-edge sectors in the Fourth Industrial Revolution, and achieve remarkable successes in the field of science and technology in record time, have depended, to a large extent, on its ability to cultivate and implement an ambitious public policy plan aimed at building an innovative, sustainable economy with greater weight given to high value-added activities.

In light of Chinese achievements, it is of great interest for Mexico to learn about the strategies that China has been implementing in the development of S&T (science and technology), its efforts to successfully invest in R&D, and the incorporation of new technologies into the industry to address innovation challenges and other difficulties it faces. This brings broad possibilities and opportunities for bilateral collaboration.

Just to note a few of China's recent achievements in these fields, I would first like to point out that according to the 2022 Global Innovation Index, China ranked 11th, up from 43rd two decades ago. And now, for the first time, it has positioned itself as one of two countries with the largest number of S&T clusters in the world.

Secondly, over the last two decades, China has implemented technological megaprojects, such as the C919 commercial aircraft, which is slated to compete in the aeronautical market, the development of maglev train technology, the announcement of the most powerful computer in the world Tianhe-3, the construction of the world's longest bridge, landing on the far side of the moon, and the recent landing of the Zhurong robot on Mars.

Third, I would like to underline China's goal to become a scientific and technological powerhouse by 2049. In pursuit of this goal, China has allocated significant resources and support to initiatives designed to attract and ensure the development of talent in S&T related fields. According to the National Bureau of Statistics, the government invested $441.3 billion, or 2.4% of China's GDP, in R&D in 2020, an increase of 14.2% from the previous year. And according to the Organization for

Economic Cooperation and Development (OECD), China is the second-largest R&D spender in the world.

For Mexico, which is looking to boost and enhance its technological capacity, it would be helpful to strengthen cooperation with China in areas such as Big Data, IoT (Internet of Things), digitalization, and the use of digital payments, thus helping to expand the application of technology across sectors with fewer opportunities and driving social and economic progress. This is why the governments of the People's Republic of China and Mexico, through the Science and Technology Subcommittee of the Permanent Committee, are exploring ways to develop closer cooperation, promote exchanges of students and researchers, whilst also implementing joint projects and potentially opening laboratories and research centres devoted to topics of mutual interest.

The governments of Mexico and China have all the mechanisms and opportunities to take the next step in bilateral cooperation and hopefully will continue having seminars, research, joint programs, and innovative projects that provide a great deal of added value.

Strengthening Educational Exchanges and Language Teaching to Bring People Closer

To continue strengthening the bridge of friendship, collaboration, and economic and social development between China and Mexico, we rely on educational cooperation at all levels, including researchers in the hard, social, and technological sciences. Whilst efforts have already been made in this area, including Mexico hosting five Confucius Institutes (second highest number in Latin America), there are still significant opportunities to enhance our educational collaboration. In this spirit, Mexico is currently supporting the opening of the 6th Confucian Institute at the Universidad Veracruzana, with the support of the University of Changzhou.

According to studies carried out by UNAM, at the moment most of the scientific collaboration between China and Mexico is in the fields of physics, astronomy, and astrophysics, and a significant amount of this takes place in multinational enterprises, which showcase the opportunities to generate more initiatives that enable direct cooperation between researchers and robust and intense academic exchanges between our countries.

As part of a new era of collaboration, China and Mexico are developing an initiative titled "Young people Building the Future, China Chapter" which organizes young people from Mexico to do internships in Chinese companies in Mexico or in Mexican companies with a presence in China, whilst at the same time, studying the language, culture, and history of China, all within Mexico. In a second stage, it is expected that the participants can travel to China to do similar practices. The project is supported by the Ministry of Labor and Social Welfare in Mexico, the Mexico–China High-Level Business Group (GANE), the Confucius Institutes in Mexico, and UNAM.

Additionally, it is important to highlight the Bilateral Scholarship Program launched between the two countries with scholarships from the Government of Mexico to students from China. In this context, an event on educational cooperation between the Pacific Alliance (PA) and China was held, which Mexico coordinated together with the China Association for International Exchanges (CEAIE) and the other Embassies members of the PA in China.

The Presence of Mexico in Multilateral Organizations

Mexico and China have also strengthened cooperation at the regional and multilateral levels. In forums such as the G20, which brings together the world's leading economies, both countries have promoted equitable access to COVID-19 vaccines, their recognition as a global public good, and the global approval of vaccines recognized by the World Health Organization.

Within the framework of the UN, Mexico and China have in this period coincided as members of the Security Council, an opportunity both countries have used to reflect their multilateralist positions on issues such as poverty reduction, disarmament, and non-proliferation.

At the regional level, it is important to note the joint work in the Forum of the Community of Latin American and Caribbean States (CELAC)-China, which was held during Mexico's pro-tempore presidency of CELAC. The forum allowed the exchange of experience in science, technology and innovation, agriculture, traditional medicine, poverty reduction, and development. These efforts successfully culminated in the Third CELAC-China Ministerial Meeting in December 2021.

China promotes multilateralism, while Mexico also has an old and well recognized multilateral position that recognizes the potential of fostering communication and positive engagement amongst nations. Our government has actively defended its foreign policy interests, always through a clear willingness for negotiation and strong confidence in international cooperation. This has been key in collaboration during several meetings held by international organizations headquartered in China.

We believe that China and Mexico are good friends and good partners. China–Mexico relations have developed in a holistic way, as evidenced by the sound momentum in multiple areas of cooperation, as well as the close coordination we have maintained on international and regional issues, making significant contributions to world peace and the promotion of common development.

The strong resilience of our pragmatic cooperation, including vaccine cooperation in the fight against COVID-19, both countries have an interest to better synergize development strategies, deepen people-to-people exchanges, and enhance coordination to jointly promote multilateralism.

Joint Efforts in International Development to Advance the United Nations Sustainable Development Goals in a Post-COVID-19 Context

Over the past two years, cooperation between Mexico and China has become more relevant in the fight against the COVID-19 pandemic. Amongst the most tangible results of this was the valuable support received from China in the initial stage of the crisis, which ensured access to medical equipment and supplies for the health sector and facilitated vaccine clinical trials in Mexico.

Thanks to this support, Mexico has access to Chinese vaccines produced by CanSino, Sinopharm, and Sinovac, whilst also engaging in productive exchanges on pandemic control strategies. Mexico will always remember the solidarity and support China provided during the most difficult parts of the pandemic. Mexico and China are two dynamic countries that can "challenge" existing normative views on regimes, governance, and institutions.

We now need to consolidate our significant but still modest trade and investment relationship, and to that end, we hope to increase capital flows to contribute to a sustainable and innovative development.

Strategically, China is a global leader in the effort to tackle climate change and achieve UN Sustainable Developmental Goals (SDG), paving the way for recognition, both domestically and internationally. Mexico, for its part, is also committed to developing initiatives that pave the way for achieving the SDGs, such as issuing the world's first sustainable sovereign bond linked to the UN SDGs.

Mexico and China share a mutual commitment and unique expertise in sustainable, low-carbon transformation, which has increased participation by both countries in environmental forums. This includes events led by the UN and the China Center for International Economic Exchanges (CCIEE), which explore how financial instruments can help tackle climate change, whilst also promoting cooperation between China and Mexico based on best practices and global advancements that are leading the transition towards a net zero emissions economy.

Future Perspectives

Mexico and China should recognize the fundamental strategic value they have for each other. Despite the distance between them, they are ideal partners as they are located at the centre of opposite halves of the world.

2023 will be essential in consolidating the new global sphere in the emerging post-COVID context. Mexico and China are perfect allies to work within this new reality, expanding and consolidating their association in global and regional supply chains, particularly where new technologies are involved, which will increasingly be key for economies to develop and their peoples to thrive.

Each country has its own strengths. By combining our efforts, the achievements we can make are limitless. For example, China's progress in developing its strategic science and technology sectors is a milestone that should be recognized. With vision and determination, in a few short decades, China has become a major global technology leader and generates the most patents of any country annually. It has the world's second-largest nominal GDP in current dollars and in terms of purchasing power parity (PPP). Of particular note is how China has successfully achieved a digital financial revolution, thus making the country a pioneer in the digital economy. All of this has contributed directly to the phenomenal economic growth China has seen and its admirable eradication of poverty.

However, reflecting its economic size, China needs to continue diversifying its production geographically, and Mexico is an outstanding prospective strategic partner in the Western Hemisphere, with its competitive labour force, thanks to its role as an important manufacturing nation. It is also located in the middle of the "rest of the world" as seen from China, with vast logistical links within North America and a core part of the thriving region that is Latin America and the Caribbean, not to mention its network of free trade agreements with more than 50 countries. What better base of production and operations for a Chinese company in the New World.

Mexico, its government, producers, and its people, need and are ready to strengthen our friendship and business relationship with China, which, despite already being our largest trading partner outside North America, has huge untapped potential in absolute numbers in both trade and investment.

This year, we celebrated the first 50 years of diplomatic relations between China and Mexico. And we are just a few decades away from celebrating half a millennium since the Manilla Galeon started making its round-trip passage across the Pacific Ocean twice a year, exchanging not only silver and chilies for Chinese porcelain and spices, but more importantly linking our countries and cultures, in those centuries when China's only communication with the Western Hemisphere was through Mexico. No wonder we both share fundamental tracts that define us, such as the way the Mexican and Chinese people cherish family, and how they honour their departed ancestors in their respective and otherwise unique major festivals.

The foundation for developing our business, cooperation, and cultural relations and the friendship between our peoples is clearly there. Important as 2022 was for us to celebrate the past 50 years of formal diplomatic ties with China, I am sure that this year will see even more important celebrations of moving forward, welcoming the first year of the next century of friendship with China, with both of us determined to make our links ever more substantial across the board.

H.E. Jesús Seade has had a unique and diverse career with top policy responsibilities globally as a senior officer in three important multilateral organizations, a trade and financial negotiator, and a senior official in the government of Mexico. He is also a recognized scholar and academic leader in universities in Europe, Mexico, Hong Kong, SAR, and mainland China. On 1 July 2018, Ambassador Seade was appointed to represent the then president-elect of Mexico in the negotiations for the new USMCA trade agreement between Mexico, USA, and Canada, after which he served as Mexico's Under-Secretary for North America. In November 2020, he received the Miguel Hidalgo Order in the Degree of Band from President López Obrador, the highest honour the Mexican Government can bestow on a Mexican national. On 13 July 2021, Mexico's Senate appointed him as Ambassador Extraordinary and Plenipotentiary to the People's Republic of China, taking up his post on 8 October, 2021.

Open Access This chapter is licensed under the terms of the Creative Commons Attribution-NonCommercial-NoDerivatives 4.0 International License (http://creativecommons.org/licenses/by-nc-nd/4.0/), which permits any noncommercial use, sharing, distribution and reproduction in any medium or format, as long as you give appropriate credit to the original author(s) and the source, provide a link to the Creative Commons license and indicate if you modified the licensed material. You do not have permission under this license to share adapted material derived from this chapter or parts of it.

The images or other third party material in this chapter are included in the chapter's Creative Commons license, unless indicated otherwise in a credit line to the material. If material is not included in the chapter's Creative Commons license and your intended use is not permitted by statutory regulation or exceeds the permitted use, you will need to obtain permission directly from the copyright holder.

China's Economic Resilience, and Jordan's Potential

Hussam A. G. Al Husseini

Understanding the economic development of any country cannot be made in isolation of its social and cultural background, since they are the basis and foundations on which the goals and targets of the economic policies are set and developed.

And when the country is as big as China, the relations between these factors are not only sophisticated but they are also indicative of the long and rich history of its diverse population.

The recent COVID crises remain a global crisis that has affected each and every country in the world. But unlike others, this crisis has affected all the segments and communities of each society, and put into test all their systems and sectors.

No doubt that the COVID crisis was a stress test to each and every country and their economies, and that very few could hardly manage such a test, though with tangible losses. Nevertheless, only China could pass the test that was stretched over three years, with relatively minimum losses, and positive annual economic growth.

It is worthwhile mentioning that the measures taken by China during the COVID crises included a massive use of digital applications that helped the nation to overcome the daily challenges of the crisis in almost every area. Such a technology not only managed to have everyone on board, but it also kept them all connected through the same procedures and protocol.

The ability of the industrial sector of China to adapt itself to the emergency needs of the nation in a very short time, was significant, and helped China to transfer itself in few months from the import to the export zone, and to become the main source of medical supplies and equipments to the rest of the world. For a giant country like China, it needs to check on its readiness and preparedness before the next step on its journey ahead, and the COVID crises were definitely that test.

Ambassador of the Hashemite Kingdom of Jordan to the People's Republic of China.

H. A. G. Al Husseini (✉)
Beijing, China

It is a worthy experience to observe and to learn from, however, it is still one of many major achievements that China has accomplished in recent years.

Poverty eradication, the world's most pressing challenge, and once, China's wildest dream, became a reality in a remarkably significant time in the history of the country.

The lifting of hundreds of millions of people from extreme poverty up to a higher income level is not just a social miracle in terms of its improving the livelihood of these millions of people of the population, but it is also a giant move to elevate a huge economic class into a higher level that is a step closer to widen the already largest middle class in the world, and by that, ensuring a steady growth for the whole economy for many years to come.

By eradicating extreme poverty on its land, China contributed to eradicating 75% of the Global figure,[1] in other words, the size of its local achievement is reflected clearly as a global achievement, something that will not only put China ahead of the world, but will also raise the bar higher for other countries, when comparing their delivery on their commitments toward the SDGs.

Eradicating poverty is a continuous process that has to adapt and adjust to the developing conditions on the way forward. And with new technologies emerging almost every day, we should expect that new forms of poverty will also be rising and evolving, unless adjustment process is carried out to ensure everyone is on board, and keep them attached to the latest development.

During my visits to areas and towns in the south of China that used to live under extreme poverty, and now lifted to a new life, and a new level of livelihood, I've witnessed twenty-first century being delivered at the doorsteps of these communities rather than just efforts to improve their living conditions; I've seen state of the art school classrooms; I've seen 4G and even 5G towers covering those areas; and I've reached these towns on modern Highways much similar to the ones in major cities.

Through the ongoing education process, and with the widespread digital connectivity, I have no doubt that these communities will soon join the middle class, and contribute to the country's growing share of global economy.

The trade figures between China and the rest of the world increased enough to make it the largest trading partner to many countries, which helps creating a safety net, that makes the stability of the Chinese economy, a stability to many of these countries' economy, and as such, contribute to the stability of the world's economy as a whole. Nevertheless, the Chinese outbound FDI is not growing enough to keep this share rising on the long run, especially with the fierce competition that is also increasing from different parts of the world. This is a high time for China's international cooperation to include investments aimed at local production, and ensure a sustainable market share for the benefit of both countries.

The recent COVID crisis uncovered the vulnerability of the supply chains worldwide, both for food, medical supplies, and manufacturing sectors in general, shipping

---

[1] FOUR DECADES OF POVERTY REDUCTION IN CHINA, © 2022 International Bank for Reconstruction and Development/The World Bank.

also faced disruptions that raised the freight costs to unprecedented levels, such difficulties could disturb the market shares, and eventually create new realities, and new market players. I think that the ability of the Chinese economy to adapt and respond to the pandemic needs enabled it not only to keep its share in the global market but also to increase it.

I believe that new challenges require new way of thinking, for instance, local production, and trading hubs could provide immediate solutions that lessen the impact of disruptions on the supply chains, like the ones during the pandemic, something my country Jordan succeeded in during the first year of the pandemic, when in few months it could transfer from importer of medical masks and gears to exporter to many countries in the region and beyond.

The vision of His Majesty King Abdullah II Ibn Al Hussein, to make Jordan a regional hub for logistics, proved to be feasible and timely, given Jordan's strategic location in the heart of the Middle East, in a spot where it connects the three continents of Asia, Africa, and Europe, makes it an ideal hub for logistics, including shipping and transportation, as well as storage and redistribution. This has always been a role that Jordan played throughout history, including at the time of the great Nabatean kingdom of Petra, when it was an important destination and trading hub on the Silk Road more than two thousand years ago.

History plays an important guide for the future, and the foot prints of the history can always draw a road map to the future.

Throughout history, China has always been a source of knowledge, science, philosophy, as well as literature and arts. And today's role of China in human development and advancement is even stronger and wider, that also includes technology & innovation, as well as industry and services.

The long history of friendship and exchanges in many different fields between both the Chinese Civilization and the Arabic Civilization that includes Jordan, paved the way for a wide area of cooperation.

The relations between China and Jordan were elevated to a strategic partnership and was sealed by an agreement that was signed in 2015 By His Majesty King Abdullah II and His Excellency President Xi Jinping, and ever since, the bilateral relations have been growing, and trade is increasing, making China Jordan's second largest trading partner.

China's global role is increasing, especially in the economic field, and so is the role of the Middle East, though it is still plagued with conflicts and instability, at the heart of this region, and in the middle of its turmoil, there is an oasis of stability, safety, and security that is still shining with hope and wisdom, and standing ready as a stable and reliable hub for business, trade, and investments to the region and beyond, and that country is Jordan, and its shared history with China is indicative of the promising future and the potential of the great opportunities ahead.

H.E. Mr. Hussam A. G. Al Husseini has been the Ambassador of the Hashemite Kingdom of Jordan to China since September 2019. Previously, he was Ambassador to Austria, Non-Resident Ambassador to Hungary, Slovakia, Slovenia, and Czech Republic, as well as a Permanent Representative to UNOV, IAEA, UNIDO, OSCE, and IACA. He has also previously served at the Jordanian Embassies in Belgium, Geneva, Pretoria, and Tokyo. Hussam A. G. Al Husseini joined the Ministry of Foreign Affairs in 1991 and has occupied several positions working in the areas of human rights and human security, European affairs, international relations and organizations, Asian and African affairs, and peace process coordination. Born in 1965, Hussam A. G. Al Husseini holds a B.A. in Public Administration from Yarmouk University. He is married with three children.

Open Access This chapter is licensed under the terms of the Creative Commons Attribution-NonCommercial-NoDerivatives 4.0 International License (http://creativecommons.org/licenses/by-nc-nd/4.0/), which permits any noncommercial use, sharing, distribution and reproduction in any medium or format, as long as you give appropriate credit to the original author(s) and the source, provide a link to the Creative Commons license and indicate if you modified the licensed material. You do not have permission under this license to share adapted material derived from this chapter or parts of it.

The images or other third party material in this chapter are included in the chapter's Creative Commons license, unless indicated otherwise in a credit line to the material. If material is not included in the chapter's Creative Commons license and your intended use is not permitted by statutory regulation or exceeds the permitted use, you will need to obtain permission directly from the copyright holder.

Education, Equality and Resilience—Finnish Recipe for Success

Leena-Kaisa Mikkola

During my almost two years in China, I have witnessed the determination and dynamism of the Chinese people that drive the development across this country and its society. At the same time, I have deepened my understanding of China's history and traditions. China is a vast country that often escapes simple truths.

Finland and China differ in many respects, starting with size and geography. Our social and political systems are different, but we both share accountability under the international obligations that our governments have accepted. Furthermore, there are factors that connect us and bring us together. One of them is the rapid, tremendous transformation that has taken place in Finland after World War II and the similarly drastic change in China during the last forty years.

A hundred years ago, newly independent Finland was a poor agrarian nation. Its per capita GDP was only half of that of the Unites States of America and Great Britain. Finland was still receiving development aid from the World Bank as recently as the early 1970s.

However, Finland transformed quickly in the decades after the war, first into an industrialised country and then into a post-industrial information-based society. This transformation followed a path familiar to other countries across the world. Some features in our experience—namely a well-functioning and transparent society, investments in education and focus on equal opportunities and empowering individuals—were clearly the cornerstones that facilitated our transformation. For us, a model of development based on a liberal democratic society and free market economy has clearly been essential.

One of the main factors behind Finland's progress was the understanding that we were a small and remote country. We had to focus on further opening to the world and building an open market economy. This understanding has defined our policies,

---

Ambassador of the Republic of Finland to the People's Republic of China.

L.-K. Mikkola (✉)
Beijing, China

and creating linkages with international markets has been of utmost importance to our citizens, companies and political leaders.

Globalisation can be defined as a byproduct of the international trading of goods, ideas and capital driven by industrialisation and shifts in monetary practices. The intensification of globalisation can be traced back to late twentieth century when the Uruguay Round of negotiations ended in the creation of the World Trade Organization (WTO). Global development since then has been immense, and globalisation has functioned as an enormous driving force for changing societies.

Intense globalisation in recent decades has produced considerable increases in well-being and other clear benefits—but it has also increased a sense of inequality and resulted in phenomena that are challenging for societies to tackle alone. As an open, trade-oriented country, Finland has benefited from a globalised world. Yet, our societal transformation was sometimes painful as we adapted from an agrarian to an industrialised society and then on to a post-industrialised service and technology-driven economy. This has been particularly true for the different realities of urban and rural areas. Our democratic structures and political competition through elections have helped to manage this adaptation and encourage our society to commit to sometimes difficult reforms. Government is often in the lead, but always held accountable to the people.

As for China, change has been tremendous. Driven by the initiation of economic reforms in 1978, China became one of the world's fastest growing economies and emerged as a global economic and trade power. The opening up of China benefited from rapidly globalised trade and actually made China one of its engines. China's accession to the World Trade Organization was a milestone in this process. As China becomes a high middle-income country with a highly educated workforce, it faces new development challenges. For China, in the years to come, further investment in sustainable reforms, both political and economic, are important and also necessary.

Whilst globalisation has contributed to increased well-being and made the world appear smaller, it has not necessarily made it simpler. Over the past decades, there has been a strong belief that global interdependence ties us together and has put us on a path of even closer and stronger cooperation. However, more recently, this belief has been challenged by increasingly inward-looking nationalist and populist tendencies and shifts in international relations.

Global tensions have been mounting, and multilateralism has struggled to deal with them. Last year, Russian aggression in Ukraine fundamentally shook the framework of European security, and the war still continues to dominate our part of the world. Climate-related threats are imminent and visible to everyone. Energy and food crises afflict especially the most vulnerable, who already suffer. We live in unpredictable times.

But the world is still interconnected. There are many challenges we cannot solve alone. We need well-functioning multilateral mechanisms and clearly articulated international rules to hold countries accountable to each other, and to hold governments accountable to the people and the market. This requires continuous work. The only way to ensure this is to engage in dialogue and strive for solutions.

In many areas, the European Union and China are competitors. Competition can be a good and positive driving force. However, at the same time, we are witnessing ongoing changes in global dynamics. New, strong economies and powers have appeared, and a more multipolar world is emerging. But changing times should not mean that we shift away from common rules. Multilateralism should not be an area of competition only. We may have differing views but we need to work together to uphold existing rules and the rules-based order.

So, regardless of how we have arrived at the present situation, we need to make shared choices to prosper together. In international trade, the reform of the World Trade Organization is key. We need rules that address the challenges of the twenty-first century and a dispute settlement system that upholds existing rules and a commitment to transparency. This all comes back to the need to strengthen an open multilateral trading system, the benefits of which are clear and concrete. Common rules enhance predictability and transparency. They foster trade, economic growth and well-being for all. If we deem this multilateral system to be valuable, we must make reforms happen. This is a massive task, and our focus should be on ways we can advance this together.

As a global power and the world's second largest economy, China plays a fundamental role in this process. China can make a difference and harness its power to tackle some of the world's most pressing global challenges, such as climate change. The response to this and other global problems is only possible if all key states are involved. China's role, last year at COP15 in Montreal in reaching the UN agreement to halt biodiversity loss, was decisive. The process showed that it is important to continue dialogue and jointly recognise that there are areas where collaboration is not only desirable, but a necessity.

Lastly, let me come back to the example of my own country. In a globalised, sometimes complicated world, a key factor that has brought us stability and contributed to our growth, is a resilient society that fosters equality and equal opportunities as well as a strong educational basis providing individuals and companies alike opportunities to develop and grow. We are a society that lifts you up, but also carries you when you are in need, with a strong culture of trust. The success story we have created did not happen overnight. It has taken many decades to achieve. Through determination and openness to the world, as well as trial and error, Finland has built its successes. This will be our recipe for the future, too.

 **H.E. Leena-Kaisa Mikkola** is the Ambassador of the Republic of Finland to the People's Republic of China. She has served in this position since September 2021. Ms. Mikkola is a career diplomat, first joined the Ministry for Foreign Affairs of Finland in 1992 and was later transferred to Beijing from the position of Director General of the Department for Africa and the Middle East at the Ministry for Foreign Affairs. She has previously served as Finland's Ambassador in Israel and also worked at diplomatic missions in Brussels, Canberra, Athens and Budapest. Ms. Mikkola has two grown sons. She holds a Master's degree in Law from the University of Helsinki.

Open Access This chapter is licensed under the terms of the Creative Commons Attribution-NonCommercial-NoDerivatives 4.0 International License (http://creativecommons.org/licenses/by-nc-nd/4.0/), which permits any noncommercial use, sharing, distribution and reproduction in any medium or format, as long as you give appropriate credit to the original author(s) and the source, provide a link to the Creative Commons license and indicate if you modified the licensed material. You do not have permission under this license to share adapted material derived from this chapter or parts of it.

The images or other third party material in this chapter are included in the chapter's Creative Commons license, unless indicated otherwise in a credit line to the material. If material is not included in the chapter's Creative Commons license and your intended use is not permitted by statutory regulation or exceeds the permitted use, you will need to obtain permission directly from the copyright holder.

Multilateralism Versus Unilateralism in International Economic Governance: How to Deal with the "Tech War"?

Jan Hoogmartens

The international economic governance architecture established after the Second World War has come under pressure. The reason this has happened is more complex of course, but an important contributing factor is that over the last couple of decades, many emerging economies with a variety of political and economic systems representing over 3 billion people have been added to the world economy. At the same time, although nothing in economic theory has changed to justify why market economies should no longer pursue profit maximization and efficiency through international economic openness, globalization as the principal paradigm of international economic governance is also being questioned. It raises fundamental questions about economic leadership and multilateralism, and it heralds a return of unilateralism and isolationism.

The difficulties in which the international economic governance system finds itself today have had an impact on multilateralism as a tool to address economic governance issues. It has resulted in an uptick in unilateralism as recent examples in the technology sector have shown, including measures by the US to restrict China's access to semiconductors. Unilateralism should not be condemned per se, and every entity subject to international public law should be entitled to pursue its own development model. However, a multilateral consensus is more likely to prevent geoeconomic tensions from becoming geopolitical flashpoints. Compromising over hard-fought national sovereign rights is not easy, though, and there are also different views on multilateralism among major contenders, which complicate efforts toward effective multilateralism. By nature of its institutions, the EU's experience in multilateralism is unique and Belgium's historical contributions to it hold important lessons.

Views expressed in this contribution are purely personal and do not necessarily reflect any official government position.
    Ambassador of Belgium to the People's Republic of China.

J. Hoogmartens (✉)
Beijing, China

International Economic Governance Today

The challenges that international economic governance wanted to address have not fundamentally changed since 1944, when the bulk of the present multilateral framework currently used for this purpose was devised. There is nothing in economic theory that has changed to justify why market economies should no longer focus on improving efficiency and profit maximization supported by economic openness. What has changed though is the addition of about 3 billion people and a growing number of emerging markets in the international economy. This has changed the process of how international economic policy is made, mainly due to the increase in participants and a wider diversity in Bretton Woods Institutions, such as the IMF and World Bank, as well as newly-created forums such as BRICS.

Over the same period, international economic governance has tried to become more rule oriented. A good example of this evolution is the WTO (World Trade Organization) which expanded its membership in recent decades, developing out of GATT in 1995, which had been founded in 1948, into a full-fledged organization including a two-step Dispute Settlement Body. However, a firm foundation of rules is only useful if they are flexible enough and can adjust to changing circumstances. This explains why new modern forms of international cooperation have sprouted as can be seen in international finance, including banking, insurance, and capital markets, as well as in areas of health and safety, such as environmental protection. With each transition, as has been happening in response to climate change, as well as intermittent crises, such as the 2008 global financial crisis, it is important for economic governance to adapt.

Whereas in certain areas, such as in international finance, more multilateral cooperation has been observed in recent times, the multilateral process has stalled in others. This is presently the case with WTO reform, where multilateralism and international cooperation has failed to make progress. This often adds to the difficulties and tensions that the world is witnessing. This lack of reform will undermine the fitness to govern the economic challenges for which the organ was set up. It does not always have to be a subject of international law, such as an organization with categorized as a legal person. Sometimes, an ad hoc political forum, such as the G20 can be equally effective.

These days, many observers agree that the world is moving away from a consensus about globalization to a new era of great power competition with a renewed focus on industrial policy. The notion that economic interdependence because of globalization is much less likely to spark major conflicts has been nonetheless the dominant paradigm since the end of the Second World War. It has been commonly believed that cross-border trade will make countries more dependent, increasing thereby the costs of any conflict between them. With geopolitical tension rising and with calls for decoupling economies from each other, this paradigm has started to shift. Nowadays, more countries are focusing on their own security, power, and influence again to strive for greater autonomy. The recurrence of unilateral actions in these areas may further undermine global economic governance. There is even talk of the "weaponization of trade".

Today, there are countries and certain groups in societies that believe a free and open world has not benefited them. They hold the view that globalization equals economic turbulence and that migration and international enterprise presents threats rather than opportunities. They want to protect themselves from injustice and insecurity. These tendencies are not restricted to the developing world, they are also present in countries of great wealth. Of course, globalization has not created a borderless egalitarian world as some would dream of. Nonetheless, many East Asian nations can testify that the internationalization of trade and the globalization of the economy have the potential to lift people out of poverty and to create prosperity. A successful development model allows for economic openness.

For international economic openness to work properly, variations of legal and economic systems must be interfaced through harmonization and standardization. Within a continued diversity of states and political systems, a certain degree of order is needed. Therefore, a broad consensus on market economic policies and some minimum requirements on a country's legal system are necessary preconditions to actively participate in the current complex international economy. Some practices are good, and others should absolutely be avoided. The Organization of Economic and Cooperation Development (OECD), of which the EU Member States and the US are members, and of which China is a strategic partner, has been able to develop especially useful guidelines and good standards, which in many cases have become globally recognized best practices.

The issue of international economic governance, however, should not focus on the divide between political systems in the West and in the East. The real issue is how to create prosperity and fairly distribute wealth. Macroeconomic gains of globalization are often diffuse, whereas the losses are often very tangible on the microeconomic level. The question of the matter is therefore how to solve the divide between the haves and the have-nots, or alternatively between the developed and the developing world. The need to ensure sufficient growth and share it with the entire world, is a compelling reason why the world needs economic governance.

Change Unseen in a Century

If governments and their stakeholders no longer wish to believe that international economic governance should focus on the creation of inclusive growth, or that economic interdependence or globalization can prevent major conflicts, then the world will enter a whole new chapter. The world will become more selfish and inward looking. This will also affect the way in which the world is already transitioning in the fields of climate, energy, and technology for instance.

For the first time in a long time, the world is witnessing more states that want to claw back control. The sovereignty of states is the bedrock of international law and it is assumed that in international and multilateral contexts, national governments always exert effective control. However, national governments do not always have sovereign control over the economic interdependencies and the effects of globalization. Factors of production, such as capital and labor, are now increasingly globalized and multinational enterprises have also freed themselves from sovereign control. Furthermore, where central bank independence exists, it does not give governments control over their own interest rate. In an international and globalized economy, much escapes the sovereign control of a nation state. This loss of control frustrates governments, which can cause them to pursue policies of unilateralism and protectionism to please particular stakeholders within their territory. For the EU and the US, this return to economic nationalism has been something recent, while China has for decades consistently controlled the commanding heights of its economy.

The industrial policies that China has pursued for decades are today being amplified by the US and the EU in a whirlwind of subsidies and trade defense measures. Where China has been accused of giving cheap energy handouts, subsidizing land-use rights, and implementing local content requirements in manufacturing, the US Inflation Reduction Act (IRA) as well as the CHIPS Act put in place similar policies to favor Made-in-America nationalism. Likewise, the EU has taken unprecedented measures to support its economy by accelerating the transition into digital and green growth. While the COVID-19 pandemic and the energy crisis in Europe have been the main drivers for the EU, the spur in the US mainly comes from its strategic competition with China. If this reawakening of industrial policy is true, what does it mean for international governance? It raises fundamental questions about economic leadership and multilateralism, and it heralds a return of unilateralism and isolationism.

Unilateralism in Full Swing

In putting up a licensing regime for high-end semiconductors and US technology in October 2022, the US cut China off from supplies of the most advanced chips, the tools to make them and the US human resources to use these tools. It chose not to use a multilateral agreement, such as the Wassenaar Agreement on restrictions on the transfer of so-called dual use technologies. Instead, the US used a unilateral instrument under its own national legislation. The main justification for the measures was that China's civil-military fusion strategy makes it possible for commercial companies in China to enhance military capabilities. Since advanced semiconductors are key building blocks for the world's most sophisticated weapons, the US invokes the national security exception to take these measures. Whether this exception could be held up before a WTO Arbitration Panel as a legal justification is of course debatable but not the purpose of this essay. The point of this example is that unilateral economic actions are a tool of deliberate choice, whereas a globalized economy would prefer a multilateral approach.

Unilateral actions could amount to bilateral sanctions as opposed to multilateral ones such as those under the UN. Examples of sanctions include trade sanctions, financial sanctions, travel restrictions, arms embargoes, military assistance sanctions, and there are more examples to think of like the suspension of dialogue or any other form of cooperation. Apart from the US, the EU and China also frequently utilize bilateral sanctions. A justification for the EU to use bilateral sanctions is that it lacks the ability to influence the behavior of others through military force and therefore has no other choice than the sanctions weapon. The EU also holds the view that these kinds of legal weapons are superior to the threat of military force. Recently, the EU has expanded its sanctions toolbox and increased reciprocity in public procurement, proposed an anti-coercion instrument, and devised other active tools to increase its leverage.

China too has used economic coercive measures to achieve political and strategic goals. Its sanction tools are traditionally less embedded in the rule of law and take a more informal nature. Recent cases include trade restrictions against Australia after it called for an independent panel investigation into the origins of COVID-19. Another example is South Korea's installation of the THAAD anti-missile defense system in light of North Korea's increased missile testing, which sparked unilateral action. Export restrictions of rare earth to Japan and targeted actions against Lithuania, and by extension to the EU Internal Market, in the aftermath of the opening of a "Taiwan" Representative Office instead of a Taipei Office can also be mentioned. After September 2020, China has adopted several regulations to respond to foreign sanctions, including Provisions for an Unreliable Entity List, Rules on Counteracting Unjustified Extra-Territorial Application of Foreign Legislation and Other Measures, and the Anti-Foreign Sanctions Law. So far, these legal instruments have not yet been put into practice.

Diversification Versus Decoupling

Political realists will point out that the economic success of one country will spur envy just as well as economic failure in another can equally lead to rivalry. In Adam Smith's time, it was already known that prosperity leads to power, and power leads in turn to others becoming fearful. Even if the economic growth of one country ultimately benefits others, politics tend to focus on inequalities in the short term and the fear that a shifting economic balance may render another state vulnerable to aggression. Nonetheless, economic weaknesses that result in increased political weakness do not have to be the result of misguided economic policies. Natural disasters as a result of climate change could also economically threaten the subsistence of a country, prompting it to take unilateral actions to protect its security.

Furthermore, it can be argued that economic openness is often accompanied by military expansion to control vital trade routes. It should, therefore, not come as a surprise that with China's economic rise, it has also made claims in the Taiwan Straits and other parts of the South China Sea. In fact, the entire Belt & Road Initiative (BRI) has already been interpreted by some governments as Chinese power projection. In a similar fashion, merchants and business groups around the world lobby actively to protect critical economic infrastructure, including human resources. The resulting efforts to maximize security can be seen as a projection of power with a view to changing the status quo. It is therefore important to avoid miscalculations.

It is against this background that China, the US, and the EU will need to find new ways to juggle conflicting economic policy goals. It is important that this is not only done through trade policy, but also through meaningful political and macroeconomic discussions. In the case of the EU, the Sino-European trade imbalance has become unsustainable. The EU is becoming increasingly dependent on China both as an export market and for key imports. China, meanwhile, is emancipating itself from European inputs because it is domestically producing many of the goods it once used to import from the EU. Both the pandemic and the war in Ukraine have brought to light some of the EU's critical dependencies. These examples have shown that the geopoliticization and weaponization of interdependencies can turn a promising market into a much less reliant trade partner in an instant. China has already anticipated and developed the concept of Dual Circulation as part of the 14th Five-Year Plan. It has already started to wane off from certain imports and to become more autonomous. The EU has probably no choice but to follow China's example in proportionally tackling its critical dependencies.

This need for diversification means that countries will still have to continue to source goods and services from both near and far. Therefore, this does not spell the end of globalization or international trade as such, but it may lead to a costlier version of globalization in which regulatory blocks are formed and political risk is factored in the cost of production. Regardless, a more fragmented form of globalization will still require that trade blocks look for increased openness and market access to diversify their sources of critical inputs, while at the same time, countries and economic sectors will need to plan for worst-case geopolitical scenarios. Hence, the EU is right when it speaks of "open strategic autonomy". Without market access and openness, diversification will not work. It also implies that new trade agreements should pay more attention to security of supply. This diversification is the result of a different approach to increased risks. Unlike decoupling, regaining full sovereign control of the value chain and to undo the effects of globalization are not goals in and of themselves.

Apart from the fact that it needs a renewal of industrial policy for its implementation, diversification does not yet answer the question as to what kind of global economic governance it requires. Should the world continue along a path of increased unilateralism, or should we try to mend existing multilateral instruments to deal with the challenges ahead? Of course, multilateralism and unilateralism are matters of degree from the start and their respective use depends on varying circumstances. They are never absolute. Countries and governments need a mix of unilateral and multilateral approaches in developing foreign policy. If we are seeing more unilateralism in dealing with China, it is because there is widespread resentment in the EU and the US based on the perception that China has enjoyed a strategic opportunity thanks to an open and liberal economy for many decades that was the result of multilateral economic consensus building in the form of institutions such as the IMF, the World Bank, and the WTO. Current frustrations also arise from China's lack of reciprocating this openness and from the belief that China has been unilaterally maximizing its self-interest to serve its own sovereign policy choices under the goal of Great Rejuvenation. However, since the US and the EU are clearly mesmerized by China's unilateral industrial policies, is it right that they should also find inspiration in China's vision on multilateralism?

About Multilateralism and Multipolarity

China has always presented itself as a staunch defender of "true multilateralism". In fact, this version of multilateralism cannot be understood without reference to China's concept of multipolarity. This concept has been frequently used since the end of the Cold War and the demise of the USSR. Deng Xiaoping, Jiang Zemin, and Hu Jintao spoke about the multipolar world which emerged from an international balance of forces where, according to their view, US military, economic, and technological power had become too great. However, Deng, Jiang, and Hu still tied the emergence and ambition of China to play a role in a multipolar world to the concept of *tao guang yang hui* (hide your strength and bide your time). It was only after the 2008 global financial crisis hit that China became confident enough to state that the process toward a multipolar world had become irreversible and that it would have to gradually revise its practice of *tao guang yang hui*. Thanks to the global financial crisis China's status and influence improved significantly. In 2014, President Xi remarked that the advancement of multipolarity in the world would not change. Ever since then, he has viewed the multipolar world as making deep changes to the international rules-based order. According President Xi, we are living in a world experiencing "profound changes unseen in a century" and heralding a new era in the international balance of forces.

China's understanding of multilateralism is tied to the multipolarity of the world that emerged after the end of the Cold War and it intends to rebuild it based on its concept of a Community of Common Destiny, or nowadays more often referred to as a Community of a Shared Future for Mankind. To build this Community, the Xi Government focuses heavily on infrastructure investment, new financial instruments, and new security concepts that borrow from its own holistic national development strategy. This embodies China's concept of globalization in which its own experience on the path of economic and social development is central.

The Community of a Shared Future for Mankind is the foundation for a loose political and economic block. By providing it with public goods, China aspires to build a "One Belt" and "One Road" and in so doing, provide the world with economic development, peace, and security. The Global Development Initiative (GDI) and the Global Security Initiative (GSI), in conjunction with the aforementioned BRI, are programs that provide these public goods to the world. Arguing that the West, under the leadership of the US, has lost its impetus to promote global governance, China has put itself in a leadership position to create a new world order by stating that it is better qualified to solve the problems and to meet global challenges. It goes as far as to set this direction and rules for others. It uses both consensual and coercive leverage in the UN system and it is actively involved in displacing liberal values that originated in the West. At present, 4 of 15 UN specialized agencies are led by Chinese nationals (UNIDO, ICAO, ITU, and FAO), demonstrating the ever-rising influence of China within the multilateral system. In addition to the UN and other multilateral institutions, such as international development banks, China also uses other forums for the roll out of public goods through action plans with regional groupings such as CACF, CEEC, China-CELAC, and FOCAC.

Notwithstanding the noble cause of building a Community of a Shared Future for Mankind, China's multipolar approach by no means equals multilateralism as viewed and practiced by the EU. The essence of multilateralism is that stronger countries accept to be bound by the exact same rules as weaker countries. China, by contrast, wants a multipolar order with its own loose coalition of support revolving around its own development and modernization concepts. This immediately and naturally limits its attractiveness for developed economies such as the EU Member States.

Moreover, where China used to be more focused on consensual elements of order-building, it is increasingly focused on punitive elements and coercion. There is nothing wrong in adding Chinese wisdom in the belief that it is better equipped to deal with global problems, but on the basis of its multipolarity, China has led outright attacks on universal norms and values, Western culture and governance systems. It should therefore not come as a surprise that this has led to a backlash in both the EU and the US. Wolf warrior diplomacy has further exacerbated these attacks on the West. It has raised legitimate questions in the EU about China's trust and reliability. It is not that the EU would be unable to accept Chinese leadership, but it questions the type of leader China might be.

Multilateralism is Based on Rules of Consent, Not Coercion

While after the Second World War, the cloak of leadership landed on the shoulders of the US and its allies, including the USSR, China has stepped into the world's limelight much later and it is no longer hiding from this light. It needs to take on new responsibilities and, therefore, must more actively participate in the formulation of international rules and institutions. The question of leadership is important. Who takes leadership in global governance and who leads within this leadership? Is it only about "might is right" or is it predominantly economic power that should account for this leadership position? Surely, to lead also means that one needs followers, and they must follow voluntarily. A country that asserts itself by coercion should not be accepted as a leader.

Leadership is born out of a collision of wills around which some consensus needs to arise. Leading by coercion by withholding food, energy, or other critical supplies from others may delegitimize the leadership altogether. With legitimacy also comes some moral component of leadership. To complicate matters even more is that governments consent on behalf of their populations and sometimes this can go against the popular will. Unfortunately, there are no clearly good or wrong answers, but sovereign nations that only serve their own naked self-interest do not make good multilateral interlocutors. Communication and persuasion are to be preferred over coercion and dictating rules. Nations should therefore avoid a world order in which consensus is the result of some form of coercion. Therefore, it seems wiser at this moment to stick to the already established rules of consent. It would be good, of course, to have some stronger elements in a group to make it more efficient, but multilateralism needs the power of inclusiveness to build consensus and enable compromise. The US and the EU both have their track records already. It will be important for China to show it also can deliver.

It should not be forgotten that without the support of the international community, China cannot realize its Great Rejuvenation and the two centennial goals. It is not enough to promote the success of its development model and to propose robust infrastructure deals or invest in security if there is the risk that those on the receiving end are possibly being coerced in a direction they do not wish to or should not take. China, for instance, may claim that it is better equipped to deal with extremism, terrorism, and populism. However, if this leads to increased surveillance and censorship, it will not easily be condoned as it will never be part of a consensus.

Likewise, if the BRI, GDI, and GSI radiate China's preference for others to become dependent on China economically and to divorce them from economic and other alliances with the West, then the Community of a Shared Future of Mankind and the goals it should serve to realize the China Dream will never be espoused by the entire world. The collective developing world may still want an alternative path to development in this conception, but it is less clear why others should join if these new instruments and concepts will only pitch the rest of the world against the West instead of rallying a broad consensus.

China still has much convincing to do and to prove that it will always play by the rules of consent, allow itself to make compromises with others and will not adopt coercive tactics. Until then, the EU is unlikely to rally around China's version of multilateralism.

International Technological Governance

Coming back to the initial question of governance, technology plays a significant role in diversification and the renewal of industrial policy. Technological progress is equally entwined with the global economy, because Artificial Intelligence, Quantum Computing, Internet of Things, among others, all intersect with international supply chains, financial power, data flows, and so forth. These are all areas where the US, the EU, and China compete to seize leadership. With programs such as Made in China 2025 and the aforementioned concept of Dual Circulation, China seeks to indigenize key technologies and to set market share targets for its domestic market. Subsidies, technology transfers, and market access restrictions are part of the industrial policies to accomplish this. China's ongoing drive to "catch up to and surpass" is a source of tension for those countries that want to remain their competitive advantage.

International economic governance should focus on the creation of a level playing field and therefore should not support acts of unfair competition. Unfortunately, a leading body or authority in the field of international competition is lacking in setting rules for anti-competitive behavior. The WTO is at present only partly equipped to this end. Technological advancement is of course part of the comparative advantage. Nonetheless, certain rules and practices could benefit from more multilateral oversight. This should become a pressing issue for trading nations around the world. This is an area where the EU, US, and China should do more together as tensions in this field are unsustainable overall.

The strengthening of transatlantic ties within the framework of the EU–US Trade and Technology Council is a step in dealing with this situation. It could make the engagement between the EU and China more complex. However, the US will have to thread carefully because the recent acceleration of US–China decoupling by means of export restrictions of strategic technologies causes unease in the EU. There are already signs that American unilateral actions are alienating partners and allies. Allies will find it difficult to reign in this unilateralism with universal values, if it outgrows certain proportions, because it will raise the question whether one can deny the right to technological progress.

It is important to discuss economic and technological capacities and to keep engaging in a more level playing field between the largest trading nations. There needs to be more room for constructive discussions on these economic and industrial policies. A lack of coordination and the use of unilateral trade sanctions could lead to serious harm and add to the existing geopolitical tensions. The EU should also not be trapped in a binary choice between trading with the US or China; neither should any other country in the world. The EU should prioritize trade and deals with partners that respect agreed norms, principles, rules, and procedures grounded in reciprocity. In addition, the EU should favor trade with partners who have stronger interests in climate change and de-carbonation of energy or in transport.

The focus on geopolitical risk should become an integral part of industrial policy dealing with microchips, batteries, and cloud systems, just to give a few examples. Getting these policies right will require a strong economic governance framework with an aim to strengthen resilience and competitiveness. At the start, it can be limited to like-minded countries or geographical trade blocks, but the aim should be to become as inclusive as possible and not to leave any nation behind. If certain existing critical dependencies are a source of geopolitical tension, it will necessitate more multilateral action to alleviate them.

After the Second World War, both steel and coal, as key supplies of the defense industry, were put under control of a supra-national authority on the European continent. Had it not been for the wisdom of the European Coal and Steel Community (ECSC), which after several stages eventually morphed into the EU, the European continent most probably would not have witnessed its longest ever period of peace. To find a true multilateral solution for the current building blocks of the defense industry like the EU did in the 1950s would be the best contribution to future world peace. Let us hope that the world does not need another devastating conflict before acknowledging again that giving up some hard-fought national sovereign rights could save the world from catastrophe.

The EU has had more experience with effective multilateralism by nature of its own institutions. Besides, the EU has always been open and oriented toward its international partners with an outward look on the world. It has been an actor of peace in Iran (JCPOA), the Sahel and recently in Armenia, to name just a few examples. The EU can speak to the world without arrogance, humbled by the numerous colonial errors of some of its Member States. It should play a role in bridging and offer a platform to find a sustainable multilateral solution to the contentions that unilateral actions by big powers are bringing to the world. The EU is not about projecting power and can lead by persuasion, without coercion. Of course, it has a defensive policy to protect existing universal norms, principles, and rules because it still believes they can work. It is time for moderate forces to invite themselves to the debate again in order to avoid extremes that could lead us to calamity.

H.E. Dr. Jan Hoogmartens was appointed Belgium's Ambassador to China in August 2020. Dr. Hoogmartens previously served as Diplomatic Advisor, Deputy Chief of Staff, and Chief of Staff in the offices of several Vice Premiers. His diplomatic postings have included Japan (Tokyo) and the European Union (Brussels) where he represented Belgium as Ambassador in COREPER (Part One). Upon his return to Brussels in 2023, he will become Chief of Staff of Belgium's Foreign Affairs Minister. Jan Hoogmartens obtained a PhD in Laws and holds several Master degrees from different universities around the globe.

Open Access This chapter is licensed under the terms of the Creative Commons Attribution-NonCommercial-NoDerivatives 4.0 International License (http://creativecommons.org/licenses/by-nc-nd/4.0/), which permits any noncommercial use, sharing, distribution and reproduction in any medium or format, as long as you give appropriate credit to the original author(s) and the source, provide a link to the Creative Commons license and indicate if you modified the licensed material. You do not have permission under this license to share adapted material derived from this chapter or parts of it.

The images or other third party material in this chapter are included in the chapter's Creative Commons license, unless indicated otherwise in a credit line to the material. If material is not included in the chapter's Creative Commons license and your intended use is not permitted by statutory regulation or exceeds the permitted use, you will need to obtain permission directly from the copyright holder.

Strengthening Australian–Chinese Collaboration in Decarbonisation and Green Economic Growth

Graham Fletcher

We are all on a journey towards a low-carbon future. Many opportunities exist for bilateral and regional cooperation on tackling the collective challenge of reducing global emissions to combat climate change.

With the world's most populous and fastest-growing economies, the Asia-Pacific region emits the largest volume of greenhouse gases, producing about half the world's carbon dioxide. At the recent 2022 Asia-Pacific Economic Cooperation (APEC) Summit, President Xi Jinping outlined China's desire to enhance decarbonisation cooperation with regional partners to protect the environment and promote green lifestyles for everyone. China has an important role to play in achieving global net zero.

China is leading the way in a number of areas of the global decarbonisation and energy transition. It is adding more renewables annually than Europe, India and the United States combined. At the same time, global efforts are being made to invest in new manufacturing technologies and build critical mineral supply chains. This will also provide new opportunities for China.

Climate Change is a Common Challenge

Most countries now have climate goals in place. In 2022, the Australian Government set a new target to reduce greenhouse gas emissions by 43% below 2005 levels by 2030. This will put Australia on track to achieve zero emissions by 2050. The

---

Ambassador of Australia to the People's Republic of China.

G. Fletcher (✉)
Beijing, China

Australian Government introduced several initiatives including, an enhanced safeguards mechanism; upgrading the electricity grid to support more renewable electricity; and tax incentives to accelerate the adoption of electric vehicles. This is a significant step up in Australia's ambition.

The Australian Government has made clear its vision for Australia, with abundant mineral resources and renewables potential, to become a clean energy superpower. To do this, policies have been adopted to foster innovation and incentivise investment to promote breakthroughs in technology, whilst also reducing emissions across all industry sectors. Australia will remain a reliable energy and resources supplier and investment partner beyond the transition.

The composition of Australia and China's bilateral trade makes us ideally suited as partners to address the climate challenge. China is Australia's largest two-way trading partner by far, and a significant source of investment. Mineral resources and energy trade is the bedrock of our trading relationship. But there is also much untapped potential.

China has an Important Role to Play in Supporting Global Decarbonisation

The Chinese government has also set its own historic carbon peaking and neutrality targets. It is committed to peaking carbon emissions before 2030 and achieving net-zero emissions by 2060. These are concrete steps in China's carbon neutrality plan.

The Australian Embassy's assessment is that, based on Beijing's current policies and trajectory, China is on track to meet its 2030 target. But we predict that achieving the 2060 target will be much harder, as it will involve a substantial transformation of China's industrial base.

China's success in developing new clean energy supply chains puts it in a prime position to invest in new manufacturing globally to support the global transition to renewable energy. This has also driven down the cost of renewables globally.

China now has the largest carbon market and the largest clean electric power generation system in the world. Despite currently being the world's largest coal consumer, China also leads the world in every zero-emissions technology. There is much for the whole world to gain from these innovations.

Opportunities for Future Collaboration

Low-carbon (energy) technology is now where the focus of governments, business and research sectors needs to be, for cooperation and innovation. China's strengths in green technology and Australia's renewable energy potential—underpinned by our energy and resources bilateral trade—can facilitate successful partnerships.

Our two governments attach great importance to addressing climate change. Following Australian Foreign Minister Penny Wong's successful visit to Beijing in December 2022, Australia and China agreed to resume dialogue on climate change as a bilateral priority. We intend to build on these discussions with a view to promoting practical outcomes that will make a difference. Our two countries are well positioned to engage in such work and make this kind of progress. Not only at the government level, but also in business and research partnerships.

New Manufacturing and Clean Energy Supply Chains

Like China, Australia has significant natural resources with huge potential in solar and wind power, as well as significant potential to develop clean energy products such as green hydrogen. Our complementary economies have much to gain by facilitating and supporting the innovation required to tap into these strengths. This will help contribute to energy and resources security for our two countries and the world as a whole.

Australia's significant natural resources also include critical minerals, which will play an important role in global decarbonisation efforts. Australia has many of the mineral elements the world needs to make advanced technology like solar panels, batteries and electric vehicles. Australia is the world's top producer of lithium, rutile and the second largest producer of zircon and rare earth elements.

China is playing a key role in the global clean energy transition. It has already made a significant contribution to Australia's energy market. This started with the supply of solar and wind systems. More recently, China became the leading supplier of battery electric vehicles in the Australian market, growing at 50% per year from a low base. Australian consumers are looking forward to more models coming to market in 2023.

Technology Sharing

China has the technology and investment power to make progress in clean power generation and supporting infrastructure upgrades. Australia's renewable energy industry is ripe for collaboration, with a strongly skilled workforce and business executives already pivoting in this direction. Australia's energy market has begun the transition—one in every three residential buildings now has solar panels. In the past five years, the proportion of Australia's electricity that comes from renewables has almost doubled, from 16.9% in 2017 to 32.5% in 2022. But a lot more needs to be done. Australia has a target of 82% renewable electricity by 2030, a substantial increase from the current level of one third.

Industry Research Collaboration

Our region can benefit from improved low-carbon industrial processes. Supply chains for clean energy technologies such as solar cells, batteries and hydrogen, improved energy and industrial efficiency and fuel switching are aimed at preventing the creation of emissions. Carbon capture, utilisation and storage (CCUS) complements the transition by addressing emissions that currently cannot otherwise be abated, including from industrial processes like steel or cement manufacturing.

China has signalled a strong desire to work with partners to find solutions to combat climate change. By seizing the opportunities before us through bilateral and regional collaboration, we can find ways to accelerate the transition to net zero. A multi-faceted approach is critical for achieving optimal low-carbon outcomes and leveraging innovation to mitigate global climate change. As we all continue on the low-carbon journey together, there will be opportunities and rewards for all. In so doing, we give ourselves a better chance to save the world.

H.E. Graham Fletcher has been Australia's Ambassador to China since August 2019. Prior to this appointment, Mr Fletcher was head of the North Asia Division in the Department of Foreign Affairs and Trade (DFAT) during 2008–2010 and again from 2015. During 2014, he led the team that completed negotiation of the China–Australia Free Trade Agreement. Mr Fletcher has served in the Australian Embassy to China on three previous occasions: as Third Secretary (1986–1988), Counsellor (1997–2000) and Deputy Head of Mission (2004–2008). He was also Deputy Head of Mission in the Australian Embassy in Washington (2011–2013) and Deputy Consul-General in the Australian Consulate-General in Noumea (1992–1994).

Open Access This chapter is licensed under the terms of the Creative Commons Attribution-NonCommercial-NoDerivatives 4.0 International License (http://creativecommons.org/licenses/by-nc-nd/4.0/), which permits any noncommercial use, sharing, distribution and reproduction in any medium or format, as long as you give appropriate credit to the original author(s) and the source, provide a link to the Creative Commons license and indicate if you modified the licensed material. You do not have permission under this license to share adapted material derived from this chapter or parts of it.

The images or other third party material in this chapter are included in the chapter's Creative Commons license, unless indicated otherwise in a credit line to the material. If material is not included in the chapter's Creative Commons license and your intended use is not permitted by statutory regulation or exceeds the permitted use, you will need to obtain permission directly from the copyright holder.

Iceland and China: Cooperating to Reduce CO$_2$ Emissions, Improve Public Health and Better Quality of Life

Thórir Ibsen

The size of both its population and economy makes China a major force in determining whether the world community achieves its common objective of halting the global threat of climate change. China is not only the world's largest emitter of carbon dioxide (CO$_2$), producing nearly one third of global emissions, but also, as the world's second largest economy, it could also be a key driver in the global green transition to carbon neutrality.

There is strong interest in many countries to work with China on combating climate change, especially in cooperation between industries that offer green solutions and climate friendly technologies. All the Nordic countries—Denmark, Finland, Iceland, Norway, and Sweden—have, for example, bilateral partnerships with China in such areas as renewable energy, electrical grids, electric power transmission, energy efficiency, and smart solutions. Together, the five Nordic countries recently completed a four-year project (2018–2021) called *Nordic Sustainable Cities* that focused on renewable energy solutions and sustainable development for Chinese cities.

Iceland and China have a long-standing bilateral collaboration in the integration and use of geothermal energy in China, which has contributed to reducing the country's carbon footprint. This cooperation started at the government-to-government level but later led to a commercial joint venture. Other Icelandic technologies developed to reduce carbon emissions have subsequently entered the Chinese market. Whilst these developments have been market driven, they have benefited from the goodwill of the governments of Iceland and China, which have actively fostered this cooperation. On multiple occasions, most recently on the occasion of the 50th anniversary of diplomatic relations in December 2021, China and Iceland have reiterated their commitment to collaborate further in areas that work towards the common goal of halting climate change.

Ambassador of Iceland to the People's Republic of China.

T. Ibsen (✉)
Beijing, China

Emissions Targets and Commitments

Both Iceland and China have made commitments to reduce greenhouse gas emissions and combat climate change. Iceland is committed under the COP 21 Paris Agreement of 2016 to cut emissions by 40% by 2030 and took on further emissions reduction commitment in 2019, pledging to cut emissions by 55% by 2030 as a part of common effort with other EEA countries (Norway and the member states of the European Union). Iceland's ultimate goal is to achieve carbon neutrality before 2040.

China has pledged, under the Paris Agreement, to reach a peak in CO_2 emissions before 2030 and achieve carbon neutrality before 2060. China intends to attain these goals by cutting CO_2 emissions per unit of GDP by more than 65% from 2005 levels, improve energy efficiency in key industries to meet international standards, implement green building standards in new structures, increase the share of new energy and clean energy-powered vehicles, enhance carbon removals through forestry, increase the installed capacity of wind and solar to more than 1,200 gigawatts, and increase the share of non-fossil energy to about 25% by 2030 and 80% by 2060.

Both countries have national action plans to attain these objectives. The Climate Action Plan of Iceland contains 48 individual actions aimed at reducing greenhouse gas emissions and increasing carbon uptake from the atmosphere. It outlines climate mitigation actions in transport, fisheries, energy, industry, chemicals, agriculture, waste management, afforestation, revegetation, and wetland reclamation. Furthermore, the Action Plan takes into account the United Nations' Sustainable Development Goals, adopted in 2015. Consistent with these goals, the action plan requires active co-operation with and participation of numerous and diverse stakeholders.

Iceland also participates in the EU Emissions Trading System (EU ETS) and aligns its actions with other members of the European Economic Area (EEA) in reducing emissions from agriculture, transport, waste management, and buildings, and in enhancing carbon removals from land use and forestry.

Climate change actions in China are guided by two policy documents, notably the *Working Guidance for Carbon Dioxide Peaking and Carbon Neutrality* and the *Action Plan for Carbon Dioxide Peaking before 2030*. These policy documents call for improved climate governance, legal and regulatory reforms, green innovation and low-carbon science and technology, incentives and constraint mechanisms, market mechanisms and sectoral policy goals for reducing emissions, and carbon removals through land-use management, afforestation, and revegetation.

The Importance of Geothermal Energy

Renewable energy plays a key role in the climate strategy of both Iceland and China. In Iceland, renewable energy supplies 85% of the energy consumed—65% of which is supplied by geothermal energy and 20% by hydropower—and all the electricity consumed in Iceland and the district heating is supplied by renewable energy. Already, Iceland has thus achieved 100% carbon neutrality in the production of electricity and energy for district heating. The next step is the transition to clean fuels in transportation.

In China, the target is to increase the share of non-fossil energy to about 25% by 2030 and 80% by 2060. China is investing heavily in renewable energy and in the production of electric vehicles. Worth noting is that energy and carbon-intensity reduction targets and non-fossil targets in energy and electricity sectors were also included in the 14th Five Year Plan (FYP).

What is unique, however, is the prominence given to geothermal energy both in Iceland and China. Both countries have taken effective steps to increase their domestic capacity to tap into this important renewable energy resource. They have also cooperated for decades in advancing the use of geothermal energy.

Iceland started assisting China in exploring and using its geothermal resources more than 40 years ago, when Chinese experts started attending the UN University Geothermal Programme (UNU GTP) in Iceland, now the GRÓ Geothermal Training Programme (GRO GTP). The programme offers professional training in the use of geothermal technology, which Icelanders have used on industrial scale for more than half a century for district heating and the production of electricity.

In 2006, cooperation between Iceland and China in the use of geothermal energy took on a much larger dimension with a joint venture between the China Petrochemical Corporation (Sinopec) and the Icelandic company Arctic Green Energy. Operating under the name "Sinopec Green Energy", the joint venture has become the largest geothermal district heating provider in the world. Today, it provides more than 70 cities and counties in China with renewable district heating. It is estimated that Sinopec Green Energy has reduced China's carbon footprint by 20 million tons of CO_2, whilst contributing to the improvement of air quality in major cities such as Beijing, Tianjin, Qingdao, Taiyuan, and Xiong'an as well as the provinces of Hebei, Shaanxi, Shanxi, Shandong, and Liaoning. The utilization of geothermal energy in district heating and cooling in Xiong'an is used as a case study in urban energy transition by the International Renewable Energy Agency (IRENA).

The Advantages of Geothermal Energy and the Opportunities of CCUS

Geothermal energy has number of advantages. Geothermal energy is renewable and provides energy systems with a base-load resource, a key attribute of geothermal energy. Its source is the molten core of the Earth, which is constantly releasing heat. This energy is often stored in the form of hot water far underground before it makes its way to the surface. With the right design to ensure heat exchange and pumping of used geothermal water back down to the reservoir, hydrothermal geothermal energy can be a very sustainable resource.

Next, there are the overwhelming environmental benefits. Geothermal installations have relatively little environmental impact if properly designed. The CO_2 emissions from geothermal plants are minimal and can be captured and stored or reused. When used for district heating in colder areas, geothermal can greatly reduce local smog and air pollution.

The cost of harnessing geothermal energy has also proven to be both predictable and stable. After initial research and investment, production costs come down quickly and the energy prices to the consumers remain stable compared to volatile fossil fuel prices.

Moreover, using domestic geothermal energy, which is a sovereign energy source, also strengthens energy security. By using domestic geothermal energy resources, countries can substantially reduce their energy supply risks by reducing their dependency on imported fossil fuels. Finally, geothermal energy is a dependable form of renewable energy that is available 24/7 and is the only renewable that is baseload.

Geothermal technologies also have a multitude of secondary benefits, some of which have become more profitable than electricity generation. Geothermal energy is used in Iceland for heating green houses, for horticulture, aquaculture, algae Omega-3 cultivation, and for microorganism research. It is used for leisure activities and sports, such as for swimming pools and spas. Geothermal water is also used to make daily life easier by melting snow in parking areas and sidewalks. Geothermal water is moreover used in medical treatments and for producing food supplements, silica supplements, skin care products, cosmetics, and various other industrial uses.

One of the fastest developing climate-related technologies growing out of the geothermal sector are Carbon Capture, Utilization, and Storage (CCUS). Icelandic companies are world leaders in developing these high-tech cutting-edge technologies. One technology involves Direct Air Capture (DAC), capturing CO_2 from industrial plant emissions and/or from the atmosphere and storing the carbon dioxide in the bedrock. Another leading technology involves capturing CO_2 from industrial processes and recycling the carbon dioxide into green methanol for industrial use or as fuel for cars, trucks, buses, and ships. Both technologies help to reduce greenhouse gas emissions from industrial facilities, and thus reduce the impact of industrial carbon emissions on the environment.

China emits some 11.5 billion tonnes of CO_2 per year and will clearly have to complete a major energy transition to renewable energy and apply effective energy efficiency measures to reduce its carbon emissions. However, even so, there will still be significant industrial emissions to deal with. In such instances, Carbon Capture, Utilization, and Storage (CCUS) technologies can help China in reaching its carbon neutrality target of 2060.

The Icelandic company Carbon Recycling International (CRI) has brought its technology for recycling carbon into green methanol to China. With this technology, industrial facilities in China can capture their carbon emissions and transform them into methanol for use as fuel or for industrial processes. The first plant to use this technology in China is in the city of Anyang in Henan Province, where CRI has constructed the largest CO_2-to-methanol reactor in the world. Two other such plants are currently under construction in Lianyungang (Jiangsu Province) and Guxian

County in Shanxi Province. With rapidly growing interest in this technology, CO_2-to-methanol technology has the added advantage of providing both road and sea transport with more climate friendly fuel whilst other technological alternatives are being developed.

Global Geothermal Cooperation

By using geothermal energy for district heating and cooling and for production of electricity, many countries can significantly reduce their carbon emissions, as well as their dependence on imported energy; this has been the experience of Iceland. The long-term economic and environmental benefits of geothermal energy outweigh the initial high costs, because the use of geothermal energy provides the general public with low and stable energy prices; it reduces air pollution and thus improves public health; and it ensures that public and private utilities generate stable and profitable income.

It is widely recognized amongst experts, however, that geothermal energy is an underutilized renewable resource. Electricity is produced using geothermal energy in some 26 countries and for district heating in 70 countries. With constantly advancing technologies like heat pumps, geothermal and thermal energy can become an even larger part of the global electricity production as well as the heating and cooling of cities, which is perhaps its greatest value.

Considering the many advantages of geothermal energy, it is surprising how little attention has been given to the utilization of this resource. Part of the answer is found in the lack of awareness of policymakers and lack of technical expertise. Part of the answer is also found in the competitive advantage that subsidised carbon fuel has over renewable energy. To increase the share of geothermal energy in the global energy profile, these two thresholds need to be levelled. Iceland has worked actively to address this issue and promote geothermal energy by raising awareness, capacity building, and initiating multilateral funding to lower the initial costs and risks of building geothermal operations on industrial scale.

Iceland's experience shows that in order to reap the long-term economic benefits of geothermal energy, effective government support is required to apply geothermal energy on a large scale. In Iceland, the Government played a major role in advancing the exploration and use of geothermal energy, supporting institutions to generate the knowledge necessary to use geothermal resources and geothermal power in Iceland, and by directly supporting geothermal projects by providing drilling insurance as well as grants and direct funding of geothermal exploration projects.

As a result, geothermal energy has today become a highly competitive industry in Iceland and much of the research costs, investment, and operational costs have been transferred to private and public companies that operate on the energy market on a competitive basis. Furthermore, the renewable energy sector in Iceland has fostered the development of robust and diverse expertise, businesses and companies that cover all aspects of geothermal energy and hydropower utilization from exploration and assessment to consultancy, design, engineering, energy production, and designing of secure high voltage energy transportation systems. Many of these companies have entered the global market, offering their services, expertise, and investment resources in geothermal projects in many countries in Africa, Asia, Central America, and Europe.

Based on this experience, the Government of Iceland, Icelandic experts, and Icelandic geothermal energy companies work actively at promoting the use of geothermal energy through such international fora as the International Renewable Energy Agency (IRENA), the Global Geothermal Alliance (GGA), the European Geothermal Energy Council (EGEC), the International Geothermal Association (IGA), the Iceland Renewable Energy Cluster and the Geothermal Research Cluster (GEORG). The Government of Iceland also hosts the GRÓ Geothermal Training Programme (GRO GTP) (formerly the United Nations University's Geothermal Energy Training Programme), which is a postgraduate training programme that offers capacity building in geothermal exploration and development. The programme offers training courses for practicing professionals from developing and transitional countries with significant geothermal potential. The programme also offers MSc and PhD scholarships in Icelandic Universities to former fellows, and short courses and workshops in Africa, Central America, and Asia.

Iceland has also initiated a special fund created through the World Bank to provide grants to cover the initial exploration costs of geothermal projects, known as the Global Geothermal Development Plan (GGDP) and led by the World Bank's Energy Sector Management Assistance Program (ESMAP). The objective of the GGDP is to assist developing countries in scaling up the use of their geothermal power. The GGDP differs from previous efforts in that it focuses on the primary barrier to geothermal expansion: notably the cost and risk of exploratory drilling, by providing substantial new concessional financing.

Iceland also supported the *East Africa Geothermal Exploration Project* in partnership with the Nordic Development Fund (NDF) to enhance knowledge and capacity building in geothermal exploration, as well as to finance the early stages of geothermal development, specifically test drilling. Iceland also works closely with IRENA and UNEP, as both organizations have dedicated workstreams on geothermal.

However, more can be done to promote geothermal energy, especially in Asia. The Icelandic capacity building programme has been brought to China through an initiative by Arctic Green Energy, launching the first Sino-Icelandic geothermal training programme in late 2019. Delayed by COVID-19, the geothermal training programme is planned to be re-launched in the autumn of 2023. The university level training programme will be particularly useful for cultivating expertise in the use of geothermal energy in China's neighbouring countries. Arctic Green Energy has also initiated the establishment of the Sino-Icelandic Geothermal Technology R&D Centre, to conduct high-level joint research, enhancing the training of and exchanges between researchers to encourage technology transfer and strengthen the geothermal capacity building in Iceland and China. Finally, the company has partnered with the Beijing Research Institute of Uranium Geology (BRIUG) to work together to develop high-temperature geothermal fields in China.

In addition to such capacity building and research cooperation, Iceland and China could join hands in encouraging Multilateral Development Banks (MDBs) such as the Asian Infrastructure Investment Bank to devote more resources to assist countries with installation of necessary infrastructure to develop their geothermal energy resources and for CCUS installations.

Conclusions

Iceland is a successful example of the commercial development and application of geothermal energy and Icelandic businesses and experts lead the way in cutting-edge research and development. As a leader in geothermal energy, Iceland is committed to sharing its experience and knowledge with other countries and to work with China to promote the use of geothermal energy and new climate-related technologies, such as carbon capture, utilization, and storage.

China has taken an important step in further embracing and promoting geothermal energy and related carbon reducing technologies by hosting the World Geothermal Congress (WGC) in Beijing in September 2023. The Congress is scheduled every two to three years and was last held in Reykjavik, Iceland, in 2021. The Congress is attended by leading experts as well as policymakers, business leaders, investors, and NGOs who come together to discuss and exchange information about geothermal technologies, policies, regulations, and markets throughout the world. There are also field-visits, exhibitions, and workshops as well as hundreds of enterprises that showcase their businesses.

By combining their knowledge, technologies, and business resources, Iceland and China can continue to work together within the international arena to raise awareness amongst policymakers and build support for the development of geothermal resources and for a more extensive use of carbon capture and reuse technologies as alternatives to carbon-based energy resources.

Geothermal energy is destined to remain a vital contributor to a global green energy future—a future Iceland wants to share with China and the world.

 **H.E. Thórir Ibsen** is currently Ambassador of Iceland to the People's Republic of China with accreditation to Mongolia, Thailand, and Vietnam. Prior to this, he held positions in the Icelandic Foreign Service including Chief Negotiator for the Free Trade Agreement and post-Brexit relations between Iceland and the UK. He was also Representative of Iceland in the EEA Grants Financial Mechanism Committee. He has served as Ambassador to the Czech Republic, Slovakia, and Hungary as well as to Indiathe European Union and Belgium with accreditation to the Netherlands and Luxembourg. He also served as Ambassador to France with accreditation to Italy and Spain. He has also acted as the Permanent Representative of Iceland to the OECD, the Council of Europe and UNESCO, served as Chief Negotiator and Ambassador for Climate ChangeDirector of the Defence Department, Deputy Permanent Representative of the Delegation of Iceland to NATO Director of the Department of Natural Resources and Environmental Affairs and Senor Arctic Affairs Official.

Open Access This chapter is licensed under the terms of the Creative Commons Attribution-NonCommercial-NoDerivatives 4.0 International License (http://creativecommons.org/licenses/by-nc-nd/4.0/), which permits any noncommercial use, sharing, distribution and reproduction in any medium or format, as long as you give appropriate credit to the original author(s) and the source, provide a link to the Creative Commons license and indicate if you modified the licensed material. You do not have permission under this license to share adapted material derived from this chapter or parts of it.

The images or other third party material in this chapter are included in the chapter's Creative Commons license, unless indicated otherwise in a credit line to the material. If material is not included in the chapter's Creative Commons license and your intended use is not permitted by statutory regulation or exceeds the permitted use, you will need to obtain permission directly from the copyright holder.

Gabon's Green Forests Whisper to a Major Carbon Emitter

Baudelaire Ndong Ella

Whether it is a country that emits very little carbon dioxide or one that absorbs the most, every nation of the world today is overwhelmed by the effects of climate change and, as such, there is a pressing need for strong collaboration, in-depth exchange, and effective global governance mechanisms to tackle environmental challenges.

Gabon has been able to make history by keeping its forests green. These forests, which have been referred to as the "last garden of Eden", absorb a total of 140 million tons of CO_2 every year, the equivalent of removing 30 million cars from the road globally, making Gabon one of the most carbon positive countries in the world, with very low-carbon emission and very high absorption rate.

However drastic seasonal changes, landslides, urbanization, and illegal mining and logging, still pose a great threat to the country's forest conservation initiatives. In the face of all these, the use of satellite imagery by the government has proven to be an effective strategy. However, an effective partnership with China, both a major emitter as well as a leader in green technology, will further boost the attainment of expected results.

Climate Change

According to the Executive Secretary of the UN Climate Convention, climate change remains humanity's greatest challenge. Bearing this in mind, countries must demonstrate a transformational shift in the implementation of the Paris Agreement. A green environment is important in attaining sustainable global development today because nature provides the foundation and conditions for human survival. The objectives of

---

Ambassador of the Republic of Gabon to the People's Republic of China.

B. N. Ella (✉)
Beijing, China

the Paris Agreement include reaching net-zero emissions by the middle of the twenty-first century, to remain below a temperature increase of 1.5 °C in global warming and to cut emissions by 5% by 2030, among others. According to the Convention, the five main impacts of climate change are storms, heat waves, rising sea levels, melting glaciers, and warming oceans.

Green Gabon

The forests of Gabon represent more than green energy for the indigenous people; it provides them food, medicine, spiritual wellness, and other benefits. To preserve harmony between humanity and the environment, the government of Gabon strictly adheres to the principles of the Paris Agreement, to which it is a signatory.

From the Massaha Ancestral Forest in the northeast of Gabon to Loango Park in the Ogooué–Maritime, down to the Lope Park in Ogooue–Ivindo and back to Akanda National Park in the heart of Libreville, the model used for forest preservation and conservation is the same and aligns with the "Green Gabon" national agenda which aims to improve the productivity of agricultural and forestry activities while minimizing the ecological footprint of human activities.

The Republic of Gabon belongs to the Congo basin, the second-largest carbon sink in the world. Green forest occupies over 88% of the country, and deforestation rates are as low as 0.08%. Gabon is serving and saving the planet by keeping its forests intact, and if Gabon were to cut its trees and mismanage its biodiversity, Africa would witness far more droughts and flooding than there are today.

Cognizant of the strategic role of the forests in solving the problem of climate change and attaining the sustainable development goals, the President and Head of State of the Republic of Gabon, H.E. Ali Bongo Ondimba, is building a culture that fosters a concept of strong environmental conservation and preservation of the country's untouched natural resources. This unassailable political commitment has made Gabon an exemplary model of environmental conservation and, since 2000, the country has successfully created 13 national parks.

Thanks to government's altruistic environmental policies, Gabon has preserved its forests and oceans and pursued a consistent vision and coherent policy on deforestation. The country is also proactively addressing land degradation. In 2009, the Gabonese government enacted a nationwide ban on whole log exports.

Gabon has experienced the firsthand benefits of carbon sequestration for job creation and enhanced climate resilience. Gabon has 13 natural parks, one of which is a UNESCO World Heritage Site. Gabon has also ensured the sustainable management of its timber resources making sure that all forest concessions are FSC certified.

The Grant

Gabon is the first African country to receive result-based payment for reduced deforestation and forest degradation emissions (US$150 million) from the Central African Forest Initiative-CAFI. The reward is a clear indication that with a realistic, multi-dimensional, and holistic approach, and emission reductions can be achieved in the Congo Basin.

To maximize the impact of the award, Gabon and CAFI have agreed that the first payment of US$17 million will go toward activities that decrease CO_2 emissions and enhance sustainable development in local communities, support forest law and enforcement to combat illegal activities, support community initiatives to improve income, and promote the welfare of households in related communities, and to improve the capacity of national park staff.

Challenges and Strategies

As a continent, Africa has contributed the least to climate change thanks to the Congo Basin, in which Gabon lies. It is responsible for less than 4% of global emissions, but is still the most impacted by climate change. Gabon, like every other African country, still feels the effects of climate change in the form of soaring temperatures, seasonal flooding, landslides, and rising sea levels, which affects lives, causes loss of shelter for millions, and increases poverty in a range of communities. As a result, Gabon feels a sense of urgency to enact smart climate strategies rather than delay and proffer crisis responses to the impact of climate change.

Today, there is a need for Gabon and Africa to continue to put in greater efforts that will result in more realistic, multidimensional, and holistic approaches and build a resilient framework at all levels in order to meet the challenges of climate change. Consequently, smart climate strategies have to be aligned with government policies and budgeting by all countries to combat this phenomenon.

According to an October 2022 World Bank report, climate change could result in GDP annual losses ranging between 2 and 12% by 2050 in Africa. Meanwhile, in the Sahel Region, 13.5 million more people could be affected by poverty by 2050. Therefore, it is against this backdrop, that Gabon is seeking lasting solutions toward the development of smart climate policies, at the national, sub-regional, and international levels.

At the national level, the greatest threat to forests is illegal mining and logging. To put an end to these dangerous activities, the Gabonese government has set up a satellite observation center and uses satellite imagery to achieve targeted results.

Urban development is also an increasing threat to protected areas. For instance, the size of the Mondah Forest north of Libreville has been decreasing, losing 40% of its total area over the past 80 years.

In 2010, the government established a national climate council, which serves as a facilitator to align climate change issues with sectorial development policies

It is against this backdrop that we have developed a sustainable forest management strategy to improve and enhance efforts to counter climate change, which is of paramount importance to the Gabonese government. According to Gabon's Minister of Water, Forests, the Sea and the Environment, Prof. Lee White, Gabon's forest management strategy is based on science based and robust. The ministry is making strides to develop and lead the implementation of forest policies, to protect and restore forest ecosystems and preserve biodiversity in the country.

This ministerial department has also set an agenda to ensure sustainability in the production of forest resources, promote the industrialization and marketing of forest products, and develop policies on wildlife and protected areas. Similarly, other areas such as regional and international cooperation have not been left out. The ministry actively seeks to inform people and raise awareness about the exploitation of forest resources, wild life and protected areas.

The government of Gabon is also working to influence public opinion and foster smart forest development by empowering local and indigenous communities, and promote the sustainable use of natural resources. In addition, government policy in Gabon is also moving toward a climate-smart mode of agriculture in order to ensure food security for Gabon.

Most importantly, Gabon is investing to ensure its participation in the carbon market. According to Minister Lee White, Gabon is hoping to produce 187 million carbon credits that can be sold. These credits would be sold as carbon that Gabon has removed from the atmosphere.

At the sub-regional level, African governments have concurred that, regional collaboration and in-depth exchange remain a driver of global progress. African Climate Week was held in Gabon from August 29 to September 2, 2022, and serves as a platform for governments and other stakeholders to generate positive opinions and set agendas for a durable response to the challenges of climate change.

Gabon used the opportunity during African Climate Week to position itself as an African leader in environmental development and offered to assist other African countries working in the same direction.

The forum was also an avenue to empower stakeholders to drive climate action across countries, communities and economies. About 2,300 actors in the domain converged in Libreville to discuss engagement and action in the context of the Paris Agreement. Discussions during the Libreville convention centered on three main issues—resilience against climate risk, the transition to a low-emission economy and partnerships to solve pressing challenges.

Gabon-China on Green Development

The Republic of Gabon and the People's Republic of China have both ratified the Paris Agreement on Climate Change and thus are working with other nations to proffer solutions to current climate issues. Both countries are investing resources and intelligence to develop a holistic and systematic approach in the development and improvement of their climate response initiatives. The report of the 20th Congress of the Communist Party of China (Oct 2022) stated that China seeks to promote a green and low-carbon economy, intensify pollution prevention and control measures, accelerate the transition to a model of green development, enhance diversity, stability and sustainability in the ecosystem and work actively and prudently toward the goals of reaching peak carbon emissions and carbon neutrality.

As a major emitter of CO_2 as well as a leader in green technology, China is a unique partner for Gabon in green energy transition and sustainable low-carbon and carbon positive development of our countries and continents.

Gabon as the planet's most carbon positive country would like to assess the possibility of linking our carbon credits to the Chinese carbon exchange. Perhaps we can introduce net carbon sequestration credits created through logging concessions operated by Chinese companies on the Chinese carbon exchange.

It is our firm belief that green economies are vital for sustainable development and low-carbon economies will benefit generations to come.

H.E. Baudelaire Ndong Ella is currently the Ambassador Extraordinary and Plenipotentiary of the Republic of Gabon to the People's Republic of China. Prior to his appointment, he was Gabon's Permanent Representative to the United Nations in New York and Geneva. Mr. Baudelaire Ndong Ella was President of The Human Rights Council of the United Nations in 2014. A career diplomat, Mr. Ndong Ella has held various posts at the Ministry for Foreign Affairs, Cooperation and the Francophonie of Gabon, including as Ambassador and Deputy Director-General for International Cooperation and Head of the United Nations Division. Mr. Ndong Ella has a postgraduate degree in international law and human rights from the University of Nantes in France and a postgraduate diploma from the National Administration School in Gabon. He also has an M.A. in public law and a B.A. in public law from the University of Omar Bongo in Gabon.

Open Access This chapter is licensed under the terms of the Creative Commons Attribution-NonCommercial-NoDerivatives 4.0 International License (http://creativecommons.org/licenses/by-nc-nd/4.0/), which permits any noncommercial use, sharing, distribution and reproduction in any medium or format, as long as you give appropriate credit to the original author(s) and the source, provide a link to the Creative Commons license and indicate if you modified the licensed material. You do not have permission under this license to share adapted material derived from this chapter or parts of it.

The images or other third party material in this chapter are included in the chapter's Creative Commons license, unless indicated otherwise in a credit line to the material. If material is not included in the chapter's Creative Commons license and your intended use is not permitted by statutory regulation or exceeds the permitted use, you will need to obtain permission directly from the copyright holder.

Swedish Security Policy in a New Security Environment

Helena Sångeland

On 18 May 2022, Sweden decided to apply for membership in NATO. This marked the end of 200 years of neutrality and non-participation in military alliances. This policy was put in place to guarantee Sweden's independence and self-determination, to safeguard our sovereignty and our fundamental values and preserve our freedom of action in the face of political, military and other pressure. During two centuries and under this policy, Sweden was able to develop and prosper.

Sweden Continues to Build its Security Together with Others

However, Sweden has never been, nor is it now isolated, or solely relied on its own capability. Defence cooperation with other countries has been and remains essential to strengthening Sweden's military capabilities to respond to armed attacks and to raise the conflict deterrence threshold. Today, Sweden takes part in approximately twenty defence cooperation initiatives, which have created the conditions for, and contributed to, a high level of interoperability with strategic partners. It has enhanced the ability to act together in a crisis and ultimately in war.

Over the last decade, the Nordic countries have further intensified their foreign, security and defence cooperation. Within the framework of the Nordic Defence Cooperation, NORDEFCO, defence cooperation in the region has been enhanced through extensive training activities, exchange of air surveillance information, easier access to each other's territories, a crisis consultation mechanism and secure communication systems. Defence ministers of Nordic countries hold regular crisis consultations.

Ambassador of Sweden to the People's Republic of China.

H. Sångeland (✉)
Beijing, China

Sweden's defence cooperation with Finland is of particular significance. In a deteriorating security environment, the importance of Finnish-Swedish cooperation has become increasingly clear. Specific areas of cooperation include joint operation planning, exercises, combined military units, the establishment of secure communication systems, air and maritime surveillance, defence material, mutual use of military infrastructure as well as personnel exchanges. In 2020, the Swedish parliament granted the Government extended rights to provide and receive operational military support within the framework of defence cooperation between our two countries.

At the same time, Sweden maintains close defence cooperation with our other neighbours Norway and Denmark on a bilateral basis. Bilateral cooperation also extends to the Baltic countries in the defence and security policy arena.

In addition, Sweden maintains defence and security cooperation with other countries in Europe, within the European Union, and with the United States. Sweden has a shared interest with the United States in improving the ability to act together in a crisis. Following the signing of a bilateral Statement of Intent, SoI, in 2016, cooperation between the United States and Sweden has developed and been solidified.

Sweden also has a long-standing tradition of supporting the UN and has reason to continue to be active in all areas of the UN's work, such as peace and security, development cooperation and human rights.

Sweden has since 1948 contributed with more than 80,000 Swedes to UN peacekeeping operations: from the very first group of military observers in 1948 in the Golan heights, to the Neutral Nations Supervisory Commission (NNSC) on the Korean Peninsula, ONUC in the Congo, UNIFIL in Lebanon, UNPROFOR in Bosnia and MINUSMA in Mali, to only mention a few examples. Swedish participation has been greatly appreciated, especially in light of the high quality of our personnel and skill. Sweden has unique capabilities in a number of areas that are crucial to UN peacekeeping, especially as conflicts have become increasingly complex and require specialised capabilities.

However, within the current cooperation framework, there is no guarantee that Sweden would be helped if it were target of a threat or attack. If I had been asked one and a half years ago if Sweden had any intention of joining NATO in the near or intermediate future, my answer would have been that I could not foresee it. Russia's large-scale aggression[1] against Ukraine, launched a year ago, on February 24, 2022, was of a nature and scope that Europe has not experienced since the Second World War. The fabric of European Security was torn apart and was an order that was based on the fundamental principles of the Helsinki Final Act, the Charter of Paris and the other commitments of the Organisation for Security and Co-operation in Europe, OSCE, and includes territorial integrity, every state's right to independently determine its security policy and the right to self-defence. Through its actions, Russia

---

[1] General Assembly adopted a definition of "aggression" (see UN General Assembly Resolution 3314 [XXIX]). The definition specifies what constitutes an act of aggression, for example, the invasion or attack by the armed forces of a state of the territory of another state. This definition also provides the basis for "crime of aggression" as defined in the Rome Statute of the International Criminal Court.

failed to adhere to the rules-based international order despite its commitments to do so.

It was a watershed moment because Russia's actions immediately gave rise to a structural, long-term and significant deterioration of the security environment in the region around Sweden, in the rest of Europe and globally. It raised questions about how Sweden could best guarantee its national security. The Government concluded that Russian provocation and retaliatory measures against Sweden could not be ruled out.

NATO Application and its Implications

Global developments require an active, broad-based and responsible foreign and security policy. It is Sweden's view that challenges and threats should, as far as possible, be met in cooperation with other countries and organisations. Political, diplomatic and international dialogue contributes to Sweden's security and national interests.

The United Nations plays a central role in the multilateral, rules-based international order. The principles and rules of intergovernmental cooperation set out in the UN Charter form the basis of the global collective security system. However, the UN's ability to act to resolve crisis affecting permanent members of the Security Council is limited by the right of veto.

The significant deterioration of the security environment has highlighted the importance of continuing to deepen Sweden's defence and security cooperation frameworks. Cooperation with the Nordic countries and other partner countries with engagement in the Baltic Sea region is especially important. While Sweden welcomes the development of the EU's civil and military crisis management capacity, as well as the cooperation to strengthen the resilience and capability development in the Member States, in line with the objectives of the Strategic Compass adopted in 2022, the necessary conditions are not in place to able defence obligations to be provided within the EU. Such arrangements were not comparable to NATO membership.

In this rapidly deteriorating security environment, the Swedish government took the decision to apply for NATO membership on 18 May 2022. This decision enjoys broad support in the Swedish parliament. NATO membership is in line with the solidarity-based security policy that has been the basis of Sweden's security policy for a long time.

NATO membership will not affect Sweden's ability to continue to promote the basic values of Swedish foreign and security policy. Membership would be complementary to Sweden's engagement in the EU, the UN and the Organisation for Security and Co-operation in Europe, OSCE. Several European countries have driven the development of multilateral formats with increased intensity in recent years. For NATO allies, these cooperation formats are complementary to NATO membership. In these, Sweden will continue to be able to push for security-related issues based on its own decisions and respect for democracy, human rights, the rule of law, women's political and economic participation, and the fight against climate change. Sweden will remain a driving force in international efforts for gender equality and the women, peace and security agenda.

As this article is written, Sweden's NATO membership is still awaiting ratification by all NATO members. The Swedish Government's report to the parliament,[2] which preceded the decision to join NATO wrote that for Sweden, the primary effect of NATO membership would be that Sweden would become part of NATO's collective security and be covered by the security guarantees enshrined in Article 5 of the North Atlantic Treaty.

The report also stated that Russia (or the Soviet Union) had never attacked a NATO Ally, but it has recently attacked non-NATO countries. Russia's invasion of Ukraine and the measures NATO has highlighted the distinction between the countries that are covered by NATO's defence guarantees and those that are not. The importance of being covered by guarantees increased as Russia showed its readiness to carry out a large-scale military attack on a neighbouring country.

As a NATO member, Sweden would be obliged to consider an armed attack on an Ally as an attack on Sweden and to assist that Ally by taking such action as it deems necessary, including military, should a situation in accordance with Article 51 of the UN Charter arise.

NATO takes decisions by consensus and, if Article 5 is invoked, each individual member country reserves the right to determine the form of assistance to provide to other allies.

Sweden would be expected to contribute to NATO's deterrence and defence posture. Like all allies, Sweden would be expected to contribute in a spirit of solidarity to operations to defend individual NATO countries.

Given its strategic geographical location, Sweden would primarily contribute to NATO through defence of Swedish territory and its neighbourhood. Swedish NATO membership would raise the threshold for military conflicts and thus have a deterrent effect in northern Europe.

With both Sweden and Finland as NATO members, all Nordic and Baltic countries would be covered by collective defence guarantees. The current uncertainty as to what form collective action would take if a security crisis or armed attack occurred would decrease. From a security perspective, the Baltic Sea region and the Cap of the North constitute a single area, and, as members, Sweden and Finland would be fully involved in NATO defence planning for that area. Through NATO membership, Sweden would not only strengthen its own security, but also contribute to the security of like-minded countries.

As already being a partner, Sweden has had long-standing cooperation with NATO within the framework of NATO's operational planning. Membership would however substantially improve the conditions for integrated defence planning. NATO has a command structure with a unique capability to lead large-scale and demanding military operations. The integrated command structure enables the allies to operate together more effectively and swiftly than what would otherwise be possible. NATO

---

[2] Deterioration of the security environment—implications for Sweden Ds 2022:8.

also provides an infrastructure that incorporates air surveillance and defence and advanced logistics cooperation.

The United States is the most important factor for security in Europe. The United States has made clear that European countries outside NATO do not receive bilateral defence guarantees. Regardless of administration, the United States has pushed for European countries to assume greater responsibility for their own security. Even if Sweden does not receive formal guarantees or become a NATO member, the United States is important for Sweden's defence.

Swedish NATO membership would make Sweden—as a member of a multilateral organisation with formal collective commitments—less dependent on its bilateral, and in this context, non-formalised relationship with the United States. NATO membership would mean that Sweden would receive collective defence guarantees from NATO's member countries under the North Atlantic Treaty.

NATO membership also entails committing to the organisation's nuclear doctrine and strategic deterrence policy. At the same time, NATO decisions are taken by consensus, and every member has the right to take a position on decisions concerning the deployment or use of nuclear weapons on its own territory as, for example, Denmark, Lithuania, Norway and Spain have done. NATO has stated that the Alliance will work to reduce strategic risk as long as nuclear weapons exist.

A number of NATO countries are committed to disarmament and non-proliferation of nuclear weapons and this will remain a foreign and security policy priority for the Swedish government. The work will be carried out not least within the framework of the Non-Proliferation Treaty for nuclear weapons (NPT) as well as through the Stockholm Initiative for Nuclear Disarmament, with a view to strengthening the implementation of the NPT, reducing polarisation between countries and achieving concrete steps on the way towards the ultimate goal of a world free of nuclear weapons.

Due to military-strategic and military-geographical factors, Sweden would inevitably be involved if a military conflict arose in northern Europe. NATO would expect support and collaboration, based on Sweden's partnership and Modalities for Strengthened Interaction, MSI, that were activated in response to Russia's invasion of Ukraine.

Similarly, Russia's defence and security structures essentially already include Sweden in NATO's sphere. Sweden had the status of an Enhanced Opportunities Partner of NATO, which is a framework for an individually designed partnership that focuses on political dialogue, training and exercises, and information exchange. Cooperation with NATO has been key to developing the capabilities of the Swedish Armed Forces, both for national defence and for operations in our neighbourhood and beyond. Following Russia's illegal aggression against Ukraine in 2014, NATO's cooperation with Sweden and Finland deepened. Following the invasion of Ukraine in February 2022, Sweden and Finland activated Modalities for Strengthened Interaction, MSI, which intensified information exchange and coordination of activities and strategic communication linked to the crisis.

The UN and NATO cooperate on peacekeeping operations, training, mine clearance, the fight against terrorism and in the area of women, peace and security. In a

Joint Declaration in 2018, the two organisation set out plans for their joint efforts in these and other areas. The UN Security Council has given a mandate for NATO crisis management operations in Bosnia and Herzegovina, Kosovo, Afghanistan and Libya, as well as NATO Training Mission in Iraq. As a partner country, Sweden has also participated in a number of NATO-led operations, including the International Security Assistance Force (ISAF) in Afghanistan, Operation Unified Protector (OUP) in Libya and Kosovo (KFOR).

Russia assumes that Sweden will cooperate with NATO on a deep and broad basis if a crisis or war involving both Sweden and NATO countries arises (or only NATO countries in Sweden's neighbourhood). On the other hand, Sweden would lack the defence guarantees that NATO membership provides, which would potentially be associated with a low risk for Russia if it took unilateral action against Swedish territory early in a conflict, for example, by attempting to take control of the Swedish island Gotland in the Baltic Sea. Sweden would therefore need to have greater military capability to defend itself and assert its territorial integrity without NATO support. This would require major investments and, in addition to the announced two percent of GDP, an increased defence budget for years to come.

The report also noted that if both Sweden and Finland became NATO members, their bilateral cooperation would also develop within the framework of NATO, where bilateral operational planning for certain situations or specific geographical areas could complement or become part of NATO defence planning. Interoperability with NATO member countries would increase further if Sweden were fully integrated into different NATO structures. Ongoing cooperation would continue, including air surveillance information exchange, territorial surveillance and the assertion of territorial integrity, but it would need to be adapted—to varying degrees—to new circumstances.

NORDEFCO could be deepened within NATO. This applies to joint planning, capability development and logistics solutions within both NORDEFCO and Nordic trilateral and bilateral cooperation.

Nordic-Baltic cooperation could also be deepened and include a greater focus on practical collaboration and joint planning. Sweden would be able to maintain the same bilateral security cooperation arrangements under the military leadership of Western countries such as the United States, the United Kingdom and France. Sweden's bilateral cooperation with the United States would benefit through greater scope for advancing bilateral defence cooperation. This is especially important, as Sweden has ambitions to, and is interested in, furthering its cooperation with the United States.

Bilateral defence cooperation with leading European countries, such as the United Kingdom, France and Germany could deepen. If Sweden and Finland joined NATO, regional defence cooperation initiatives such as the JEF and EI2 would only comprise NATO countries, which could facilitate coordination and complement NATO's other operations in times of conflict.

All in all, the report concluded, it can be said that Sweden's existing bilateral and multilateral defence cooperation could be enhanced if Sweden joined NATO. Cooperation with countries in Sweden's neighbourhood could serve as a platform for shared responsibility within NATO for the Baltic Sea region and the Cap of the North. Sweden's extensive defence and security policy dialogue and high level of interoperability with other countries in the neighbourhood would contribute to this.

Hence, through the membership Sweden's national security will be significantly strengthened. At the same time the entire responsibility of NATO will be Sweden's responsibility—an attack on one member is an attack on all. Or, as recently expressed by the Swedish Prime Minister, through an equally well-known phrase: one for all, all for one.

H.E. Helena Sångeland has served as Ambassador of Sweden to China and Mongolia since 2019, before which she served as Ambassador to the Islamic Republic of Iran 2016–2019 and to Malaysia 2005–2010. Ambassador Sångeland was posted to Vietnam 2002–2005 and to Finland 1992–1995 (secondment to the Ministry of Foreign Affairs of Finland 1999–2000) and to Italy 1989–1992. Ambassador Sångeland has held various positions at the Ministry for Foreign Affairs of Sweden. She was Ambassador at the European Union Department in charge of Baltic Year 2011, Head of the Department for Asia and Oceania, ASEM senior official and Special Representative for Afghanistan and Pakistan 2011–2016. Ambassador Sångeland has a degree in business administration and economics from Göteborg School of Economics and Business Administration and has studied both political science and German at Sweden's University of Göteborg.

Open Access This chapter is licensed under the terms of the Creative Commons Attribution-NonCommercial-NoDerivatives 4.0 International License (http://creativecommons.org/licenses/by-nc-nd/4.0/), which permits any noncommercial use, sharing, distribution and reproduction in any medium or format, as long as you give appropriate credit to the original author(s) and the source, provide a link to the Creative Commons license and indicate if you modified the licensed material. You do not have permission under this license to share adapted material derived from this chapter or parts of it.

The images or other third party material in this chapter are included in the chapter's Creative Commons license, unless indicated otherwise in a credit line to the material. If material is not included in the chapter's Creative Commons license and your intended use is not permitted by statutory regulation or exceeds the permitted use, you will need to obtain permission directly from the copyright holder.

Ireland on the UN Security Council—Our Work on Women, Peace and Security and Women's Participation in Decision-Making

Ann Derwin

Introduction

Ireland is recognised as a longstanding champion of the Women, Peace and Security (WPS) Agenda. Mainstreaming the WPS Agenda was a golden thread running through all of our work on the United Nations Security Council, during our most recent term as an elected member in 2021 and 2022. In this article, I will reflect on some of our achievements on the Council, as well as the challenges we faced, with regard to our work on WPS and women's participation in decision-making.

As recent events in the Middle East, Ukraine, Afghanistan and Ethiopia have reiterated, the rights of women and girls are a peace and security issue. Now, more than ever, we need to promote the Women, Peace and Security Agenda: the proliferation of armed conflicts around the world serves as a stark reminder of its importance and the role the UN and the international community must play to ensure women's full, equal and meaningful participation at all decision-making levels.

Ireland's commitment to gender equality and women's participation shaped our work right across the Security Council agenda, where we consistently sought to translate high-level commitments into practical reality. As a result, we sought to promote greater collective efforts to mainstream WPS throughout the work of the Security Council.

We continue to urge current and incoming Security Council members to maintain the momentum on implementing the Women, Peace and Security Agenda. We must redouble our efforts to prevent rollbacks and build upon the gains made since the adoption of the original UN Security Council resolution 1325 on Women, Peace and Security. This is not only an end in itself, but will also help us to achieve a more peaceful and equal world.

Ambassador of Ireland to the People's Republic of China.

A. Derwin (✉)
Beijing, China

As we heard from Mary Robinson, Ireland's first woman President and current Chair of The Elders, speaking during Ireland's Presidency of the Security Council in September 2021, *"Women's rights are not western rights. They are fundamental human rights"*.

Ireland's Election to the Security Council

The year 2022 marked one hundred years since the establishment of the Irish Free State. One of the first acts of the Irish Free State was to seek membership of the League of Nations (often considered the predecessor of the United Nations). The principles we articulated over one hundred years ago on joining the League of Nations and continue to inform Ireland's approach to our foreign policy today—the belief that all countries, large and small, have an equal right to live in peace and to contribute to international peace and security, and the belief that all people have the right to live in dignity, and to have their human rights and fundamental freedoms respected.

Our term on the UN Security Council coincided with this centenary of Ireland's independence, allowing us to reflect on our principles and ideals as a nation. This inclination—to look outwards, to work with others, to be part of agreed global systems and structures that shape and regulate how we act as nation states—remains at the core of Ireland's foreign policy today.

In seeking election to the Security Council, we believed that Ireland, as a small, independent country with a deep and longstanding commitment to the UN, could make a difference. Above all, we wanted to help the Security Council fulfil its critically important mandate, as laid out in the UN Charter: the maintenance of international peace and security.

Our 2021–2022 term on the UN Security Council was underpinned by three core principles that guided our work and engagement:

1. Building peace, including strengthening UN peacekeeping and peacebuilding globally;
2. Strengthening conflict prevention, by addressing factors that drive conflict;
3. Ensuring accountability, through working to end impunity for those responsible for serious violations of international humanitarian and human rights law.

These principles came not only from our own foreign policy priorities, but also from the UN Charter itself which gives the Security Council its mandate on the maintenance of international peace and security.

The Importance of Partnerships

Partnership is always essential in diplomacy and none of our work on the Security Council would have been possible without the partnerships we built, maintained and nourished—with other governments, with the UN system, with civil society partners, with analysts, journalists and academic partners, with the Oireachtas (Irish parliament) and with the Irish public.

Partnership becomes all the more essential at times when geopolitical tensions are high. In this environment, Ireland's role as an elected member of the Council—as a country that is clear in its principles, committed to the UN Charter and to multilateralism, and convinced by the value of cross-regional partnerships—became even more important.

Ireland's experience was that a constructive relationship with all Security Council members was critical to achieving progress on key files at the Council. Throughout our term, we sought to be a constructive and thoughtful member, focused on solutions and working openly with all partners.

Our investment in partnership and dialogue went beyond the Council chamber in New York—our then Foreign Minister Simon Coveney travelled to meet with counterparts from all parts of the world, including a visit to China in May 2021 to meet with Foreign Minister Wang Yi, to discuss key issues of importance for Ireland and China on the UN Security Council agenda, and areas for collaboration.

As I will outline in further detail below, working closely with Mexico and Kenya on the Women, Peace and Security Agenda was a further illustration of how our partnerships have been key to making progress on issues that matter at the Council.

Ireland's Work on Women, Peace and Security at the UN Security Council

Ireland has built a strong international reputation as a leader in the Women, Peace and Security (WPS) Agenda, and it remains a central priority of our foreign policy. We worked hard to ensure that the WPS Agenda was at the heart of the Security Council's work, and we delivered key results in this area.

Ireland has broad and longstanding experience in WPS—we are currently implementing our third National Action Plan (NAP) on Women, Peace and Security (2019–24). This has received special recognition by the UN Secretary-General for including in its design women from conflict-affected areas living in Ireland, and rural and minority women.

Ireland is also a board member of the WPS-Humanitarian Action (WPS-HA) Compact that emerged from the Generation Equality Forum (GEF), a multi-stakeholder, inter-generational global initiative to accelerate the implementation of the WPS Agenda and further strengthen gender equality and women's rights, convened by UN Women and launched in June 2021.

In addition, Ireland is a WPS champion within the Action for Peacekeeping (A4P) initiative and supports the UN Secretary-General's efforts to ensure women's full, equal and meaningful participation in peacekeeping.

The WPS "Presidency Trio" and the "Shared Commitments"

Throughout our term on the Security Council, we worked to move the WPS Agenda forward in a number of clear and practical ways.

In partnership with Mexico, we championed the full, equal and meaningful participation of women, through chairing the Informal Expert Group on Women, Peace and Security, a Working Group of the Council. This working group facilitates a more systematic approach to WPS within the Council's work and enables greater oversight and coordination of implementation efforts.

In September 2021, at our initiative, Ireland together with Mexico and Kenya formed a "Women, Peace and Security Presidency Trio", committing to using our respective Security Council Presidencies to integrate WPS fully into the Council's work, across all thematic and country files. This involved developing a set of "Shared Commitments", which outlined tangible actions to advance the implementation of the WPS Agenda.

Over the three months of the "Presidency Trio" (September to November 2021), we oversaw a number of key achievements. We achieved significant improvement in the gender balance amongst briefers to the Council, ensuring that half (49%) were women, who spoke to a range of areas relating to peace and security. We also encouraged UN briefers to include substantive gender analysis in their briefings to help ensure that Council members heard detailed reporting and analysis on the situation on the ground for women and girls. We strengthened WPS language in Council products such as mandates, resolutions and Presidential Statements. We pushed for geographic debates to include a WPS focus. Ireland also led two WPS-focused press briefings (known as "stakeouts") during our tenure—since then, it has become commonplace for Member States who have signed up to the Shared Commitments "group", numbering 17 current and former UNSC members (as of December 2023), to undertake joint press stakeouts.

Wherever possible, we tried to build on the momentum by highlighting the importance of WPS in discussions with other member states. A summary report outlining the achievements of the WPS Presidency Trio initiative was circulated to the UN Security Council (S/2022/91) encouraging future presidencies to continue finding tangible ways to implement the WPS Agenda.

It is clear that the WPS commitments launched by the Presidency Trio proved to be a very effective way of progressing change at the Council. We were deeply heartened by the fact that so many other member states have since built upon this initiative and adopted the "WPS Shared Commitments" during their subsequent presidencies. As a result, we have seen a sustained commitment to bringing greater gender parity to the Council, and more collective action to draw public attention to the need to accelerate the full implementation of the WPS Agenda.

Peacekeeping and WPS

In 1958, just three years after Ireland joined the United Nations, while we were still a very poor nation, our service as international peacekeepers began. I know China also shares this commitment to peacekeeping, being the largest troop contributor amongst the permanent members of the Security Council, and the second-largest contributor to the UN peacekeeping budget.

In fact, Ireland today has the longest unbroken peacekeeping record of any nation in the world. We take great pride in this commitment, although we must never forget the dangers that come with this work, or how the members of the Irish Defence Forces serving on peacekeeping missions risk their lives every day in order to build and maintain peace in conflict zones across the world. We pay particular tribute to those Irish Defence Forces personnel who have died serving in UN peacekeeping missions, including most recently Private Seán Rooney who was tragically killed in Lebanon in December 2022 when serving with UNIFIL.

Reflecting this longstanding commitment to peacekeeping, our work on the Security Council included efforts to ensure that peacekeeping mandates were clear, credible, realistic and adequately resourced. A particular highlight was Ireland's leadership to secure the adoption of Security Council Resolution 2594 on Peacekeeping Transitions, which aims to help to the UN better prepare and manage transitions, after peacekeepers leave. We worked hard to ensure this resolution contained strong WPS and human rights language, including requesting the UN Secretary-General ensure the mainstreaming of a gender perspective, and that gender analysis and technical gender expertise are included throughout all stages of the transition process. We hope this resolution will be one of the lasting legacies of our time on the Council.

More broadly, we also sought to ensure that the Security Council's Resolutions on Women, Peace and Security were implemented effectively across the UN's peacekeeping and political missions. Our role as co-chair of the Informal Expert Group on Women Peace and Security also allowed for close engagement with the senior leadership of UN missions in monitoring actions to implement the WPS Agenda on the ground.

Peacebuilding and WPS

As well as recognising the vital importance of peacekeeping, we also understand the importance of investing in peacebuilding. In particular, as we know from our own experience of conflict on the island of Ireland, the participation of women is essential to building sustainable peace. Women can make an indispensable contribution to peace-making when they have a seat at the table. Yet, all too often, they are prevented from participating and from being part of decision-making. Ireland has therefore been a consistent advocate for ensuring women are included at all stages of peace negotiations.

Over the period of our Security Council tenure, Ireland pushed for the full, equal and meaningful inclusion of women in UN-led peace processes. As we saw from an Arria-formula meeting on ensuring women's participation in UN-led peace processes that we convened with Mexico at the Security Council in March 2021, there was a strong call across Member States for the UN to take a lead on this—indeed, that women's participation should be a requirement for UN-led peace processes.

The Arria-formula meeting followed a commitment in 2020 by the UN Secretary-General to ensure women are better represented in peace processes. However, we remain concerned that despite commitments, not enough progress has been made in this area. According to the UN Secretary-General's report on WPS in September 2022, although women participated in all peace processes led and co-led by the UN in 2021, representation of women in peace processes has in fact been decreasing (from 23% in 2020 to 19% in 2021). Urgent political leadership is still required to turn this trend, and we are encouraged that it was the focus of the Secretary-General's WPS report to the Council in 2023.

Engaging with Civil Society on WPS

Amplifying the voices of women in conflict and post-conflict settings remains key to promoting and safeguarding gender equality. In this regard, Ireland worked hard to ensure that women's voices were heard at the Security Council, and we maintained an ongoing dialogue with grassroots women peacebuilders throughout our tenure.

During the WPS Trio Presidency (September to November 2021), 35 women civil society briefers participated in Council meetings, representing almost half (49%) of all civil society briefers in 2021. This is significant given that as recently as the 1990s, there were no women from civil society briefing the Council in any meeting. In September 2021, during Ireland's Security Council Presidency month, we brought the voices of 16 women civil society briefers to the Council table—a record number for any Security Council Presidency.

In the case of Afghanistan, since the Taliban takeover of Kabul, we have seen an alarming and unacceptable regression in respect for human rights. This has had a particularly devastating impact for women and girls, including their right to education, employment, movement and other activities in public spaces. In this context, Ireland used its seat on the Security Council to stand by Afghan women and to push for accountability for the actions of the Taliban.

During our Security Council tenure, we met regularly with Afghan human rights activists and women leaders. Our leadership on Afghanistan at the Council was directly informed by the courageous activism of these and many other Afghan women. Their advice and concerns informed Ireland's engagement—from pushing for strong language on gender and human rights in the Council's statements and resolutions on Afghanistan to galvanising support for Afghan women and girls amongst other member states. In particular, we helped to ensure that the mandate for the UN Mission in Afghanistan included strong provisions on women's rights.

Standing alone, we refused to agree to an extension of the exemption to the UN travel ban that senior members of the Taliban enjoyed—we believed that the Taliban, like others responsible for abuses or violations of human rights, must face accountability for their actions.

Conclusion

There is no doubt in my mind that Ireland had a sustained, positive impact during our time on the Council—we lived up to our pledge to be an inclusive, ambitious and responsive Security Council member.

Thanks to Ireland's leadership on Women, Peace and Security at the Security Council, during our tenure, we saw greater collective efforts to ensure the WPS Agenda was better reflected throughout the work of the Council. We are very proud of these achievements.

Since the end of our term, Ireland has continued to build on the legacy of our work on the Council. We remain guided by our three principles—building peace, preventing conflict and ensuring accountability. We have maintained our engagement on many of the priorities we worked to advance during our tenure, including on WPS and in particular on ensuring the full, equal and meaningful participation of women in all aspects of peace and security.

At the UN General Assembly, we continue to work towards the implementation of the UN initiative "Our Common Agenda", as well as the achievement of the Sustainable Development Goals (SDGs). We are running for a seat on the UN Human Rights Council in Geneva for the 2027–2029 term. We will continue to play an active role in regional bodies such as the OSCE and the Council of Europe, where we held the Presidency in 2022. And of course the European Union will remain at the centre of our foreign policy, and indeed who we are as a country, as we celebrated fifty years of EU membership in 2023 and look towards our next EU Presidency in the second half of 2026.

The partnerships we developed while on the Security Council continue to be crucial, particularly with Small Island Developing States, and countries in Africa, as well as our strong ongoing engagement with civil society.

Despite its flaws, the Security Council continues to play a pivotal role at the heart of the multilateral system. When the Council can find a common cause and take action, it can deliver outcomes that can have an immense impact on the ground. We cannot address global challenges—like conflict, climate change and food insecurity—without it. We have seen first-hand that, with political will and with partnership, multilateralism can deliver results.

Turning again to the words of Mary Robinson, speaking during Ireland's Presidency of the Security Council in September 2021, *"A united and purposeful Security Council is needed now more than ever"*.

H.E. Dr. Ann Derwin was appointed as Ambassador of Ireland to China in January 2021, having previously served in the Department of Foreign Affairs in 2017 as Director of Global Irish Services. In this role, she oversaw the digitisation of Passport Services, the provision of consular services to citizens including in response to the COVID-19 pandemic and Ireland's diaspora policy development and implementation. Prior to this, Ann held a number of positions in the Department of Agriculture, Food and the Marine including Assistant Secretary-General for Corporate Affairs, Chief Economist and Senior Veterinary Inspector as well as serving as Agriculture Attaché at the Embassy of Ireland in Madrid, Spain. Ann holds a Doctorate in Governance from Queen's University in Belfast and a Masters in Agricultural Economics from Imperial College London.

Open Access This chapter is licensed under the terms of the Creative Commons Attribution-NonCommercial-NoDerivatives 4.0 International License (http://creativecommons.org/licenses/by-nc-nd/4.0/), which permits any noncommercial use, sharing, distribution and reproduction in any medium or format, as long as you give appropriate credit to the original author(s) and the source, provide a link to the Creative Commons license and indicate if you modified the licensed material. You do not have permission under this license to share adapted material derived from this chapter or parts of it.

The images or other third party material in this chapter are included in the chapter's Creative Commons license, unless indicated otherwise in a credit line to the material. If material is not included in the chapter's Creative Commons license and your intended use is not permitted by statutory regulation or exceeds the permitted use, you will need to obtain permission directly from the copyright holder.

Global Development and a Future with China

Working for Change: Brief Observations by a Brazilian Diplomat

Marcos Galvão

Twenty-five years ago, in the second half of 1997, I finished a dissertation titled "Globalization: heralds, skeptics and critics". It was an overview of the then recent, and at times raging, debate on globalization, a very lively and trendy discussion in those days.

As the title indicates, I tried to group the various positions on the issue into three main groups. I described the heralds of globalization as those who were arguing in favor of the phenomenon and saying that it was irreversible, inevitable and positive.

The skeptics were those who questioned the transformational potential of globalization in areas such as international relations and who qualified supposed trends such as the diminishing relevance of nation states. In that group, for example, I placed realist thinkers who continued to maintain that relations and power differentials between states would continue to be the main determinant of the global order.

Finally, the critics were those who, while coming from varied ideological backgrounds, focused on what they saw as the adverse effects of globalization. They adopted a critical view regarding the notion, for instance, that a world primarily organized by markets, rather than by national political decisions, would be a better place.

In those days—and for at least a decade after that—pro-globalization positions and arguments were dominant in most developed countries, a trend that had started in the late 1970s and early 1980s. The fundamental premise was the belief that a smaller government presence in managing the economy was far better than a model in which the public sector played a larger role in deciding the course of and setting up of incentives for economic activity.

It was obvious that behind that notion was a sense that market players were prone to do a better job than elected and non-elected public officials, provided they

---

Ambassador of the Federative Republic of Brazil to the People's Republic of China.

M. Galvão (✉)
Beijing, China

were given greater latitude to make choices and were unencumbered by regulation and restrictions. The concept therefore ultimately involved, to a smaller degree, a negative attitude toward politics and political decision-making.

The idea of globalization was also associated with the emergence of a supposedly borderless world, in which limits between national jurisdictions were not to interfere with the establishment of chains of production, investment and trade. On the contrary, the activities of corporations and banks should be permitted to freely develop across borders, in order to completely fulfill their potential.

This was not, of course, a merely ideological construct. It did, in fact, also correspond to extraordinary and accelerated technological transformations that obviously enabled—and to an extent called for—economic activity to be increasingly global, or globalized.

We also know, however, that certain aspects of economic liberalization and deregulation went too far and ultimately led to the great global financial crisis that began in 2008. It was a crisis caused by excesses resulting from the notion that markets required no adults in the room to establish and enforce minimum requirements of discipline, transparency and responsibility.

Countries caught in that crisis, which ended up affecting the world economy as a whole to varying degrees, paid a high price for those excesses and for the fact that governments, as well as supervisory and regulatory agencies, had seriously failed to live up to their responsibilities.

While pro-globalization policies and narratives were still dominant, there was a growing sentiment, particularly in certain developed nations, that the social costs of globalization were rising. Much was said, for example, about the export of jobs and investment. Increasingly, the idea that insufficient attention was being given to those segments of society that were paying a higher price for this reorganization of the world economy also gained ground.

In some countries, those concerns brought about a backlash against what we could call a supranational element of the globalized economy, frequently tied to the view that national governments were no longer concerned with the plight of their own citizens; that governments prioritized the interests of large companies and economic interests regardless of where the benefits of their activities would finally land.

As we know, that reaction fueled political forces that brought back, with greater strength, arguments in favor of what has been called economic nationalism. Recent trade wars are an expression of that.

Over a period of approximately three decades, therefore, we have moved from an environment in which there was a demand for depoliticizing economic decision-making to a situation of growing politicization—and even geopoliticization—of decisions in areas such as trade, investment and flows of information regarding science and technology.

We are not going to return in technological terms to a pre-digital era and it is highly unlikely that we will return to a pre-globalization world. As it is often said, what we have been calling globalization since the 1990s is not an entirely new phenomenon. In other ways, in other stages of scientific progress, the process of globalization has been present ever since people began to travel long distances and different societies established contact and began to trade with each other.

In the current environment, however, new expressions that have appeared and gained currency—such as nearshoring, friendshoring and deglobalization—are as relevant a sign of the times as the word *globalization* was when it was on everybody's lips; as can be seen in the very name of the Center for China & Globalization that now supports the book in which this article will be published.

Globalization never was, nor could it have been, the panacea that many proclaimed. But is economic nationalism the solution to all the social and other problems frequently associated with globalization. If the 2008 financial crisis was the crisis of the excesses of liberalization—and of what some have described as market supranationalism—the context we are at present living in is also the result of what we could call a crisis of the excesses of economic nationalism and of the contamination of economic decision-making by reasoning increasingly derived from political, geopolitical and ideological considerations.

The most preoccupying aspect of our present global environment is that the world has become a much more dangerous place. The possibility of a nuclear conflict between major powers, for example, is now mentioned as a considerable scenario, as a clear and present danger. This has not happened for the last sixty years and is not a minor fact.

Those that I referred to as the heralds of globalization of course exaggerated the extent to which it would transform national realities and the conduct of international relations; there was a mixture of naiveté, wishful thinking and intellectual obfuscation in their claims. The same judgment applies, therefore, to the surprise and frustration they professed when their lofty forecasts failed to materialize. They should have known it was simply never going to happen.

What is going on now clearly heads in the opposite direction. Just as in those earlier days when the heralds of globalization painted unrealistic rosy pictures of where the world was supposed to be heading, now it's mostly about doom and gloom. The kumbaya of a globalized paradise has been replaced by the permanent drumming up of supposedly irreconcilable differences and by the adoption of policies that actually reinforce those differences, as well as the potential for conflict.

If in the recent past, there was a clear overestimation of the possibility that differences could be overcome, or ideally even eliminated; today, there is a tendency to underestimate or even deny the possibility that different political, social and economic models can and should coexist in peace.

This not only makes the world a more dangerous place, but also drains resources that could be invested in a manner not related to perceptions of inevitable competition and conflict.

Curiously, therefore, just as globalized liberalization has been linked to growing inequality within and among different countries, the current excesses of economic nationalism and politicization will also probably further delay efforts to overcome inequality, particularly between different nations and regions of the world.

In that regard, if there are words whose coming and going are a representation of the different historical settings we have experienced, the almost complete disappearance of references to development with no adjectives—and also to the very notion of development as an overarching goal—should be a source of great concern.

Yes, we certainly still speak about sustainable development; with an emphasis on the imperative that human development take place in a manner consistent with the preservation of our natural environment and of the very survival of our planet. Fortunately, there is now a hard-won and necessary consensus regarding the need to stop and reverse climate change and global warming.

But we no longer see a similar concern or consensus regarding the imperative of development as a means to eliminate hunger and poverty, and to ensure better education, healthcare, clean water and opportunities. This is happening at a time when, among other plights, food insecurity, in some cases extreme food insecurity, is becoming more serious in many places of the globe. The notion of a moral, political and economic imperative in that regard has sadly faded into the background of international debate, and of multilateral deliberations.

This reality not only hinders the path to the social and economic well-being of humanity as a whole, but also makes the world more unstable and dangerous; even more so in our digitally connected era, when individuals all over the globe can literally see with their own eyes the conditions in which others live and the contrasts, some of them scandalous, between those different realities.

We must bring back to the fore the concept and the cause of development. Prioritizing development is an affirmation of the belief that things can change and must change. It is almost shocking that after the extraordinary transformations, we have gone through in recent years, such as progress in the field of connectivity in this entirely new digital world, many players continue to behave as if wars, poverty, hunger and inequality are somehow inevitable.

It is as if some things can be changed and others cannot. As if the future is condemned, at least to an extent, to reproduce many of the core problems of past and present.

In that regard, I am reminded of an expression coined by the late professor Fred Halliday, who spoke of "megalo-presentism" when referring to the possibility that certain conclusions—such as Fukuyama's "End of History"— in fact incur an exaggeration of the impact and relevance in the future of contemporary occurrences or trends. In other words, a historical overestimation of facts that we witness and experience in our lifetime.

There was a lot of megalo-presentism in certain analyses and proclamations regarding globalization in the recent past. A quarter of a century ago, for instance, very few people, if anybody, would have imagined that today would be speaking about *deglobalization.*

The worst part of such proclamations, however, is not the fact that they are not confirmed in the medium and long run, but rather that they bring about a notion that current realities and trends cannot and will not be reversed or transformed. Even more regrettable is the fact that there tends to be an incentive for uniformity rather than dissonance, for passive adherence rather than healthy intellectual and political debate.

Individuals and societies must free themselves from such notions of inevitability. This is essential if we are to move from either joining or remaining passive in the face of negative and dangerous trends and instead adopt an attitude based on the belief in the possibility of change and in the will of people to join the struggle for change.

In my case, I joined the Brazilian Foreign Service more than four decades ago not primarily for the experience of being involved in the diplomatic projection of our interests abroad. In truth, I entered Brazil's Foreign Service as a means to work for the development of my country and even more so for the improvement of the living conditions of my compatriots who did not have the opportunities I had and who legitimately aspire to a much better life.

Development—our national development and that of other nations—has always been at the core of Brazilian foreign policy. It is our main objective. An objective that we permanently seek while, at the same time, preserving our respect for international law and promoting multilateral institutions as the *fora* where international law is negotiated, written and enforced.

Brazil has always defended international law and multilateral institutions, not as instruments for preserving the *status quo,* but rather as the only path for development, for change, for building a world of peace and prosperity accessible to all humanity.

For more than 150 years now, Brazil has had no armed conflict with any of its ten neighbors. Very few countries in the world can claim such a track record. What we preach, therefore, is what we practice.

That is an essential basis of our credibility. It reinforces our credentials—as one of the world's leading countries in terms of territory, population, economy, natural resources and biodiversity—to play an increasingly more relevant and always constructive role on the international stage, particularly in a world that is becoming, as previously stated, more dangerous and even more unequal.

Rather than a statement of official positions, I have chosen to share a few personal thoughts in this book wherein the Center for China and Globalization once again gathers the contributions of numerous ambassadors now serving in Beijing.

I hope that readers, be they many or few, will at least get an idea of how an individual Brazilian diplomat sees the world we live in and of the values upon which my country has traditionally based its objectives and conduct on the international scene.

It is also a statement of the values, spirit and goals that move me—as I believe they moved previous Brazilian ambassadors and their teams—in our work devoted to building broader and deeper relations between Brazil and China. Ours is a partnership that will continue to benefit the development of both our peoples and nations.

H.E. Marcos Galvão has been Ambassador of Brazil to the People's Republic of China since August 2022. An experienced diplomat with more than forty years of dedicated service to Brazil's diplomatic corps, he has served as Deputy Foreign Minister and MFA Spokesperson. Prior to this, he served as Ambassador of Brazil to Japan, Permanent Representative to the WTO and Head of the Mission of Brazil to the European Union. Other positions he has held include Secretary (vice-minister) for International Affairs at the Ministry of Finance and the head negotiator for the Ministry of Finance for the G-20 (2008–2010).

Open Access This chapter is licensed under the terms of the Creative Commons Attribution-NonCommercial-NoDerivatives 4.0 International License (http://creativecommons.org/licenses/by-nc-nd/4.0/), which permits any noncommercial use, sharing, distribution and reproduction in any medium or format, as long as you give appropriate credit to the original author(s) and the source, provide a link to the Creative Commons license and indicate if you modified the licensed material. You do not have permission under this license to share adapted material derived from this chapter or parts of it.

The images or other third party material in this chapter are included in the chapter's Creative Commons license, unless indicated otherwise in a credit line to the material. If material is not included in the chapter's Creative Commons license and your intended use is not permitted by statutory regulation or exceeds the permitted use, you will need to obtain permission directly from the copyright holder.

Prospects for Mozambique-China Partnership in the Context of the Current Global Environment

Maria Gustava

Introduction

The foundations of relations between Mozambique and China can be traced back to the 1960s, during the time of Mozambique's struggle for national independence from colonialism and imperialism. At that time, China fully supported our liberation and was the first to recognize Mozambique as state on our Independence Day, June 25, 1975. Consequently, on 2 July of the same year, the two countries signed an Economic and Technical Cooperation Agreement, covering areas ranging from the political-diplomatic to the social-economical, and cultural. On the same occasion, China opened its diplomatic embassy in Maputo.

Over time, our bilateral relations, based in friendship, solidarity, and cooperation, have continued to consolidate and flourish. The consistent spirit of trust, friendship, and shared vision embedded in this traditional relationship and constitutes the basis for the building of a common bright future. In fact, in 2016, the heads of state of the two countries decided to elevate Sino-Mozambican relations through establishment of a Global Strategic Cooperation Partnership (GSCP). From then on, there have been unrestrained and legitimate expectations and hope that in the next two decades, our bilateral strategic cooperation will further enhance the synergies between both countries.

In this globalized and interdependent world, characterized by rapid and dramatic changes and uncertainties derived from, among others, pandemics, poverty, conflicts, terrorism, strains in the relationships between world powers, and the redrawing of geopolitics, the two countries should further unite their efforts and deepen their relationship to high level in all aspects, in order to form a common front and help and assist each other in addressing these old and new challenges. In fact, is expected

---

Ambassador of the Republic of Mozambique to the People's Republic of China.

M. Gustava (✉)
Beijing, China

more practical and programmatic bilateral cooperation with tangible results from the implementation of the Global Strategic Partnership Cooperation, especially in the areas with great potential.

The Prospect for the Mozambique-China Partnership in the Context of Current Global Environment

The current global environment presents enormous opportunities that have emerged from the advances in innovation and technology and trends in globalization, but there are also huge challenges in the form of poverty, climate change, food insecurity, public healthcare, conflicts, cyber-security, and debt crises, among others, which require a collective response. Indeed, the deep interconnections and interdependency among countries highlight the importance of common efforts and international cooperation in finding solutions to common concerns. The negative impact of the COVID-19 pandemic is still being felt in every corner of the globe and has undermined the development and progress of many countries, particularly in the developing world.

It is in this context that China plays a crucial role in assisting and working with its friends and partners in the developing world, like Mozambique, to take hold of existing opportunities and respond to the challenges they face in terms of socio-economic recovery, progress and well-being of the people.

In looking at bilateral cooperation between China and Mozambique, one can see a tremendous increase over the last two decades. The existing bilateral Global Strategic Cooperation Partnership between the two countries has provided the necessary legal framework for broadening this relationship and produced mutually beneficial results. I believe that this partnership has created and enhanced a positive environment for more dynamic cooperation policies and programs that can boost institutional development and financial mobilization in relevant areas. However, this success will depend on strategic guidance, effective operational arrangements and a strong mechanism for knowledge development, learning and accountability. This reinforces the need for an Action Plan in the implementation of the GSCP.

The success or failure of this partnership will depend on a number of factors both on the domestic and global levels. Some of the preconditions for success include common vision, deepening mutual knowledge, trust, confidence, commitment, open communication, accessibility, flexibility, pursuing mutual interests and benefits, and setting goals and tangible results.

Open communication is the backbone of any effective partnership and regular consultations at all levels are of extreme importance. Therefore, the two sides must be ready to continue mutual visits, promote open discussions, work together, and commit adequate resources to the implementation for projects that have been agreed upon.

I am positive about the future of Mozambique-China bilateral cooperation. I believe that both sides will make efforts to jointly continue to manage a combination of factors and circumstances both in terms of domestic developments and unforeseeable global events.

Areas of Potential Success and Development

As mentioned earlier, the beginning of the future of relations between Mozambique and China was agreed upon by President Xi Jinping of China and Filipe Jacinto Nyusi of Mozambique as "supporting each other in matters of vital interest and of great importance" in range of vital issues areas including political-diplomatic, social-economic, peace and security, tourism and culture, infrastructure, industrialization, and many others. This is a clear indication of the political will and mutual understanding between both parties. In the current global environment, the following scenarios for partnership between Mozambique and China are of particular relevance:

Scenario I: Areas with Strong Potential of Success and Development

This scenario is supported by existing political will and mutual understanding. Our political-diplomatic relations are excellent and based on shared values and principles, profound friendship, trust, mutual respect and support and collaboration. These are the pillars of our bilateral relations and serve as a driving force for the success. Also our "ideologically driven" wills feed and sustain our bilateral relations on both the political-diplomatic and socio-economic level. Indeed, the preconditions for success in Mozambique-China strategic cooperation are already in place. Programs and projects are also in place and are in an advanced stage of maturation. This is the case for political-diplomatic and to some extent trade.

(a) **Political-Diplomatic**

We expect that the two sides will continue to strengthen their cooperation in this field, namely at the governmental level through both legislative institutions and local governments. Our high-level political dialogue has been the backbone of the bilateral relations, with frequent contacts between the leaders of the two countries and regular coordination, which have remained undisrupted even during the COVID-19 pandemic. The two countries also conduct visits at different levels, annual bilateral political consultations as well as meetings and consultations of a Bi-national Commission and various working groups.

In this context, we hope that the two sides will continue to support each other in matters of vital interest concerning national sovereignty, territorial integrity, security, and stability. Mozambique will continue to defend the "One China" principle and China will continue to support Mozambique against external interference. In governance, the two countries will also encourage "ties between cities and provinces" and cooperation between local governments.

(b) *Cooperation in Regional and Multilateral Forums*

Mozambique and China have been engaging in close consultation and coordination within the framework of different forums, particularly at the United Nations, the Forum for China-Africa Cooperation (FOCAC), the Forum for Cooperation between China and Portuguese Speaking countries (Macau Forum), the Belt and Road Initiative and others on issues of common interest, such as international peace and security, poverty reduction, climate change, development and multilateralism. We have also supported each other on issues of vital importance like human rights, non-interference in internal matters, and promoting fruitful economic cooperation.

The election of Mozambique as a non-permanent member of the United Nations Security Council for the period of 2023–2024 represents another window for our two countries to coordinate and defending the importance maintenance of multilateralism and world peace and security.

(c) *Peace and Security*

On this topic, the two sides will continue to support each other in "resolving territorial and maritime disputes", and in safeguarding "national security and stability". Likewise, the two sides will continue to cooperate on promoting institutions dealing with law and order and defense and security such as the armed forces, police, intelligence services, and migration services.

We have also decided to cooperate in the area of national defense, including increasing our capacity to safeguard stability, share information, and train staff, specifically to fight extremism in Cabo Delgado. We hope that China will continue to provide equipment, technology, and military industry knowledge to augment our security and defense capabilities.

Scenario II: Areas with Potential for Success and Development

The current global situation provides both challenges and opportunities for strengthening bilateral cooperation. New areas have emerged and others present enormous potential to be explored in order to generate success and development. These include health and sanitation to prevent future pandemics, social protection policies, actions to ensure economic recovery, technological research and development, trade, investment and finance, human development, peace and security, as well as tourism and culture and people-to-people exchanges.

(a) *Health and sanitation issues*

COVID-19 has highlighted the need for regular and close cooperation in the health sector, especially in increasing the production capacity of developing countries, like Mozambique, in terms of protective and medical materials, capacity building, and training to secure access to resources for diagnosis, prevention, and treatment in the case of a future pandemic.

Reinforcement of training and human capacity in the health sector is of paramount importance now and represents a huge opportunity for bilateral cooperation. In this context, China is committed to continue sending Chinese medical teams to Mozambique. Apart from that, my county is looking forward to maximizing the use of the new Center for Exchange and Cooperation for the Prevention of Pandemics between China and Portuguese Speaking countries in Macau as well as the promotion of exchanges on traditional medicine.

(b) *Economic Recovery, Investment, and Trade*

A fruitful partnership in the economic field is central to a win-win and mutual beneficial forms of cooperation, since it generates profits, jobs, and wealth for both sides. Therefore, measures and efforts for the promotion of trade and investment continue to be essential for economic recovery on both sides.

Mozambique is reviewing its policies to improve the environment for business and trade. In this context, Mozambique has decided to abolish tourism and business visas for all types of Chinese passports. Apart from that, an e-visa has been introduced for the remaining visas, which is aimed at facilitating Chinese people to travel to Mozambique to explore business opportunities and enjoy the fantastic and exotic tourism atmosphere of the country.

We welcome the Chinese decision to grant zero tariffs to Mozambican products exported to China, for 98% products of all taxed items. This provides opportunities for Mozambique to increase and diversify its exports to China. Nevertheless, flexibility is necessary in order to remove and ease all non-tariff and administrative barriers from the Chinese side and allow companies to register and export their products. At the moment, the trade balance is in favor of China.

China and Mozambique have also agreed to encourage more Chinese companies to invest in Mozambique to increase the production capacity of Mozambican products entering the Chinese market. In this process, China and Mozambique also recognize the need for assistance and encouragement in the development of small and medium enterprises, specially, in agro-processing, taking into the account their importance to the livelihoods of people in Mozambique.

(c) *Human Development, Tourism, and Culture*

Both sides are expected to expand human and cultural exchange and promote cooperation in areas of culture, education, health, youth, academia, and media. It is also expected that China will provide more scholarships to Mozambique. There is a positive record in this area and it is expected to continue in the same way. In fact, the two sides are expected to promote efforts conducive to the resurgence of tourism, especially after the COVID-19 pandemic. This includes conducting cross-border promotions of tourism and visa abolition and making it easier for people to travel between the two countries.

China is willing and committed to encouraging Chinese citizens to travel to Mozambique. The Chinese authorities are also ready to support national companies to invest in Mozambique, particularly in the building of hotels, tourist facilities, and other tourist infrastructure. The good news is that four years after signing the GSCP, Mozambique-China Cultural Center and the Confucius Institute, were built in

Maputo and are ready to be used. This mutual effort also culminated in the construction of additional infrastructure that will soon be operational. These will be useful in promoting exchanges between young people, academics, and media from both countries. This is one of the few issue areas that presents huge potential to flourish in the near future.

(d) *People-to-people exchanges*

A part from political, economic, human resources development and health, people-to-people exchanges have been defined as central to the partnership between the two countries as a guarantor for mutual understanding and a legacy for future relations. From this perspective, Mozambique and China are eager to foster the cultural exchange and connectivity, education, and tourism and youth cooperation.

Scenario III: Strong Potential Success in the Long term

This scenario is supported by the existence of the preconditions for successful strategic cooperation coupled with shared values and principles rooted in the traditional bilateral relations between Mozambique and China. These features serve as an important driving force for future development of both countries since the strategic cooperation partnership has been promoted in a contest of "mutual understanding". The issue areas are for long-term execution lie in productive capacity, manufacturing, railway infrastructure, industrialization, and modernization.

These are Mozambique's priorities and, therefore, are of paramount importance. But because of their dimension and financial resources involved, it is very unlikely that they will be implemented over the short term. However, some projects could start at any time.

(a) *Financial, Investment, and Infrastructure*

In financial matters, both countries will continue to explore multiple options to improve and reinforce bilateral cooperation. However, it is expected that in the long term, both sides will remain committed to opening branches of financial institutions in each country. The idea behind this is to encourage national enterprises to use national currency in investment and trade, among other desired activities.

The agreement also states that "as a priority", both sides have agreed to encourage the Chinese business community and financial institutions to invest in infrastructure in Mozambique. This investment is supposed to be directed to issue areas with huge potential and far reaching economic and social impact. It was also highlighted that priority will be given to the construction of railways, highways, airports, power stations, communications, and IT infrastructure.

For this purpose, the investment would come in the form of public-private partnerships (PPP), or at least a Build-Operate-Transfer (BOT) framework. This has opened up opportunities for private company participation in the development and construction of strategic infrastructure in Mozambique. The hope is that over the next two decades, it will be possible to implement these two financing mechanisms.

Both sides are also determined to work together in the promotion of "Belt and Road Initiative" projects for mutual benefit, including coastal aquaculture, sea fishing, maritime transport, construction of ports and industrial parks in port areas and maritime scientific research, among others.

(b) *Industrialization, Agriculture, and Science and Technology*

In these spheres, both countries have agreed to continue to coordinate plans and policies that increase production capacity, in the fields of energy and mineral exploration and manufacturing, among others. The more important goal is to take actions to speed up industrialization and modernization in Mozambique. Likewise, it is expected that under this partnership, support will be given to Mozambique to increase agricultural production of grains, cash crops, and livestock. The development of storage capacity and the processing of agricultural products will continue to be issues of concern in the agricultural modernization of Mozambique.

The agreement on agriculture emphasizes the need for adoption of effective measures to strengthen cooperation in the areas such as entry and exit inspection and the quarantine of animals and plants, among others. These actions are aimed at allowing the entry of food and agricultural products into the two markets, expanding the scope of bilateral trade. By doing this, it is also expected that the two countries will be able to reach the goal of a "trade balance". Both sides are expected to make proper use of the Agricultural Technology Demonstration Center in Mozambique for promotion of joint research, demonstration, and training as well as for the transfer of agricultural technology to Mozambique.

China is moving for high-quality development through technology and innovation towards building a modernized society. Mozambique being China strategic partners will for sure benefit from its experiences and assistance in this sphere in order to integrate in the new era.

Conclusions

The prospect for future relations between Mozambique and China is promising considering the existing trust, political will, and commitment from both parties to building a sound strategic partnership in all areas of cooperation. The current global environment brings new challenges and opportunities for our relations in the context of our mutual understanding, plans, and programs.

In essence, the existing deep friendship, the political will, economic and trade opportunities as well as the mutual understanding we have constitute the driving forces and factors for future expansion in the relations between our two countries. It is important to note the commitment of the leadership in ensuring effective implementation of agreed upon programs and projects, including enhancement of the coordination between the teams at the regional and country levels.

Despite the existing asymmetry in development in Mozambique and China, the existing partnership is a strong and useful tool in bridging ideological gaps, enabling two sides to pursue economic and social gains. In fact, a win-win situation doesn't necessarily mean sharing the gains on a 50% basis of gains for each partner. But also it is not based on a sum zero game. Additionally, it represents a collective action with collective gain in terms of sharing values and principles, as well as the commitment offered by the parties involved in the strategic partnership.

The major thematic subjects, such as infrastructure (bridges, roads, and railways) will only be translated from paper to reality over a long period due to the institutional hurdles. The lack of a Plan of Action makes a difference in assessing this process. Therefore, its absence makes it difficult to predict subsequent actions within the context of bilateral strategic cooperation. Certainly, political will and mutual understanding are not enough to overcome budget constraint challenges (Scenario III), but we are confident that both sides will strengthen their partnership by focusing on jointly selected priorities and by leveraging institutional strengths and synergies.

Against this background, the existing strategic partnership will allow the two countries to work together and share the opportunities offered by the current global environment and pursue shared economic and diplomatic interests. The strategic partnership between Mozambique and China not only serves the interests of both sides, but it also helps to promote partnerships between China and developing countries with the view of a future of common prosperity.

Is expected that Mozambique and China will strengthen cooperation and collaboration and put more resources into economic investment, social cultural development, institutional strengthening, and longer-term development in achieving GSCP goals.

The cooperation between Mozambique and China is a long-term undertaking and should continue to be guided by common values, principles, and measurable actions. The current commitment from both sides is also expected to continue in areas such as resources (human, material, and financial) with regular evaluations and additional efforts to introduce new programs and to expand collaboration. Success, of course, will depend upon a number of factors, such as leadership, resources, management, and assessment and signals from the global system.

I am certain that, in time to come, the current domestic and international challenges will be gradually overcome, including the geopolitics interest and geostrategic aspiration of certain countries. This is the case of the wars in Africa, Europe, and the Middle East, as well as food, poverty, energy, climate change, and financial crises. Both countries will continue to jointly find common solutions towards building community for shared future.

H.E. Mrs. Maria Gustava has been the Ambassador of the Republic of Mozambique to the People's Republic of China since 2018, also serving the North Korea. She has also served as the Ambassador of the Republic of Mozambique to Indonesia with multiple accreditations to Malaysia, Singapore, Thailand, and Timor Leste as well as deputy head of the Mission in South Africa. Mrs. Gustava is a career diplomat and joined the Foreign Service in 1989. Before this, she served in the Ministry of Foreign Affairs and Cooperation of Mozambique in multiple roles such as Head of Department for Multilateral Economic Relations, Deputy Director General for International Organizations and Conferences, Deputy Director General for Studies Planning and Information, and Director General for Asia and Oceania. Mrs. Gustava was born in 1966 and holds a Master's degree in Foreign Affairs and Trade, from Monash University, Australia. She lectured at the High Institute for International Relations in Mozambique.

Open Access This chapter is licensed under the terms of the Creative Commons Attribution-NonCommercial-NoDerivatives 4.0 International License (http://creativecommons.org/licenses/by-nc-nd/4.0/), which permits any noncommercial use, sharing, distribution and reproduction in any medium or format, as long as you give appropriate credit to the original author(s) and the source, provide a link to the Creative Commons license and indicate if you modified the licensed material. You do not have permission under this license to share adapted material derived from this chapter or parts of it.

The images or other third party material in this chapter are included in the chapter's Creative Commons license, unless indicated otherwise in a credit line to the material. If material is not included in the chapter's Creative Commons license and your intended use is not permitted by statutory regulation or exceeds the permitted use, you will need to obtain permission directly from the copyright holder.

Thailand and China Amid a Changing Global Landscape

Arthayudh Srisamoot

Global Landscape

The world today is far from being static. A series of disruptors have shaken the global landscape, beset by unprecedented and interconnected changes that test every nation's strength and solidarity. As we emerge from the devastation caused by the COVID-19 pandemic, new challenges have arisen in the form of geopolitical tensions brewing across different regions and economic sanctions fueling rising inflation, which have exacerbated the already constrained supply chain bottlenecks, and jeopardized global trade and energy and food security.

We have witnessed the advent of new trends that conform to ideas of deglobalization and slowbalization,[1] forcing certain countries to delink from one another (managed-decoupling) and source from allies closer to home (friend-shoring). In Asia and Europe, most trade is already intra-regional and this percentage is continuously rising. Intraregional trade made up 58.5% of Asia's total trade in 2020, the highest share since 1990.[2] Countries have also become more inward-looking, and invisible fences have been constructed out of fear of the unknown and the unpredictable.

Against this backdrop, climate change, global warming, and natural disasters are playing out at a faster rate than we could have ever imagined. We are in a race against Mother Nature, and in a race against ourselves. While disruptions are a natural feature of history and part of the never-ending cycle of the world, the key is how each country chooses to deal with these disruptions. For a medium-sized nation such as Thailand,

---

[1] Douglas Irwin, "The pandemic adds momentum to the deglobalization trend", The Centre for Economic Policy Research, May 2020.

[2] Asian Development Bank, "Asian Economic Integration Report 2022: Advancing Digital Services Trade in Asia and the Pacific", February 2022.

Ambassador of the Kingdom of Thailand to the People's Republic of China.

A. Srisamoot (✉)
Beijing, China

we recognize that multilateralism and aiming for sustainable growth will always be the prevailing solutions in response to "black swans" in an era of disruption.[3]

The Asian Century

It is undeniable that the world's center of gravity is tilting toward Asia. China's rapid and spectacular development in recent decades, and the growing economies of India and Southeast Asia, have powered unprecedented growth, bringing new opportunities and prosperity to this region that have made Asia increasingly the center of the world economy. It is predicted that by 2040, the region could account for more than half of global GDP and about 40% of global consumption.[4]

As all eyes fixate on the world's most populous continent with the fastest growing economy, nations around the world are eager to gain a foothold in the region, deemed to be the epicenter of the most important global affairs of the twenty-first century. The emergence of geopolitical Asian-focused foreign policies, namely United States' Pivot to Asia, western countries' Indo-Pacific Strategy, and Russia's Turn to the East signaled the enhanced strategic emphasis and increased engagement in this region.

Faced with a choice between solidarity and division, and cooperation and confrontation, the international community expects Asia to play a leading role, to which Southeast Asian nations and China are actively doing their part. Home to more than 650 million people, Southeast Asia is one of the world's most culturally diverse, economically dynamic, and growth-oriented regions in Asia. With its vast endowments of natural resources, an expanding middle class, a young, dynamic, and increasingly well-educated population, a diversified economy and intensive regional integration initiatives, the region is well positioned for prosperity and will exert growing influence on global development.

For these reasons, even countries within Asia have begun to formulate new foreign policies to increase engagement with Southeast Asian nations. India's Act East Policy and South Korea's New Southern Policy are just a few examples, of increasingly strategic moves to enhance cooperation with the Southeast Asian countries.

2022 saw a significant move by Asian countries, which took to the global stage and shined a spotlight on the region to drive global diplomacy, marking an "Asian Moment". On 23–24 June 2022, China hosted the BRICS Summit; on 13 November, 2022, Cambodia hosted the East Asia Summit; on 15–16 November 2022, Indonesia hosted the G20 Summit; and on 18–19 November 2022, Thailand hosted the Asia–Pacific Economic Cooperation (APEC) Economic Leaders' Meeting.

Both Thailand, ASEAN countries, and China are acutely aware that this "Asian Moment" must not just be a laurel of glory to be rested upon, but rather a shared

---

[3] Don Pramudwinai, "Taming the Black Swan: Multilateral diplomacy for sustainable growth in the era of disruption", 2021.

[4] McKinsey Global Institute, "The future of Asia: Asian flows and networks are defining the next phase of globalization", 2019.

responsibility by all countries in the region to rise up to both the occasion and the challenge. It is with this mindset that Thailand stands ready to work with ASEAN and China to champion open regionalism and jointly uphold the common interests of developing countries; only then can peace and prosperity in this region be achieved in harmony.

Open—Connect—Balance

It can be said that the formation of APEC drew inspiration from the Association of Southeast Asian Nations (ASEAN), whose series of ministerial consultations, which began in 1967, demonstrated the feasibility and value of regular consultations. By 1989, the ASEAN ministerial consultation process had expanded to embrace 12 members (the then six members of ASEAN and six dialogue partners), which gave birth to the idea of APEC and led to the eventual establishment of the 12 founding members of APEC in Canberra in 1989.[5]

33 years later, on 18–19 November 2022, Thailand hosted the 29th APEC Economic Leaders' Meeting (AELM) in Bangkok. As the first in-person Leaders' Meeting in four years since the outbreak of COVID-19, Thailand successfully brought together leaders of 21 economies, as well as participants from international organizations including the International Monetary Fund (IMF), Organization for Economic Co-operation and Development (OECD), World Health Organization (WHO), and World Trade Organization (WTO).

To further enrich and elevate the deliverables of this occasion, two important leaders, namely the Crown Prince and Prime Minister of the Kingdom of Saudi Arabia, a global energy powerhouse, and the President of the French Republic, a key player in the European Union, were invited as guests of the APEC Chair to discuss how APEC and its external partners can work together to promote sustainable trade and investment amid on-going economic challenges. In addition to AELM, two important activities were organized in parallel—the APEC CEO Summit and APEC Voices of the Future 2022—to actively engage APEC stakeholders, business leaders, and youth from different sectors.

A theme of "Open. Connect. Balance." guided Thailand's hosting of APEC in 2022, which aimed to OPEN to all opportunities, CONNECT across all dimensions, and achieve BALANCE in all aspects. Thailand worked to strengthen partnership and cooperation both on trade and investment, which are the bread and butter of APEC, as well as emerging issues of common concern, i.e., climate change, geoeconomics, and pandemic readiness, to strengthen APEC's standing as the premier economic forum in the region and as an incubator of ideas.

---

[5] Andrew Elek, "Back to Canberra: Founding APEC", Australian National University (ANU), Pacific Economic Cooperation Council, September 2005.

A Chalom, a traditional bamboo-woven basket used for carrying goods, a symbol of trade and commerce and the logo for Thailand's APEC host year in 2022

The Chalom, a traditional bamboo-woven basket used for carrying goods, was carefully chosen as the logo for Thailand's APEC host year. A symbol of trade and commerce, it encapsulates local wisdom and creativity in transforming raw materials into innovative and practical items. As one of the founding members of APEC since it was established in 1989, Thailand recognizes that APEC's work is a long-term process that requires continual and coordinated efforts, much like the tightly interlaced bamboo strands of the Chalom, which reflects the closely-knit relationships between the 21 member economies of APEC.

Consensus was achieved on the APEC Joint Ministerial Statement and the APEC Leaders' Declaration. The leaders also jointly endorsed the Bangkok Goals on the Bio-Circular-Green (BCG) Economy to serve as a model for sustainable and green development for the global community.

The Bangkok Goals were a landmark deliverable and counted as APEC's first ever comprehensive framework on sustainability, accompanying the Putrajaya Vision and Aotearoa Plan of Action until 2040. It provided a clear path to advance inclusive and sustainable growth in relevant APEC's workstreams in a bold, ambitious, and transformative manner, focusing on four key areas: climate change mitigation, sustainable trade and investment, environmental conservation, and waste management. Upon adoption, the Bangkok Goals website was launched and can be accessed at www.bangkokgoals.apec.org. It also serves as an important springboard to the United States' APEC host year, which has adopted the theme "Creating a Resilient and Sustainable Future for All".

The BCG Economy Model was highlighted as a catalyst to shift our mindset and behavior toward more responsible business models where growth objectives are pursued in tandem with environmental sustainability. The concept also aligns with China's Global Development Initiative (GDI) to foster global development and achieve the United Nations' 2030 Agenda for Sustainable Development.

Securing strong supply chains and ensuring safe trade and travel between countries remains a high priority. Thailand proposed the implementation of the Safe Passage

Taskforce's recommendations to increase the resistance of the region's travel infrastructure to future disruptions. In addition, significant headway was also made in the Free Trade Agreement of the Asia–Pacific (FTAAP) multi-year work plan in the post-COVID-19 context, one of the key deliverables of Thailand's APEC host year, which will help drive the region toward more a sustainable and inclusive economic recovery and long-term resilience against future pandemics and other disruptions. It also reflected Thailand's efforts to pass the baton from the Beijing FTAAP Road Map, which was proposed by China in 2014.

As one of the biggest economies in this region, China's contribution to APEC was indispensable. During my tenure as Thai APEC SOM Leader from 2017 to 2018, I witnessed firsthand the constructive role China plays, as an avid supporter of the multilateral trading system, especially in the framework of APEC. In the same line, China's support contributed to Thailand's successful hosting of APEC 2022 and helped to guide APEC into the next stage of growth.

The APEC AELM ended on a high note and injected new confidence into the positive cooperation of economies in this region. This was well reflected in President Xi Jinping's speech titled "Shouldering Responsibility and Working Together in Solidarity to Build an Asia-Pacific Community with a Shared Future" whereby he quoted a Thai proverb "You reap what you sow", noting that the APEC economies have jointly sown the seed of the Putrajaya Vision and that it is time to cultivate, nurture, and foster the blossoming flower of common development in the Asia–Pacific region.

Community with a Shared Future

While the APEC Meeting was a gathering of leaders to achieve common goals on a multilateral front, it also presented the opportune setting for face-to-face bilateral meetings between leaders, that prior to this had mostly been meeting through video screens. The resurrection of in-person head-of-state diplomacy was of particular significance for Thailand and China.

President Xi Jinping's visit to Thailand, his first since assuming office, and the first of a Chinese President in 19 years, was a milestone of historic significance in advancing our bilateral relations to new heights. The visit was also most timely, as it occurred shortly after the successful conclusion of the 20th National Congress of the Communist Part of China in October 2022, and coincided with the 10th anniversary of the Thailand-China Comprehensive Strategic Cooperative Partnership.

President Xi had a private Royal Audience with His Majesty the King of Thailand, a bilateral meeting with Prime Minister Prayuth Chan-o-cha and headed a Cabinet of Ministers meeting, whereby the two countries reaffirmed their close partnership and expressed their determination to work together to build a more meaningful partnership in the future. This was evidenced by the issuance of three important documents, which were key deliverables of this visit, namely: (1) a Joint Statement between the Kingdom of Thailand and the People's Republic of China on Working

Towards a Thailand-China Community with a Shared Future for Enhanced Stability, Prosperity, and Sustainability; (2) a Joint Action Plan on Thailand-China Strategic Cooperation between the Government of the Kingdom of Thailand and the Government of the People's Republic of China (2022–2026) and (3) a Cooperation Plan between the Government of the Kingdom of Thailand and the Government of the People's Republic of China on Jointly Promoting the Silk Road Economic Belt and the 21st Century Maritime Silk Road. Apart from the aforementioned key documents, three Memorandums of Understanding were also signed during the visit to promote cooperation in areas such as e-commerce, investment, academics, and science and technology.

The visit provided a fresh impetus to chart the future direction of bilateral relations rooted in the idea that "Thailand and China are One Family" (中泰一家亲) and our long-standing friendship of over 700 years that began during the Sukhothai Era and Yuan Dynasty.[6] This year marks the 48th anniversary of diplomatic relations with Modern China, and bilateral relations today continue to take the form of a comprehensive and strategic partnership, encompassing all sectors of cooperation and involving both central and local governments, the private sector, academia, and civil society.

People-to-people exchange is considered the backbone and a solid foundation for Thailand-China relations. Thailand is home to one of the world's largest overseas Chinese communities and Chinese tradition and culture have been embraced by Thai people and become a part of their livelihood. 2022 marked the 10th anniversary of the establishment of the China Culture Center in Bangkok, the first of its kind established by China in Southeast Asia. Thailand is also home to the largest number of Confucius Institutes of any ASEAN country. Before COVID-19, Thailand was China's top tourist destination, receiving over 10 million tourists annually. Thailand looks forward to the speedy resumption of international travel and hopes to welcome Chinese tourists back to Thailand under our tourism campaign "Visit Thailand Year 2023: Amazing New Chapters".

On the economic front, China has been Thailand's number one trading partner for ten consecutive years, and the primary export market for Thailand's agricultural products, specifically tropical fruits, cassava, rubber, and rice products. In 2022, bilateral trade amounted to 134 billion USD with a three percent increase,[7] despite the negative impact from COVID-19. China was Thailand's largest source of FDI applications through the Board of Investment (BOI) of Thailand in 2022, with combined investment totaling 2 billion USD, constituting around 18% of total investment value. There remains, however, room for increased engagement to restore the economy to pre-COVID levels and drive an upward trend in bilateral and regional economic development.

---

[6] Edward Thadeus Flood, Sukhothai-Mongol relations: a note on relevant Chinese and Thai sources with translations, 1969.

[7] The General Administration of Customs of the People's Republic of China, Trade Statistics, November 2022.

In line with the global transition toward a low-carbon society, bilateral cooperation between Thailand and China in green and sustainable development has been dynamic and positive with Chinese enterprises actively participating in Thailand's renewable energy market. The Chaiyaphum wind farm, for example, has constructed 32 of China's Goldwind turbines with a total capacity of 80 MW.[8] Meanwhile, in the new energy vehicle sector, Chinese automakers such as SAIC, Great Wall Motor, and BYD have successively established production lines in Thailand, accelerating the pace of low-carbon development in Thailand.

At the same time, Thai enterprises such as Banpu, an integrated energy company with 20 years of experience in China, have helped to accelerate the transformation to greener and smarter growth in accordance with China's transition toward a low-carbon society.[9] Meanwhile, Charoen Pokphand Group, which has 40 years of pig farming experience and expertise in China, and is the first company to establish the Chinese pig farming industry chain,[10] has contributed favorably to China's food security initiative. Such achievements are not only the result of the profound friendship between our people, but also reflect the joint efforts between the Thai and Chinese governments in creating an amiable environment for business between our two countries.

To strengthen economic linkages, both countries have established strategic synergies between Thailand's Eastern Economic Corridor and key Chinese economic clusters, namely the Greater Bay Area (GBA) and the Yangtze River Delta (YRD). At the same time, steady progress has been made in the construction of the Thailand-China High Speed Railway, which will link up with the Laos-China Railway, as well as the New International Land-Sea Trade Corridor (NILSTC), to form an artery connecting the Indo-China Peninsula that will facilitate the flow of people and goods, promote economic and trade development and achieve common prosperity. Such practical cooperation is a shining testament to the positive benefits of our bilateral cooperation and translates into a substantive contribution to regional development and prosperity.

Drinking Water from the Same River

A friend in need is a friend indeed. Thailand has always underscored the importance of neighborhood diplomacy. We believe that foreign policy begins at home, and good diplomacy starts with our neighbors. It is for this reason that Thailand's foreign policies are underpinned by the notion of joint development and "leaving no one behind", which remains the main outlook in the numerous multilateral sub-regional framework that Thailand partakes.

---

[8] The Electricity Generating Public Company Limited, https://www.egco.com/th/.

[9] Banpu China, https://www.banpu.com.cn/pc/about_us_en.html.

[10] Charoen Pokphand Group, https://www.cpgroupglobal.com/en/sustainability/health-living-well/innovation.

This same concept correlates with China's firm stance to promote shared development with neighboring countries. The China-proposed Belt and Road Initiative (BRI) has created enormous opportunities for its neighbors, who are welcomed to board China's express train of development.

One important sub-regional framework that Thailand, China, and its neighboring countries have actively participated in is the Mekong-Lancang Cooperation (MLC). While differing in name, it refers to the same river, which originates in China's Qinghai-Tibet Plateau where it is known as the Lancang River, from whence it flows downstream across Myanmar, Laos, Thailand, Cambodia, and Vietnam, where it is known as the Mekong River.

I personally had the honor of attending the inauguration of the MLC back in 2015 and watched as it blossomed into one of the most dynamic cooperative mechanisms in the sub-region today. This year marks the 7th anniversary of the establishment of the MLC and despite its young age, the MLC has delivered substantial benefits to the people and played a significant role in promoting socio-economic development in the Mekong-Lancang sub-region, particularly through the MLC Special Fund.

As co-chair with China for 2023–2024, Thailand looks forward to bolstering good neighborliness and pragmatic cooperation, fostering a community with a shared future of the Mekong-Lancang countries, and contributing to greater prosperity of the region and well-being of its people.

At the same time, 2023 also marks the 20th anniversary of the establishment of the Ayeyawady-Chao Phraya-Mekong Economic Cooperation Strategy (ACMECS), a cooperation framework with reference to the region's three principal rivers that flow through Cambodia, Laos, Myanmar, Thailand, and Vietnam to promote sub-regional prosperity despite varying economic capabilities. ACMECS attaches great importance to engagement with and the contribution of external partners, such as China who is an important development partner, as well as other relevant stakeholders, to ensure that the environment in the sub-regional is conducive to productive cooperation and healthy competition.

As the original initiator of both frameworks, Thailand advocates building synergy between ACMECS and MLC to avoid duplication and to join forces in promoting sustainable development in the region. Such linkages will help to achieve a "strategic equilibrium" in the sub-region and foster a conducive environment for "win-win-win" benefits, as a win for Mekong countries is a win for development partners, and a win for the sub-region as a whole.

After all, as the Chinese saying goes, as neighbors that drink water from the same river[11] and are as close as one family, we are naturally linked and well positioned to work together and deepen cooperation.

---

[11] Lancang-Mekong Water Resources Cooperation Information Sharing Platform, http://www.lmcwater.org.cn/.

Looking Forward

The global landscape today is undergoing transformative changes and complex uncertainties unseen in a century that will far-reaching impacts on the lives of the People, the health of the Planet, and the path to Prosperity. A holistic approach with concerted and coordinated efforts is needed now more than ever to tackle global challenges.

To this end, Thailand has submitted its candidature to host the Specialized Expo 2028 in the famed paradise of the Andaman Sea—Phuket—which not only is exceptional for its scenic nature, but also for its diversified ecosystem, its pioneering people, and culture that has carried the city through various challenges only to emerge stronger and more resilient in the face of adversity.

The Phuket Expo 2028 will advocate innovative and collaborative solutions toward a sustainable and equitable future, under the theme of the "Future of Life: Living in Harmony, Sharing Prosperity" focusing on People, the Planet, and Prosperity, to help chart a new path toward achieving the United Nations 2030 Agenda for Sustainable Development.[12] It will serve as a platform for all nations to stimulate dialogue and foster tangible solutions for the benefit of all. We aim to inspire everyone to explore their own innovative and collaborative ways to a future of peace and harmony, where health and wealth are in balance, where all lives can thrive and prosper, and where the environment and nature are restored.

Amid accelerated global changes and a downward trend in the global economy, no country can tackle these challenges alone or remain immune to their impact. At such a critical moment, nations need solidarity, not division; dialogue, not confrontation. Thailand commends China's role as a responsible major country and for holding high the banner of multilateralism and friendly cooperation. Thailand, therefore, welcomes the 3rd Belt and Road Forum in 2023, which will mark the tenth anniversary of President Xi Jinping's proposal of the BRI, and sustain the shining glory of the "Asian Moment" by injecting new vitality to the prosperity of this region and the wider world.

As Thailand and China prepare for the 50th anniversary of the establishment of Thailand-China diplomatic relations in 2025, I am confident that our elevated bilateral cooperation will guide us toward the successful building of a Thailand-China Community with a Shared Future for Enhanced Stability, Prosperity, and Sustainability. At the same time, our steadfast commitment to extensive consultation, joint contribution, and shared benefits, will help us effectively navigate through an increasingly complex global landscape, and set an exemplary role for fruitful bilateral and multilateral cooperation in this region and beyond.

---

[12] Bureau International des Expositions, "Five visions for Specialised Expo 2027/28" https://www.bie-paris.org/.

H.E. Mr. Arthayudh Srisamoot has been the Ambassador of the Kingdom of Thailand to the People's Republic of China since 2019. In 1988, he started his career in the Ministry of Foreign Affairs in the Department of ASEAN Affairs. He was Ambassador Extraordinary and Plenipotentiary to the Federal Republic of Austria, Slovak Republic and Republic of Slovenia and Permanent Representative to the United Nations and International Agencies in Vienna from 2014 to 2017. Originally from Bangkok, he has also spent time in the United States where he received his Bachelor of Science in Economics from Monmouth College and Master of Arts from the University of Chicago in Illinois.

Open Access This chapter is licensed under the terms of the Creative Commons Attribution-NonCommercial-NoDerivatives 4.0 International License (http://creativecommons.org/licenses/by-nc-nd/4.0/), which permits any noncommercial use, sharing, distribution and reproduction in any medium or format, as long as you give appropriate credit to the original author(s) and the source, provide a link to the Creative Commons license and indicate if you modified the licensed material. You do not have permission under this license to share adapted material derived from this chapter or parts of it.

The images or other third party material in this chapter are included in the chapter's Creative Commons license, unless indicated otherwise in a credit line to the material. If material is not included in the chapter's Creative Commons license and your intended use is not permitted by statutory regulation or exceeds the permitted use, you will need to obtain permission directly from the copyright holder.

The Future of Algeria-China Relations in a Changing World

Hassane Rabehi

Overcoming conflicts and achieving stability in the world cannot be achieved without considering the issue of economic development, which was stressed clearly at the last 20th CPC Congress, during which China offered a new choice for humanity to economically advance outside of the current situation.

The Congress of the CPC also emphasized China's involvement in setting global network of partnerships based on new international relations should therefore be the basis for reform and development of the global governance system leading to a world with common prosperity through mutually beneficial cooperation and inclusivity.

The world strives for more development, whatever the path or the necessary political vision, taking into consideration the respect for ethics, the environment, and the unique characteristics of each country or society. In this regard, China remains an important model to follow, particularly for developing countries like Algeria.

In this context, after his meeting with his Chinese counterpart in New York in late September, the Algerian Minister of Foreign Affairs, M. Ramtane Lamamra, stated that *"The United Nations has become nowadays a space founding hopes of Nations for a better future where Justice, Peace and Equality prevail"*.

This raises the question of Algeria and China's future relations in light of the world's major transformations. Algeria and China agree on the need for a renewed multilateralism based on the principles and goals enshrined in the United Nations Charter, in order to avoid a polarized world that imposes certain cultural and social models on others. The question is how to enhance multilateralism by prioritizing issues such as nations' equality, mutual respect, non-intervention in internal affairs, and respect for sovereignty, etc. Principles shared by our two countries are rooted in our own histories as a result of foreign oppression that we have experienced in the past.

Ambassador of the People's Democratic Republic of Algeria to the People's Republic of China.

H. Rabehi (✉)
Beijing, China

Indeed, the achievement of these principles and goals could only be based on a further pacification of international relations to build on real economic development initiatives. This calls for a more realistic spirit of reform in the architecture of the United Nations, including the functioning of its different organs, including the Security Council, the General Assembly, and the institutions in charge of global economic governance. The opening of BRICS to new members as proposed by China is also highly appreciated by countries like Algeria, which is ready to strongly support this valuable initiative.

Cooperation between Algeria and China is, therefore, an integral part of this larger movement that is already very closely linked to United Nations organs as well as other international and regional fora, particularly those dealing with development matters, such as the G77+China and South-South cooperation. China and Algeria have also demonstrated their commitment to regional cooperation by maintaining a fruitful dialogue inside the Forum China African Countries and the Forum China-Arab countries.

Algeria has also joined and supported, in the past few years, key multilateral initiatives launched by China, such as the "Belt and Road Initiative" and the "Initiative for a Global Development", and has welcomed the idea of the new "Initiative for a Global Security" announced by Chinese authorities. We find in these various initiatives the expression of our own ideals for peace, security, and development in a world where gaps are becoming wider, year after year, between powerful and less powerful countries as well as between developed and developing countries.

At the bilateral level, Algeria and China enjoy strong political ties thanks to the sustainable dialogue between the leadership of the two countries, which has never stopped since China recognized the first Algerian Government in 1958, established during the struggle for its independence. Solidarity, friendship, and cooperation constitute the core of the Algeria-China relationship and the two sides have, over the course of time, expanded their partnership in numerous fields.

The close relations and deeply rooted links that have been maintained over time will provide the two countries with new horizons of a common future of cooperation in a changing world with multiple challenges. Believing that development remains one of the keys to achieving peace and security in the world, efforts must be made in fields able to guarantee progress, the well-being of populations, and respect for the environment.

This momentum should be based on existing agreements as the two countries are already bound by a Global Strategic Partnership, signed in 2014.

The focus should also be given to the Belt and Road Initiative which could have a large ripple effect in a global perspective, considering the numerous economic reforms initiated by Algeria and the adoption in July 2022 of a new Law of Investments, which is aimed at improving the business climate, diversifying the economy, and better connecting to the global market.

Algeria's development strategy has always worked to attract Chinese companies and investors, which have contributed to our efforts to create a solid basis for the whole economy by participating in huge infrastructure projects covering tremendous vital sectors like transport, highways, public works, ports and airports, housing programs, telecommunications technology, developing the digital economy and e-commerce, green development and energy transition, re-industrialization, pharmaceuticals, railway projects, food security, and agriculture…

This fruitful multi-disciplinary cooperation between Algeria and China is a testimony of the ties of friendship, solidarity, and trust forged over the years. The two countries, which celebrate in 2023 the 65th anniversary of the establishment of their diplomatic relations, are more than ever engaged to push forward their comprehensive strategic partnership to new heights for the benefit of their two friendly people.

H.E. Mr. Hassane Rabehi is Ambassador of the People's Democratic Republic of Algeria to the People's Republic of China is a great connoisseur of China. This is his second time in this position in Beijing, which he assumed in January 2022, after a first five years term of duty, from 2010 to 2015. Before his return to China, Ambassador Rabehi occupied high positions in the Algerian Government and in regional organizations. He was the Minister of Communication, official Spokesman of the Government, and the Minister of Culture (2019) and served as Deputy-Secretary General of the Arab League of States (2020–2021). During his long diplomatic career, H.E. Mr. Rabehi has assumed high-level functions in the Algerian Ministry of Foreign Affairs, as Secretary General (2016–2017), Head of Cabinet of the Minister (1994), Director General of Consular and Legal Affairs (2004), and Ambassador of Algeria to Ghana (1997–2004).

Open Access This chapter is licensed under the terms of the Creative Commons Attribution-NonCommercial-NoDerivatives 4.0 International License (http://creativecommons.org/licenses/by-nc-nd/4.0/), which permits any noncommercial use, sharing, distribution and reproduction in any medium or format, as long as you give appropriate credit to the original author(s) and the source, provide a link to the Creative Commons license and indicate if you modified the licensed material. You do not have permission under this license to share adapted material derived from this chapter or parts of it.

The images or other third party material in this chapter are included in the chapter's Creative Commons license, unless indicated otherwise in a credit line to the material. If material is not included in the chapter's Creative Commons license and your intended use is not permitted by statutory regulation or exceeds the permitted use, you will need to obtain permission directly from the copyright holder.

The Next Phase of Development in Azerbaijan-China Relations: From Infrastructure and Digitalization Toward Green Energy

Akram Zeynalli

China's Important Contributions to Globalization as a Vital Player in a Changing World

Globalization has long been considered a powerful force for global economic growth, and the great story of China's development and progress over the four decades since reform and opening-up was launched, is deeply connected to the process of globalization. China has benefited from and significantly contributed to the process of globalization by increasing the movement of goods, services, finance, data, and people across borders. China's advance and rise on the international stage form a basis to play a constructive role in to address the new challenges associated with globalization. This also includes assisting to update global governance mechanisms, acting as a catalyst for regional integration, and further serving as a locomotive for the global economy.

Four decades of growth has led to a significant increase the welfare of Chinese citizens, and China became one of the main drivers of globalization. The country's rise from the periphery of international trade to the world's trading powerhouse has been swift. China's share of global exports of goods between 1978 and 2020 is an excellent testimony of the rapid rise. Constituting only 0.8% in 1978, this figure increased to 14.7% in 2020, which was a significant achievement. With this success story, China has become the number one exporter of goods in the world.

China actively participates in and strongly supports economic globalization. In order to jointly sustain the stability and growth of the world economy and trade, China is committed to the promotion of a multilateral trading system and eager to expand its cooperation with other nations on the basis of equality and mutual respect. The fact

---

Ambassador Extraordinary and Plenipotentiary of the Republic of Azerbaijan to the People's Republic of China.

A. Zeynalli (✉)
Chaoyang District, China

that its development path is closely tied to the rest of the world, China intertwines its own growth objectives within the context of the global development. This is the foundation of China's efforts to promote and maintain a strong and sustainable community with a shared future for mankind.

Besides to being the second largest economy and the top exporter of goods, China has recently emerged as a global economic superpower and has been investing significantly in infrastructure and development projects overseas as part of the Belt and Road Initiative (BRI), which was launched by President Xi Jinping in 2013. This initiative is an important mechanism to bring nations together by improving connectivity and advancing trade routes along the Ancient Silk Road and beyond. This is a crucial step towards the realization of common development for all mankind in a globalized world. In this sense, BRI should be considered one of China' most important contributions to globalization.

However, it should also be emphasized that globalization has also caused certain inequalities in the society. Digitalization and automation in many industries has triggered unemployment, while at the same time positively affecting trends in global trade. Today, the threats of conflict, pandemics, environmental disasters, as well as calls for protectionism and other challenges are on the rise and these developments could damage consequences as the world continues to struggle to jump-start growth. In turn, above-mentioned situation could also create the real risks for China, whose economic prospects are deeply interweaved with its integration into the world markets.

China's unprecedented development, especially over the past decade, and the progress that has been achieved in many spheres, demonstrate ample opportunities this country possesses. China's global economic and infrastructure initiatives like BRI, a great anti-poverty strategy that lifted 800 million people out of poverty, environmental policies and projects that greatly affected environmental standards and many other undertakings are clear examples of China's great achievements and contribution to joint development with win-win results that many countries can learn from.

It is essential to point out the vast changes in China's economic system over the past 40 years, which paved the way to become the second-largest economy in the world. China's path of development and reform is unique and often referred as the 'China Model' of development. Today, we are still witnessing China's comprehensive development, increases of its industrial potential, achievements in space exploration, significant advance of its military-industrial complex, improved transport and logistics capabilities and growing trade and economic cooperation with the whole world. Furthermore, China's efforts to contribute to the protection of environment, its successful domestic policy in the field of social services and increasing the welfare of the people, the implementation of an effective policy of reforms and openness all contribute to the strengthening of China's international image, its rapid entry into the ranks of world economic leaders, and the implementation of a balanced foreign policy.

Generally, attention should be drawn to the fact that Chinese society exists in a flux of constant creation, with its own ups and downs, as well as trials and errors.

But this also leads to constant learning and success, which, in turn, results in new creations and new achievements.

China's further economic development has already been forecasted by several well-known financial organizations and research centers, and it is believed that China will become the largest economy in the world in the nearest future. This success means that all countries are keen to work with China to profit from mutually beneficial cooperation with China is not an exception. We are ready to work together with China in order to improve our bilateral economic ties, substantially increase trade and imporive our rapidly developing bilateral relations to a higher level.

Azerbaijan and China: Two Friendly Nations and Strong Partners Along the Ancient Silk Road

As one of China's main trade partner in the South Caucasus, Azerbaijan attaches special importance to the development of relations with China in all spheres. It is no coincidence that during the meeting between the President of the Republic of Azerbaijan Ilham Aliyev with President Xi Jinping in April 2019 in Beijing as part of the Second Belt and Road International Cooperation Forum, President Xi referred to the President of Azerbaijan as "a great friend of the Chinese people", while President Aliyev, in turn, called President Xi as a "reliable friend of the Azerbaijani people". Thanks to the efforts of our leaders and the political dialogue established at the level of the heads of state, the current relations between our states are characterized as a multidimensional partnership which is on the track to move to the level a strategic partnership.

It should be noted with satisfaction that relations between Azerbaijan and China has demonstrated rapid growth, especially over the past decade. The strong political willingness and friendship between the current leaders of our countries have ensured tremendous achievements in all aspects of bilateral relations, including cooperation in trade, energy, humanitarian, transportation and logistics and etc. spheres.

One of the most remarkable examples of this successful cooperation could be observed in the field of economy and trade, which is fundamentally a result of the partnership created by the "BRI" Initiative. Azerbaijan was among the first countries to support this very important global initiative and our country has made a significant contribution to its realization. In this context, projects like the Baku-Tbilisi-Kars railway, initiated by Azerbaijan, as well as the commissioning of the Baku International Sea Trade Port in Alat, eventually resulted in the formation of the Trans-Caspian International Transport Route (*Middle Corridor or TITR*).

The main aim of the Middle Corridor was to ensure the additional efficient alternative route connectivity between China and Europe, and vice versa, which could take much less time than sea shipping. The recent geopolitical situation proved that formation of the Middle Corridor (TITR) was very far-sighted and visionary approach. Today, companies from Azerbaijan, Kazakhstan and Georgia, as well as various shipping companies, railways and ports of Türkiye, Ukraine, Romania and Poland all participate in the TITR.

As it was mentioned above the latest global challenges and geopolitical uncertainties have made the transportation of goods through the Middle Corridor more critical than ever, which creates the need for improved efficiency along this route. To this end, a trilateral organization made up of ministers from Azerbaijan, Türkiye and Kazakhstan was established last year to enhance cooperation and optimize the effectiveness of the Middle Corridor and identify future steps to further improvement of the route. Upon its completion, the China-Kyrgyzstan-Uzbekistan railroad could also become a part of the Middle Corridor, but it is essential that all projects implemented in Azerbaijan and the Western Caspian region be synchronized. Thus, Azerbaijan is planning to increase the capacity of the Baku International Sea Trade Port from 15 to 25 million tons.

The TITR and other infrastructure projects have enabled Azerbaijan to become a regional shipping and logistical hub and opened up new opportunities for cooperation with other countries, making a tangible contribution to the rapid and high-quality transportation of goods along East-West and North-South Corridors. Despite its lack of access to worldwide sea routes, Azerbaijan has already built an important transport network, including railways, road and air transport that could be used to deliver goods to European consumers.

As early 2022, the main route connecting northeast Asia with Europe was the Eurasian Northern Corridor. Goods were transported along the Trans-Siberian railway from Russia's Far East through Kazakhstan and Mongolia. According to a preliminary report conducted by the European Bank for Reconstruction and Development (EBRD) on sustainable transport connections between Central Asia and Europe, the Eurasian Northern Corridor was responsible for transporting around 1.5 million 20-foot equivalent units (TEUs) of cargo or containers. The Russia-Ukraine conflict has negatively impacted the use of the route for an unknown period. As a result, the completion of the Middle Corridor and the transportation of goods from China to Europe through the Middle Corridor has become more relevant. In early 2022, approximately 20,000 TEUs travelled through the Caspian Sea ports of Aktau and Kuryk in Kazakhstan. This figure continued to rise throughout the year and the amount of transit cargo passing through Azerbaijan increased by 75% compared to 2021.

During the bilateral meeting between the leaders of Azerbaijan and China on the sidelines of the 2022 SCO Summit in Samarkand, President Aliyev emphasized the excellent prospects for cooperation and partnership within the Middle Corridor and Belt and Road projects. He underlined that Azerbaijan plays an essential role in transport links between China and Europe, adding that the country's transport and logistical capabilities are of great importance in international cargo shipments.

During this meeting, it was also emphasized that Azerbaijan is currently implementing large-scale reconstruction work in newly liberated territories of Azerbaijan. Many Chinese companies have also shown interest to participate in this work and of course, Azerbaijan supports the involvement of Chinese companies in reviving the Karabakh and Eastern Zangazur economic regions of Azerbaijan. In this regard,

Huawei's participation in a smart village project in the liberated city of Zangilan in Azerbaijan is a clear indicator of the mutual trust and practical cooperation between our countries.

In addition to re-establishing the shortest route between Azerbaijan proper and its exclave of Nakhchivan, the planned Zangazur corridor will play a significant role in connecting East-West and North-South transportation routes. As a transit across the Caucasus, the new Zangazur corridor will significantly reduce the transportation time between China and Europe, complementing the Baku-Tbilisi-Kars railway and facilitating trade and business. This new corridor will play an important role in terms of connectivity along the Belt and Road and create great prospects for Azerbaijan and China to expand cooperation in the transportation and logistics sectors.

However, infrastructure development is not limited to upgrading existing physical roads, railways and sea ports. It also includes digitalization and improvement of the digital networks that link Azerbaijan to the world via the Internet. One of the major tasks Azerbaijan has put forward is the "Digital Silk Way" project that includes the establishment of a digital telecommunications corridor between Europe and Asia. The project, implemented under the "Azerbaijan Digital Hub" program, envisages the transfer of digital content and internet services from European Internet centers to Asian countries via Azerbaijan. The project will enable Azerbaijan to play a central and strategic role in telecommunications, transmitting Internet services and content from major content operators such as Google, Amazon, Alibaba, Netflix, Facebook and others. In the future, with the establishment of the Internet Exchange Centre in Baku, the country will transmit this content and other internet traffic to Central and South Asia, and other neighboring countries in the region.

The "Digital Silk Way" is of great importance to countries in Central and South Asia, where internet traffic has been increasing. To this end, "AzerTelecom" and "China Telecom" signed a Strategic Memorandum of Understanding within the framework of the Second Belt and Road International Cooperation Forum, which was held on 25–27 April 2019 in Beijing, laying the foundation for cooperation between "AzerTelecom" and "China Telecom" in the creation of a telecommunications corridor (the Digital Silk Way) between Asia and Europe under the framework of the "Azerbaijan Digital Hub" program.

Future Prospects on Cooperation Between Azerbaijan and China in Green Energy Development

Since it was first proposed in 2013, China's BRI has taken on many forms. A clear-eyed strategy to connect Asia with Africa and Europe via land and maritime networks, the BRI's primary goals are regional integration and the stimulation of trade and economic growth. Yet, these goals are not limited to any singular aspect of trade, logistics or infrastructure but also include green goals through technology, investment in capacity building, and information sharing. In this context, Azerbaijan has a great deal to contribute in bilaterally cooperation with China and within the BRI in terms of energy transition and green energy development.

Azerbaijan is a country with rich oil and gas reserves, which means Azerbaijan plays an important role in terms of the energy security of Europe today. TANAP and TAP pipelines, as part of the Southern Gas Corridor, carry natural gas from the Caspian Sea reserves directly to the European marketplace. A Memorandum of Understanding on a Strategic Partnership in the Field of Energy, signed between the European Commission and Azerbaijan on July 18, 2022, states that the annual imports of natural gas from Azerbaijan to Europe will double by 2027.

Along with all these developments, while improving Azerbaijan's position as a key supplier of oil and gas, our country is also keen on contributing to the transition to green energy. More than 8% of the electricity produced in Azerbaijan today is made using renewable resources, but the Ministry of Energy of Azerbaijan has set a goal to increase this figure to 30% by 2030. The goal is attainable given the fact that Azerbaijan's geographical location creates favorable conditions for developing renewable energy. Most importantly, green energy projects are essential for the liberated territories of Azerbaijan. It is no coincidence that the Karabakh and Eastern Zangazur economic regions have been declared "green zones" by President Ilham Aliyev. These liberated lands have huge potential in terms of wind and solar energy generation, and Azerbaijan has already started implementing numerous green projects in those territories.

Azerbaijan is also planning to increase its green energy production to a level that it will enable to export electricity. An agreement signed by the leaders of Azerbaijan, Georgia, Romania and Hungary last year to build an underwater electric cable through the Black Sea will allow Azerbaijan to export electricity to the European market and further contribute to the energy security of Europe. Azerbaijan currently produces 27 GW of wind and solar power, and green projects being implemented throughout the country, especially in the Karabakh and Eastern Zangazur economic regions, will increase energy production and enable us to even greater volumes of energy to the European marketplace.

Taking all of this into account, we believe there are huge opportunities to cooperate with China in the area of green energy infrastructure, especially in light of China's considerable experience in this sector and the advanced technologies Chinese companies have developed to make energy transition easier and more achievable. It is pleasant to be witnessed that several Chinese companies are already participating in green energy projects in Azerbaijan, but we welcome even more Chinese companies to join us in our goal to reach green objectives.

H.E. Mr. Akram Zeynalli is Ambassador Extraordinary and Plenipotentiary of the Republic of Azerbaijan to the People's Republic of China. A career diplomat, Akram Zeynalli graduated from Baku State University, International Law and International Relations faculty before joining diplomatic service and starting his diplomatic career in the Ministry of Foreign Affairs of the Republic of Azerbaijan in 1998. He served as a diplomat at the Embassies of the Republic of Azerbaijan to the Kingdom of Belgium, to the Hellenic Republic and the Permanent Mission of the Republic of Azerbaijan to the United Nations Office and other international organizations in Geneva. Akram Zeynalli is the former Ambassador of the Republic of Azerbaijan to the Swiss Confederation and the Principality of Liechtenstein. Currently, he is the Ambassador Extraordinary and Plenipotentiary of the Republic of Azerbaijan to the People's Republic of China and the Democratic People's Republic of Korea. He holds the diplomatic rank of Ambassador Extraordinary and Plenipotentiary.

Open Access This chapter is licensed under the terms of the Creative Commons Attribution-NonCommercial-NoDerivatives 4.0 International License (http://creativecommons.org/licenses/by-nc-nd/4.0/), which permits any noncommercial use, sharing, distribution and reproduction in any medium or format, as long as you give appropriate credit to the original author(s) and the source, provide a link to the Creative Commons license and indicate if you modified the licensed material. You do not have permission under this license to share adapted material derived from this chapter or parts of it.

The images or other third party material in this chapter are included in the chapter's Creative Commons license, unless indicated otherwise in a credit line to the material. If material is not included in the chapter's Creative Commons license and your intended use is not permitted by statutory regulation or exceeds the permitted use, you will need to obtain permission directly from the copyright holder.

The Future of China's Development and Globalization: A View from Poland

Wojciech Zajączkowski

My first personal recollection of China as global manufacturer and international trading actor goes as far back as the beginning of 1980s when I bought a "Hero"—brand fountain pen produced in Shanghai. For a young college student from a provincial city in communist Poland, it was something magical. It was amazing that I was using a nice gadget designed and produced thousands of kilometers away in a country that I'd only heard of in geography and history class. At that time, black tea and cheap flashlights were the only other proofs of China's existence. However, reality can changes very quickly. Initially unsophisticated Chinese products were replaced by a wave of garments, initially of low quality, followed by top clothing brands and electronic devices with small, hidden geographical hints: "Made in China". Today, high-end Chinese products proudly stating their country of origin have now become a part of everyday life.

This incredible evolution from fountain pens and black tea to cutting edge IT products happened in the span of a single human lifetime and is reflected in global trade statistics. In 1980, China's share of global merchandise exports hovered around 1.0%, and in 2021 it was already 15.07%. China took advantage of globalization and made good use of it to increase the wealth of its citizens, build infrastructure, and develop research capabilities. It benefited China's economic partners as well. The question was, could it maintain this pace over the long-term?

Today this question is rather more academic than practical. The globalization that we were familiar with still a few years ago belongs to the past and the turning point came in two waves: the COVID-19 pandemic and a series of political earthquakes which culminated in Russian aggression against Ukraine. These events belonged to different realms—global health and international politics, respectively—and they had different impacts on our lives. However, despite many dissimilarities, they shared

---

Ambassador of the Republic of Poland to the People's Republic of China.

W. Zajączkowski (✉)
Beijing, China

at least one common trait as they revealed the complexity of interdependencies which emerged from globalization.

Already well before 2020, governments of some countries, including China, came to the conclusion that the globalization, which had spurred economic growth in recent decades, did not offer sufficient protection against critical shocks resulting from excessive cooperation with international partners. This discovery prompted them to look for alternative solutions and finally led to including a transition to a policy of increased self-reliance. A very good example of this approach was the "Made in China 2025" program launched by the Chinese government as early as 2015.

The outbreak of the COVID-19 pandemic, followed by intensified international tensions, only reinforced this trend. In 2022, President Xi Jinping had good reason to say that one of China's key goals was to "accelerate the realization of high-level scientific and technological self-reliance and self-improvement." Many other leaders echoed similar words.

Is this good or bad? A lot depends on the language we use to describe this phenomenon. Words such as "decoupling" or "protectionism" can have a negative tone, which is unnecessary. Nobody should feel offended by ongoing changes; they are real, and the word "adjustment" renders their meaning much better. The more complex question is what will be the long-term consequences of these "adjustments"?

Quite often, these situations are considered in terms of a zero sum game. This may be the case sometimes, but the current situation is different. This adjustment should be seen as a natural reaction to the shocks that the world has been experiencing over last few years. By definition, adjustment is future oriented and opens a new chapter in the contemporary social and economic history of the world by making development more resilient in the face of geopolitical, health, and climate threats.

It is very likely that this new social and economic environment will be characterized by a more equal distribution of manufacturing potential and more differentiated logistic chains on a global scale. Countries and companies will work to reduce dependencies, and one can imagine that new important actors will emerge, especially among Global South countries, in South East Asia, Africa, Latin America. In the decade from 2011 to 2021, China's contribution accounted for 33.4% of all global economic growth, while Africa and ASEAN countries contributed 3.7% and 8.4%, respectively. However, sooner or later, all these great regions will claim a new place in global distribution of economic potential. If considered as a single entity, ASEAN is the third largest economy in Asia, and the fifth largest in the world after the USA, China, Japan, and Germany. We cannot discount the fact that the relocation of some industrial sectors to these areas will boost future economic growth. This does not mean, however, that this process will necessarily happen at the expense of China. If global economic growth continues, China's revenues from trade and manufacturing should also keep growing even if its share in the global economy plateaus or contracts.

To better asses the opportunities and challenges that China will face in the future due to adjustments made to global economic cooperation mechanisms, it may be interesting to look at its relations with other countries. Poland may serve as a good example in this context. Both countries have maintained complex and multifaceted economic exchanges that date back to 1950. In 2021, their bilateral trade turnover exceeded 53.6 billion USD with a huge 47 billion USD surplus on the Chinese side. The majority of Polish products exported to China in 2021 were copper ore and copper products, wood, car parts and accessories, converters, textiles, machinery, and dairy products. This list of exports is neither long nor diversified, but at the same time Polish industry has gained international recognition in such sectors as furniture, green technologies, the gaming industry, yachts and recreational boats, biotech, nanotech and pharma, medical devices and services, food and agriculture, mobility, cosmetics, fashion, and tourism. Clearly, there is a great deal of unexploited potential in the Polish–Chinese trade, particularly if it becomes more balanced and less unilateral.

Polish–Chinese investment is another interesting field to look at. For decades, it remained stagnant despite the fast economic growth of both countries. Recently, however, it has gained momentum, and efforts have resulted in milestones that echo historical achievements like the founding in 1951 of the first joint Chinese—foreign company. Chipolbrok, a Polish–Chinese shipping joint venture that boasts registry number "1" in China, celebrated its 70th anniversary in 2021 and remains a source of inspiration for all those who dream of promoting business between our countries. For the time being, the share of Chinese investors in Poland make up a small part of overall foreign investment and in 2019 accounted only for 3.15% of the total investment that year, mainly focusing on acquisitions of existing enterprises and mergers. Polish investment in China also remains low.

For years, Poland has been ranked very high among Central and Eastern European countries in terms of its attractiveness to investment. In 2021, Poland moved into third place in the European Union and 14th in the world in terms of the inflow of foreign direct investments with the value of 24.8 billion USD (an 82% rise year-on-year and 86% compared to 2019). Within the European Union, only Germany and Sweden showed higher inflows. The number of greenfield investment projects amounted to 423 (11% growth year-to-year) ranking fourth in Europe and sixth in the world. Foreign investors appreciate Poland's stable economic growth, strong domestic demand, geographical and logistic proximity to other European markets, highly qualified and hardworking labour force, improving infrastructure as well as number of different investment incentives.

The economic development of Poland and the evolution of its industries have created great opportunities especially in electro mobility, including the production of electric cars batteries; electronics (production sites as well as R&D centres); renewable sources of energy; and logistics, including e-commerce warehouses and logistics centres.

The above overview of trade and investment between Poland and China suggests that there is considerable room for further growth and even at a time of global economic adjustment, both sides can benefit from deeper ties. Achieving this result, however, should not be taken for granted. The need for a change in how China works with countries like Poland seems to be eminent. A new model for cooperation should be more reciprocal and inclusive. In the long-run, economic relations founded on the assumption that one side produces and another side buys are not sustainable. To avoid a stalemate and unlock the untapped potential of economic cooperation, more attention should be paid to the following issues:

First, a level playing field and market access. Unbalanced trade remains the main challenge in our bilateral relations as well as EU–China relations. The Chinese market remains closed to many foreign goods and services. There is a need to provide the same opportunities for foreign and Chinese companies. Today, the latter enjoy more rights than their foreign competitors (public procurement is a good example) and have access to controversial state support mechanisms. Keeping one fifth of the global economy partly locked and partly open will have negative consequences worldwide.

Second, transparency and predictability. These two imperatives are crucial for maintaining economic relations in a globalized world. If you are unable to say what your trade or investment partner is going to do in the near future, you start to consider alternative options.

Third, credibility. If we want to advance or even to maintain our cooperation in the future, mutual trust is needed. This is the cornerstone of any cooperative relationship. If we face a deficit of mutual trust, then the political framework, all bilateral and multilateral meetings, become meaningless. In the case of relations between Poland and China we are very close to this point.

Fourth, geopolitics. Many believed this concept had become obsolete, but today it is back. It can be clearly seen in the case of rail freight between China and Europe. In 2015, 18,900 containers passed through Malaszewicze—a border crossing between Poland and Belarus, and the biggest railway terminal along the EU border; in 2021 this number grew to 227,000. However, this may not be sustainable. Based on border data from Malaszewicze, the projected volume of containers transported from China to EU plummeted 25% year-on-year in April 2022. This is mainly due to the impact of the Russian war in Ukraine, which have forced some producers and exporters to redirect their containers from rail to sea routes due to possible risks of border closure, sanctions, and the rising costs of insurance.

Unfortunately, geopolitics has broader implications for economic cooperation than just the flow of goods through a railway border crossing point, even if it is the biggest one in Europe. It is about understanding the basic rules of international relations, including territorial integrity, non-use of force, non-interference in domestic affairs, and respect of sovereignty. It is clear that differences of opinion in this area between European countries, including Poland, and China, particularly in the case of Russian aggression against Ukraine, do not contribute to better trade and investment climate. On the contrary, they foster distrust and lack of confidence in the logic of economic development. Therefore, while speaking about trade and investment, we must keep in mind that respect for UN Charter principles an essential precondition for a safe and stable international economic environment, where globalization was born.

It is hard to underestimate China's potential contribution to the redefinition of globalization. If China takes the current trend of economic adjustment as an opportunity to improve its economic relations with foreign partners and becomes more open and reciprocal in its policies, it will benefit the world and itself. It will play a pivotal role in the global post-pandemic recovery and bring economic cooperation a new level on par with its "high quality development" formula. If the focus is to defend old positions, we can expect only more tension and disruption, which will have negative consequences all over the world.

H. E. Wojciech Zajączkowski has been the Ambassador Extraordinary and Plenipotentiary of the Republic of Poland to China since 2018. Before taking up his post in Beijing, he was the Director of the Department of Foreign Policy Strategy at the Polish Ministry of Foreign Affairs. He joined Poland's Ministry of Foreign Affairs in 1998, and during his earlier diplomatic career he was posted to Russia, Ukraine and Turkmenistan. From 2008 to 2010, he was Poland's Ambassador to Romania, and then from 2010 to 2014, he served as Ambassador to Russia. From 2004 to 2007, he headed the Department for Eastern Policy and in 2008 became the Chief Advisor to the Prime Minister of Poland and Head of the Working Group on Energy Security. He has also worked as an editor, advisor to the Senate of the Republic of Poland, and analyst. He is also the author of multiple books and articles on international politics focusing on Russia. He holds a Ph.D. in Political Science.

Open Access This chapter is licensed under the terms of the Creative Commons Attribution-NonCommercial-NoDerivatives 4.0 International License (http://creativecommons.org/licenses/by-nc-nd/4.0/), which permits any noncommercial use, sharing, distribution and reproduction in any medium or format, as long as you give appropriate credit to the original author(s) and the source, provide a link to the Creative Commons license and indicate if you modified the licensed material. You do not have permission under this license to share adapted material derived from this chapter or parts of it.

The images or other third party material in this chapter are included in the chapter's Creative Commons license, unless indicated otherwise in a credit line to the material. If material is not included in the chapter's Creative Commons license and your intended use is not permitted by statutory regulation or exceeds the permitted use, you will need to obtain permission directly from the copyright holder.

Appendix

CCG Ambassadors' Roundtable—In Conversation with Nordic Ambassadors[1]

Paths Toward Common Prosperity: The Nordic Model and Beyond

In an era of globalization, countries everywhere face daunting socioeconomic challenges. Inequality is rising. Cohesion is weakening as societies undergo identity crises. As governments in search of role models for governance, equality, and social and economic policy, the so-called Nordic Model often ranks at the top. Practiced in Nordic countries, including Sweden, Norway, Denmark, Finland, and Iceland, the Nordic Model is characterized by a state welfare system, access to quality education, and low income disparities, which contributes to the countries' continued growth and prosperity.

China shares the Nordic countries' drive to combine market economy and government intervention. As the country seeks to transform its economy and address challenges due to unfettered growth in the past decades, the Nordic experiences may shed light on possible pathways toward the national goal of common prosperity. This event provides highly contextualized accounts of the Nordic Model and a discussion about its relevant applications for the future.

At the Center for China and Globalization (CCG), the Ambassadors of the five Nordic countries, namely Denmark, Finland, Iceland, Norway, and Sweden, presented different aspects of Nordic governance and practices, including fiscal policy, education, parental leaves, demographic policy, resource management and sustainability, and exchanged views with Chinese scholars and officials on how China can learn and build on Nordic experiences and practices as it works to meet its national goal of common prosperity.

---

[1] This roundtable was held on 7 June, 2023, full video at http://en.ccg.org.cn/archives/79556.

© The Editor(s) (if applicable) and The Author(s) 2024
H. Wang and M. L. Miao (eds.), *The Future of China's Development and Globalization*, China and Globalization, https://doi.org/10.1007/978-981-99-7512-9

Feature Presentations

H.E. Helena Sångeland, Ambassador of Sweden to China

The topic of my intervention today is addressing the demographic challenges in Sweden from an economic perspective. When we talk about demographic challenges, over-population is still a major problem, and human population has grown beyond a sustainable means. We are consuming more resources than our planet can regenerate with devastating consequences, and this goes particularly for richer countries, like my own. More people mean an increased demand for food, water, housing, energy, house care, transportation and more, and all that consumption contributes to ecological degradation, and increase conflicts and a higher risk of large-scale disasters like pandemics.

This is a very important topic—how to grow the world population in a sustainable way. But, the demographic challenge that I wish to talk about today is from an economic perspective, because many countries are grappling with lower birth rates, and aging populations, which increases costs to the economy, pressure on health services, competition for jobs, or decreased participation in the workforce, potentially less funding for young people, and an increased dependency ratio.

Population growth, on the other hand, will lead a higher tax revenues, which can be spent on public goods, such as health care and education. By that token, it can be a good thing to have an increasing population. Sweden is just like our Nordic neighbors, one of the richest countries in the world, but we are also rich country whose population still grows, and ages, and this picture illustrates by year 2100, Sweden's population is estimated to grow from today's 10.5 million to 13.7 million, and in a Chinese perspective, that is quite laughable, it is the size of a fourth tier city in China, but it is still growth.

Sweden is one of the few countries which will continue to grow, whereas others will decrease. Population growth in Sweden basically comes down to two factors: there are more births than deaths, and more people move to Sweden than move out. The policy challenge is to sustain a comparably higher degree of labor market participation, in order to support both our children and our elderly.

So what are the measures that Sweden has taken? In the 70s, which indeed was a decade of many reforms, we came to political consensus that we needed to create possibilities for women to both work and raise a family. The economy grew fast, and we needed all hands on deck, in our manufacturing sector and service industry. We also needed the population to keep on growing. So, what was introduced in the 1970s was a number of reforms, the provision of heavily subsidized childcare, equal for all. Municipalities have to provide for all children regardless of what hours their parents work, meaning provision of nighttime childcare for those who works as nurses and doctors and others who work nightshifts.

School is free so as to provide equal opportunities for all. There are also provisions of after school care, so that parents can work full time. Parental leave has gradually been increased to what we have today. A child can have one parent on paid leave for almost one and a half years, and with 80–90% of the leave paid. This parental leave must be shared, so at least one parent needs to take out a minimum of three months of the one and a half years and the fathers' share of all parental leave days has increased tremendously.

For instance, when I get new staff at my embassy, young men in their 30s, if they are married or living with a partner, I can be assured that they will ask for six months of leave, although they are posted abroad and they are entitled to it. Just as mothers they are also entitled to take their leave for six months.

Universal child allowances are also provided and increase with the number of children that we have. Maternal and under-five mortality rates are low, and we have laws in place to hinder employer discrimination against pregnant women or to-be parents. We do not discriminate against men or women, although it is the case that women still taken more parental leave than men, but the difference is shrinking.

What these reforms did, apart from allowing women and men to both work and have children, was that they transferred a lot of work from the informal to the formal sector. Such as household chores have become jobs, which has a lot of spin-off effects like increased taxation and revenue. As a bonus, people do not need to save up for day care, school, universities, and elderly care. Thus they have more money and incentives to spend on consumption, in turn driving economic growth. Labor participation of women is today 71%. It is still lower than that of men, which is 76%, but from an international perspective that is rather high.

That is not to say that we do not have a lot of challenges, women still work more part time than men, they have lower salaries and higher unemployment, but we have come far during the past 50 years. Another factor affecting the labor force is how long we work; we are fortunate enough to have people living longer and healthier lives. Life expectancy has increased by almost 10 years for men and 7 years for women over the past 50 years, to 81 and 85 years, respectively. But that also means that older people need to be supported financially for a longer time, unless they work longer, which exactly what they are doing in Sweden. The earliest you can retire today and to receive public pension is 63, and you have the right to choose to work until 69 and if you and your employer want, you can also continue longer than that.

Retirement age is constantly raised in pace with life expectancy and you have economic incentives for working as long as possible. The longer you work, the higher your pension will be. A remaining challenge is to improve working conditions for those carry out physically demanding occupational activities. For example, women who work as nurses, with long hours and heavy lifting of patients, we have to ensure that they have bodies and minds in shapes to enjoy retirement after 45 years of working.

And, of course, we also have immigration. Despite all our advances, the fertility rate in Sweden is 1.6 per women, and higher than that in most developed countries, but still not high enough to tip the scale in favor of population growth in the long run, even if there are more babies born than those who die.

In the 60s and 70s, during our manufacturing boom, we would never have been able to make it without immigrants from our neighbor Finland and southern Europe. Today we have newly arrived refugees from war zones such as Afghanistan, Iraq,

Syria, Eritrea, and Ukraine, who are working in our services sector, taking care of our elderly and our children. Others are highly skilled immigrants advancing our technological and scientific development.

Although there is no lack of challenges, they largely contribute to how we have overcome the demographic challenge that so many countries meet at a certain stage of economic development. About 20% of Sweden's population is born abroad (i.e. if you have two parents born abroad). I, for instance, am part of that immigrant population, because my parents were born abroad, they were born in Finland and came to Sweden to find a work in the 50s and 60s.

There is no one simple solution to address demographic challenges, but there are many measures can be taken that combined come a long way. Thank you very much.

H.E. Leena-Kaisa Mikkola, Ambassador of Finland to China

I will talk shortly about Finnish education system and in particular about educational equality. I will concentrate on the Finnish system, but the issue of equality is very important for all of us in every country's educational system.

During the last years, my country has often been in the headlines when it comes to quality education. According to many international surveys and studies, we have indeed done quite well in improving equal and quality education for all. But before highlighting the aspects of educational equality, let me start with a few words about historical background and the Finnish educational system in general. I will also address the issue of vocational education, which I think is essential when building the society for all, a society of equal opportunities.

It is perhaps of interest for you to know that Finland was among the last countries in Europe to make education compulsory. We became independent from centuries of Swedish and Russian rule in 1917, and the act concerning general compulsory education came into force in 1921. Schooling was common even before that, especially in the urban areas, however, in the countryside, where majority of Finns those days lived, schooling of children was less common. And this also relates to my own family background; my grandmother was born in a village in 1906, and she never went to school. The act from 1921 aimed to do away with the educational inequality between towns and countryside, and the idea of educational equality has remained one of the guiding principles in our education system ever since.

Equality consists of two dimensions—fairness and inclusion. Fairness means reducing the social-economic barriers, while inclusion is to ensure basic standards of education to all. We do not live in a perfect world and it would be hypocritical to claim that we, or somebody else, has achieved complete equality through education. But while not perfect, I would say that Finland and other Nordic countries have done quite well. Finnish youth have universal and free access to education. Students' gender or school's language of instructions explains a very small part of the difference in skills during his or her educational path. Whether the student comes from the capital area or from the sparsely populated northern part of the country does not make a real difference when evaluating skills, or academic achievements.

The successes that we have had did not happen overnight 102 years ago. It has taken many decades to achieve. There has been a series of reforms and responses also to changing economic needs. But through trial and error, Finland has built successes in education. Of course, broader societal factors have also been helpful. The overall commitment to equality, various welfare services, and the question of strong cultural trust have always been fundamental when developing our road. There has always been a kind of whole society approach, but what works for us, might not always be 100% copy pasted for others.

However, there are some ideas free for copying.

Firstly, education for all approach has been a hallmark for Finnish education policy since its onset. There has always been and there still is a broad political consensus to build a public school system that will serve every student without costs. As a result, every Finn has a subjective right to participate in quality schooling, cost free from early childhood education, all the way to obtaining a university diploma. The equality aspect is supported by investments, for example, in free school meals, free school rides, but also in investing in special education. The Finnish education system is in many ways very flexible. We know that students' and pupils' preferences change as they grow older. Education also needs to be able to respond to the fast-paced changes taking place in the labor market and the society. To allow for this necessary flexibility, there are no dead ends in our education system. A student entering and graduating a vocational school, for example, is still able to pursue later on a university-level education. In recent years, efforts have been made to increase possibilities of personalizing studies, also already at the secondary education level, something that has been very much the case at the tertiary level of education.

Coming back to the culture of trust. At the primary and secondary level, there are no ranking lists compiled of Finnish schools. The most important thing is the system of trust based on the qualified and committed educational staff. Educational policy development is to a large degree headed by professional educationalists, rather than politicians. Teaching is a sought-after career that people respect. Entry into that profession is quite hard—often only one out of 10 applicants is accepted into teachers' training programs in the universities. But the high standard of our staff means also greater independence. The schools are able to supplement the national curriculum with locally important topics and independently decide how the teaching is carried out.

Now a couple more words about vocational education and why. We think good quality vocational education is not only about equality in education, but also about equal opportunities in the society as a whole. The development of Finland's vocational education system has roots in our history. After the Second World War, Finland had to pay huge reparations to the Soviet Union, which were basically paid in goods, machinery, and ships, which we did not have. In order to have all these, we needed to significantly adjust our industrial production, which meant we needed a significant amount of skilled and qualified workers. That was the stepping-stone for our vocational education schools and appreciation of them. Nowadays, it takes about three years to get a vocational education degree. The training is to provide the necessary skills for working life. But not only that, the education also supports students' growth as individuals and responsible members of the society. It is characteristic to the Finnish system that about half of the students choose vocational education as their secondary education.

To conclude, we Finns are quite pragmatic and levelheaded people. We are equally levelheaded and realistic about the challenges and problems facing our educational system. The picture is not always rosy and one must admit that in recent years, regional differences in educational inequality have grown. Also, the differences in the skills of students in different schools have grown somewhat. However, from an international perspective, the differences between schools and students are still quite moderate in Finland. When we see inequality, we take it very seriously, because it mirrors very much the equality in the society as a whole and also the social cohesion that makes us the happiest country in the world for the sixth time, which we value so much.

On a personal note, which explains educational thinking in Finland: during my previous postings, an educational expert from that country asked my older son, who was 15 at the time, what is the difference between the international school he attended at the time and the Finnish school he attended previously. My son explained that in this international school, we prepare for academic excellence, but in my Finnish school, we prepare for life.

H.E. Signe Brudeset, Ambassador of Norway to China

First of all, I would like to say thank you very much to CCG for organizing this event. The topic of today, *the Nordic Model*, generally refers to similarities in economic management, the organization of working life, focus on human rights and universal welfare services in the Nordic countries. It is not a uniform model, but we share similarities.

We have a long tradition of valuable exchanges with Chinese and Nordic experts on our respective society models. In the late 1970s, the Norwegian Ministry of Energy and the state-owned energy company Statoil shared experiences with CNOOC on management of the petroleum sector. Later we have had valuable exchanges on pension reform and gender equality. Now green financing is a topic.

Making relevant comparisons between China and the Nordic countries may not intuitively come across as relevant. The governance models are very different, the size of the populations are miles apart, but still, we share some of the same challenges—aging population, how to tune our education systems for the future labor market, how to avoid increased inequality. Today, I would like to touch on three topics central to the Norwegian governance model. The first is taxation, the second is management of petroleum resources, and the third is state ownership.

If you want to understand how a country works, you should study its tax system. This is certainly true for Norway, where taxation issues are among the most hotly debated issues. And I believe the same is true for China. Recently, I had a look at a very interesting book called "Governing and Ruling: The political logic of taxation in China". The author (Zhang Changdong) points to important dilemmas around taxation and economic growth, taxation and representation, as well as relationships between central versus regional and local authorities.

For Norway, our tax system is indispensable for securing strong government finances that fuel a sustainable welfare state. Openness and transparency in the tax system are essential values. Although Norway has been blessed with abundant petroleum and natural resources, our workforce is seen as the country's most important resource. The main goal of the Norwegian employment policy is to ensure that as many people as possible participate in the labor market and contribute to society. This is a prerequisite for the sustainability of Norway's welfare schemes; *we must create value before we can share value.*

A broad tax base founded on a high level of participation in the labor force is necessary to ensure sufficient revenue. But we also believe it promotes fair distribution, value creation, and work incentives. Tax revenues are also used to redistribute and to reduce inequalities between people socially, economically, and geographically.

The Norwegian system and culture expect that all who are capable of participating in the labor market do so, and seek—through free training and education—to facilitate everyone's inclusion in the workforce. Norway has thus a relatively high retirement age, normally 67 for both men and women. Norwegian policymakers are working for an inclusive labor market that makes it possible for men and women, immigrants, the young, the elderly, and people with disabilities to find gainful employment and continue working longer.

Our high labor market participation, together with a broad tax base, generates income to the state, which in turn can be redistributed for the common good of society. Again—*we must create value before we can share value.*

Making sure that those with the highest incomes and most wealth contribute most helps generate sufficient revenue and a fair tax burden, but it also fosters trust. Trust in our society is incredibly important.

Income, wealth, and opportunities are often unevenly distributed geographically. To even out these disparities, successive Norwegian governments have developed policies that promote geographical redistribution. Subsidies are offered to various industries located in the periphery, such as agriculture, where national food security is an important aim.

In general, today's public welfare schemes in Norway include free healthcare (beyond a small deductible) and education, generous maternity and paternity leave, retirement and disability pensions, unemployment benefits, 100% sick pay, and other welfare services and benefits. In addition to ensuring a strong social safety net, the interaction between the welfare system and a well-functioning labor market with small wage gaps has contributed to a high employment rate, low income inequality, a high degree of transparency, equal opportunities, and social trust.

Another important factor for a good and stable Norwegian economy has been responsible management of petroleum revenues. When oil and gas were discovered on the Norwegian continental shelf in 1969, it sparked discussions about how revenue should be handled in order to benefit all Norwegians, including future generations.

In 1990, Norway established a sovereign wealth fund, today known as the Government Pension Fund Global. The state's revenues from oil and gas extraction are now kept in the fund, together with the returns on the fund's investments. The fund's statutes and investment rules are regulated by the Parliament, and the organization of the fund is supervised by the Ministry of Finance. But the fund operates independently and free from political interference. The majority of investments are made in low-risk international equities and bonds. The current size of the fund is around $1.4 trillion, which makes it the second largest sovereign wealth fund in the world.

To avoid the so-called resource curse, we have established "the budgetary rule", which says that "transfers from the fund to the central government budget shall, over time, follow the expected rate of return on the fund". This is today estimated to about 3%. As significant emphasis is placed on evening out economic fluctuations and contributing to sound capacity utilization and low unemployment, the annual transfers may exceed 3% in difficult times and be well below that in normal times. The transfers are thus used in a counter-cyclical manner into the Norwegian economy. The fiscal policy framework has aimed to preserve the real value of the fund for the benefit of future generations. The revenues that we get today are not for generations today, but also for future Norwegians.

State ownership has also been an important tool for making sure that our common resources benefit all. Private ownership is, as a rule, preferred in Norway's mixed market economy and direct state ownership requires a special justification. In the area of common resources, the state owns a higher share in the domains of energy and the extraction of natural resources, but private companies also participate in this sector and contribute to a competitive business environment.

It is, however, worth underlining that state-owned companies in Norway operate at an arms-length distance from the government and are subject to the same rules and objectives as privately owned companies. The state can exercise its rights as a shareholder, but the company is managed and operated independently by its management personnel and board of directors. Typically, the government focuses on the rate of return with many state-owned companies listed on the stock exchange and include private shareholders as well.

Creating a perfect system for economic and social governance is nearly impossible, as most variations on any system have their advantages and disadvantages. Nevertheless, economic systems need to be well adapted to the changing situation in the countries that have adopted them, and a fair balance between competing ends and considerations must be found.

Although the Norwegian and Chinese systems and realities differ, we find it to be highly valuable to engage in discussions and experience sharing with Chinese counterparts on such issues. So, thank you very much again to CCG, my Nordic colleagues and the other distinguished participants. I look forward to further exchanges on these topics. Thank you!

Appendix

H.E. Thomas Østrup Møller, Ambassador of Denmark to China

The first thing that came into my mind when I heard about today's topic was the concept of trust. Of course, trust is not inherently a Nordic idea, or a foreign concept in China. Nor is trust a concept with a single meaning. We can talk about several types of trust.

One type is individual trust, a trust in someone you already know. An evolutionary trait that most likely dates back to the primitive hunter-gatherer societies. If you were injured during a mammoth hunt, you could trust your small clan to care for you. This makes sense, and we all have family members that we trust dearly. Those who are close to you, you trust. Another type is institutional trust, your confidence in public bodies such as courts, police, and the administration. I will get back to that in a bit.

But let me start by telling you about our take on trust in the Nordic countries. Although there may be variations, we trust each other—almost by default. This is a third kind—societal trust. This is trust in strangers you have never met before. And I believe that this is quite fundamental to the Nordic Model and Nordic way of life.

Let me give you an example. Many Danes will remember a story from 1997, when a Danish woman left her 14-month old daughter asleep in a baby carriage outside a coffee shop in New York City. The mother was sitting inside and could see the baby through the window, so everything to her was in perfect order. But soon a concerned citizen called the police, who took the baby into custody and arrested the woman.

Luckily, she got off with a warning, and mother and child were soon reunited. Yet, if you have ever been to Denmark, you have without a doubt noticed there are many baby carriages outside local coffee shops. In Denmark, we routinely leave sleeping babies outside, without any direct supervision other than a sound recorder, so we can hear when they wake up. This is a very concrete example of societal trust. We simply trust others—people we have never met—enough to leave our children sleeping alone.

And this leads me back to institutional trust. We also have great trust in our government, legal system, police, and administration. Do not get me wrong, one of our favorite pastimes is complaining about politicians or the bureaucracy. But in the end, we generally trust them to do the right thing. And we trust that our public institutions and authorities act in a fair and impartial manner.

Both societal trust and institutional trust is crucial to our welfare model. Denmark and the other Nordic countries are strong welfare states. This model relies on redistribution of tax revenues between strangers, not among people with mutual individual trust relations. Such a system does not work if you do not trust institutions to divide the cake fairly. And it does not work if you do not trust your neighbor enough to expect her to do her share.

In other words, this model means that everyone is expected to contribute and to have a sense of duty. But it also means that everyone is sure to receive care and help if anything happens to you. If you get sick or when you get old, you do not have to worry about sick bills or whether your kids live close enough. You can trust the system to take care of you.

An added benefit of trust is that it lowers transaction costs in the economy. With trust, it is easier to get things done. You do not need to provide excessive legal hedging to foster joint action or to promote exchanges between economic agents. Some would argue that this is a significant part of the explanation of why Nordic welfare states are also fairly wealthy states.

But why do we have such a high level of trust in Nordic countries? It is not because we are inherently different from everyone else.

I believe one reason is our political system. Through transparency, oversight and separations of powers, people trust that policy outcomes and the public administration are run in a fair way. Laws and rules are clearly defined and fairly and impartially implemented, no matter who you are or how much money you have in your bank account.

Another reason is the process by which we make laws. For instance, we have a very strong consultation mechanism for hearing public demands. This leads to a sense that rules are there to promote and protect the interests of every individual. We have a sense that following the rules is both in your own interest as well as the overall interest of society and the nation.

This does not mean that we do not, from time to time, experience irregularities among public authorities or politicians. But when cases like this happen, we deal with them through due process in a transparent manner. And the almost certain debate about the issue contributes to a sense that such problems are not allowed to take root.

From the outside, our political system or debates in the public sphere about politics may seem disorderly, or even chaotic. Maybe you get the sense that our society is brimming with discontent and antagonism. But to us, debate—sometimes fierce debate—is seen as strength and a sign of a well-functioning, healthy system. As such, debate and diverse opinions do not undermine the system. Rather, it actually contributes to trust in the system and between all of us.

H.E. Thórir Ibsen, Ambassador of Iceland to China

I will devote my presentation to two observations.

Firstly, a general observation about the Nordic approach, and secondly a more specific observation about Iceland's experience of sustainability.

As for the general observation, the Nordics are pragmatic. We avoid using strong words in our analysis of state-of-affairs. We believe that dramatized language is not helpful and in fact can be dangerous as it can encourage reactions and solutions that are neither useful nor peaceful.

Thus, instead of drawing up a dramatic picture of the challenges that the world community is facing, we approach these challenges in a pragmatic and analytical manner with a view to solving the problems.

As a Nordic, I thus take issue with such broad stroke generalization that we are living an era of crises.

We are certainly facing important challenges and changes. But we are not facing crisis and certainly not multitude of crises. Our institutions, society and economy have not become dysfunctional. And neither our societies nor the world order are at the brink of collapsing or being transformed into a new social or world order.

On the contrary, we have, at least in the Nordic countries and in Europe, efficient democratic governance that constantly address income disparity and other socioeconomic challenges through fiscal policy, the education system, health care, and the welfare system.

We like diversity and we have a long-standing democratic tradition, institutions, and independent media that foster cohesion through free and transparent political discussion.

We have decades of experience of resolving environmental problems. And we lead international cooperation to protect the environment and promote sustainable development.

And our security architecture, especially NATO has proven to be one of the most cohesive, capable, and committed collective defensive alliance in the world. It safeguards our way of life, our freedoms, and our security. This has been especially important since Russia's brutal and illegal invasion of Ukraine and war of aggression.

Turning to Iceland, and our experience of sustainability.

Iceland is an affluent, dynamic, and democratic island country. We enjoy one of the highest living standards in the world, and as a Nordic country, Iceland has an egalitarian society, characterized by social inclusion, economic fairness, and gender equality.

We built our affluence by adopting an open export-oriented market economy and by developing the use of our natural resources into successful competitive export industries.

Relying as we do on our natural resources, we have learned the importance of protecting our environment and using our natural resources sustainably.

With sustainable resource management, we secure a more stable economy and long-term economic growth, as well as more equal distribution of economic rewards and social benefits.

Moreover, by focusing on sustainability, we unleashed innovation and growth of green practices and low carbon technologies that have brought Icelandic companies to the global market and indeed to China.

However, transforming the economy to sustainability is often easier said than done.

In our experience, for sustainable policy to be successful, it must have a broad support among businesses and citizens alike. It must be justifiable and based on reason. And the policy and its implementation must be clear and transparent.

In other words, both businesses and citizens must understand the need for the policy, see their interest in implementing the policy, and be able to trust that its application is equitable, inclusive and just.

Thus, the policy must bring win–win for businesses and people as well as for the environment.

The regulatory framework must encourage sustainable business practices including through economic rewards. And the social and economic needs of communities must be met with secure employment.

Businesses and people must have ownership of the policy. That is, policies and measures must be developed with direct involvement of representatives of the relevant interest groups and stakeholders and be subject to public consultations.

The policy must be justifiable and based on reason. Thus, the environmental measures and decisions related to the management of natural resource must be based on the best available scientific knowledge.

The policy and its implementation must be clear and transparent. Citizens and businesses must be able to see and verify that the sustainable policy is working and applied in a just and equitable manner. Number of tools secure such transparency, including:

- Publicly available environmental data.
- Peer-reviewed environmental performance reviews of government policies.
- Corporate environmental disclosure.
- Reliable labeling for consumers, including eco-labels. And
- Environmental impact assessment of projects.

To conclude with a few thoughts on sustainability:

- requires independent and peer-reviewed science,
- has to be economically efficient and beneficial,
- has to be socially equitable and just,
- must involve ownership and direct participation of all stakeholders (citizens, businesses, and interest groups), and
- must be transparent to ensure trust.

Appendix

CCG Ambassador Dialogues

As one of China's leading think tanks, the Center for China and Globalization (CCG) is committed to bridging gaps in communication and understanding between China and the world. From day one, telling China's story and listening to the world has been our unwavering vision and greatest endeavor.

Following CCG's release of the book China and the World in a Changing Context: Perspective from Ambassadors to China in March 2023, we have received great praise and support from intellectuals, government agencies, entrepreneurs, and the public, who find the insights provided by ambassadors to be incredibly helpful in terms of better understanding China and its place in the world.

This inspired us to carry on the discussion with a program that we have called the **"CCG Ambassador Dialogue"**. *These regular events invite ambassadors to China from around the world for an in-person video interview at CCG where they can share their insights, experiences, and hopes for their own countries and relations with China.*

Taking China–Brazil Relations to the Next Level

H.E. Marcos Galvão
Ambassador of the Federative Republic of Brazil to the People's Republic of China

Dr. Henry Huiyao Wang
Founder and President of the Center for China and Globalization (CCG)

Trust has been the foundation of the friendship between Brazil and China for over half a century, and is reflected in their bilateral relations as well as their cooperation on multilateral agendas like the BRICS platform. On January 10, 2023, in the discussion between Dr. Henry Huiyao Wang and Brazilian Ambassador to China, Marcos Galvão, we gain key insights into bilateral relations between China and Brazil, as well as the latest developments in Brazil domestically.

Henry Huiyao Wang: So, good morning Ambassador Marcos Galvão, Your Excellency. Welcome to CCG's Global Ambassador Dialogue. I know that you just assumed your post in China a few months ago in August. What is your impression so far? I know that COVID restrictions are being relaxed, so you are coming at the right time.

Marcos Galvão: Thank you very much Dr. Wang for this welcome and for having me here. Coming to Beijing was an old dream. I have been in the foreign service for over 42 years now, in active service, as you said. I have served in many places all over the world and also in Brazil, not only in the Foreign Ministry, but also in the Finance Ministry, in the Environment Ministry, and in the President's Office. And coming to Beijing was a dream that I have had for a long time, at least for the last

10 years when I was Ambassador in Japan, I thought of coming here, and finally, this dream has come true.

Why was it a dream? Not only because I wanted to be in China, because the emergence of China was the most relevant fact in the world. During these 40 years, I have been a diplomat, because I believe in our relations, in what the relevance they can have to our peoples and countries and want to work for those relations. So this was an aspiration that I had. Now it is an aspiration that I have to live up to. Now my dream has come true, and I have to, let us say, render the best service I can to the Brazilian taxpayers and to the Brazilian government.

Henry Huiyao Wang: China and Brazil have such great relations and China is Brazil's largest trading partner. China imports a lot of agricultural products from Brazil every year. Bilateral relations have really been on very good terms. So tell us a bit about your views on bilateral relations between China and Brazil.

Marcos Galvão: One element of our relations with China over almost half a century is that there has never been a breach of trust. We each have our views of the world. We each have our interests, but we have always respected each other and treated each other considerately. And we have always had trust in each other. This is a fundamental element in human relations in general, in personal friendships and in friendship between countries. There has to be trust. I think trust is an element that has always been there in our relationship.

More importantly, I think this has been very clear since the 2008 crisis, which was a changing point in recent world history, including the place of emerging economies in the world. We have, respectively, played a relevant role in each other's development. And our relations with China, be it in trade, be it in investments, be it on the international scene, have had a permanently positive impact on Brazilian development. We like to see ourselves also as a contributor to the development of China.

Brazil has now inaugurated a new political cycle. President Lula was elected on October 30 last year in the second round of elections. He was president twice before from 2003 to 2006 and then from 2007 to 2010. He has become, in a way, the Pele of Brazilian politics. So he has also become a face of Brazil. It is curious because I have been in China, as you mentioned, for five months. When Pele unfortunately passed away recently, I could see how many people in China knew and liked Pele, but I could also see how many people in China know and like President Lula. The other day, I went to a restaurant here. It was playing Brazilian music. I spoke to the owner. He did not know the music was Brazilian, but he mentioned President Lula. He was president during a particularly critical period of China and Brazil's international life—2008 and 2010. This was the period following the great global financial crisis of 2008 in which both of our countries, both China and Brazil, rose to play a much more relevant role on the international scene. This was when the G7 had to step back and the G20 stepped forward, because the G7 countries recognized that without us, the large emerging economies, they would not be able to face the problems they had to face. We made a very important contribution in this respect, including the reform of international financial institutions aimed precisely at strengthening the voice of countries like China and Brazil on the international scene and on decision making regarding financial and other matters.

Appendix

Henry Huiyao Wang: We are a think tank that focuses on globalization, but we know globalization has seen many setbacks, and people are talking about deglobalization as well as populism and nationalism. It is also probably very sad to see what happened recently in Brazil on January 8 with the storming of the parliament and a high court and government houses. So what do you think about that? What has happened in Brazil for that to happen now?

Marcos Galvão: January 8 was a very sad day for Brazil. Basically, we had a mob of radicalized people who stormed, as you said, the places where the executive branch, the President's office, the Congress, and the Supreme Court are. There was a lot of destruction and vandalism. And these people, these were strongly anti-democratic people, extremists, were radicalized, but I think that the conclusion will be, and this has already begun to happen, that the preceding democratic institutions, including those three branches of power, are very strong and resilient. The rule of law did prevail and will prevail. These people that did this will be punished according to the law, to the extent of the law; not only those who were there actually vandalizing public buildings and stealing things, but also those who helped finance and inspired what happened. All of them will have to pay for what happened. And I think that in the end, both Brazilian society and the international community will see that once again, this was a test for Brazilian democracy. But the all political forces in Brazil have rallied behind democracy and behind the established institutions. I think very quickly it will be made very clear that these institutions will prevail.

Henry Huiyao Wang: China and Brazil are key members of BRICS and, as you said, the two largest emerging economies in Asia and in the Americas. You were actually involved in the early days when BRICS first started. Tell us a bit about the BRICS phenomenon and your prediction for the future development of BRICS countries and how we can really work together.

Marcos Galvão: BRICS is a very curious phenomenon. You know better than I. This comes from an acronym that was created by an economist and stood for Brazil, Russia, India, and China. South Africa came onboard somewhat later. The four countries, I think, did not dislike the acronym. The foreign ministers of the BRICS began to meet on the side of the UN general assembly. The first meeting of foreign ministers was held in 2008. The global financial crisis came on September 15, 2008, and in November in Brazil, in São Paulo, the finance ministers and central bank governors met for the first time. After that, we worked a lot together, as I said before, in international financial institution reform. Basically, it was about getting seats in some entities, such as the Financial Stability Forum that became the Financial Stability Board, where no emerging economies had a seat until 2008 and in raising our voice and vote and quotas in organizations, such as the IMF and the World Bank, which we managed to modestly reform.

We had a common agenda, basically, that aimed at reforming international governance. And this is an agenda that is still there. All of the BRICS members are countries that wish that the world be governed by international law, by rules that are negotiated multilaterally. We want these, but that does not mean that we want to keep things as they are. We want the international rule of law to function as the basis for international reform in order to make the world a more fair place for all and to provide opportunities for all.

One last point is we have to restore, I think, the centrality of the notion of development in the world. People talk about sustainable development. Climate change is a challenge that we have to work together on. Development has to be made sustainable, but in order for development to be made sustainable, that there has to be development to begin with. Development was something that people spoke about in the 60s and the 70s, perhaps until the 80s somewhat, then this was forgotten. Food insecurity is out there, and it is growing, and poverty is still out there, and it is growing in some places. We have to take care of the more vulnerable in the world, because otherwise the world will never be stable and the world will never be fair. So, we have to bring back this notion of development. Yes, sustainable development, but development also. And I think that China and Brazil, who are, let us say, advanced developing countries, have a role to play in order to strengthen the concept of development within the broader framework of globalization.

Henry Huiyao Wang: What is your prediction for 2023 and for bilateral relations as the new ambassador? What are your hopes for the future development of Brazil–China relations?

Marcos Galvão: There is a new political cycle in Brazil. There is a very important thing happening, which is the opening of China after the pandemic, which will allow person-to-person contacts. All this video conferencing that went on for years is fine. It is very good, but it does not replace person-to-person contacts. I think there will be a flood of foreign delegations coming to Beijing and China from all walks of life from now on. Certainly there will be many Brazilian delegations, from government and the private sector to business and social and academic delegations. This is crucial to overcome. I think the most important elements of our relations with China is that ultimately, Brazilians know what China is, what it stands for, the importance and centrality of China. But we know very little of each other's daily lives of what we do, of who we are. I think this is the greatest challenge that we have to work on. I think that ultimately we like each other as peoples but I think we will like each other even more when will see what we can do together.

There are many things. We have a common space program already. We have academic cooperation. But there is a lot more that we can do together. And in order to do that, we have to get together to begin with. 2023, I think, will mark the reopening of China after the pandemic and our ability to visit each other's countries. I think that as an ambassador, this will make me work more because many Brazilians will be coming to China, but I will be very happy to help them go around in China, and we will certainly be in contact with your organization to do that.

Henry Huiyao Wang: OK, great. Thank you so much, Ambassador Marcos Galvão, and it is been a really great pleasure to have you on this episode of CCG's Ambassador's Dialogue series. I look forward the further collaboration with our Brazilian friends. Thank you very much for coming.

Marcos Galvão: Thank you very much.

Africa and China: Natural Partners Choosing Their Own Development Pathways

H. E. Teshome Toga Chanaka
Ambassador of the Federal Democratic Republic of Ethiopia to the People's Republic of China

Dr. Henry Huiyao Wang
Founder and President of the Center for China and Globalization (CCG)

China and Africa are natural partners. African cooperation with China has played a unique role in promoting much needed basic infrastructure in Ethiopia, driving forward sound industrialization and pulling millions out of poverty. The beauty of the partnership between China and Africa is that it allows both sides to choose the development pathway that suits each side best, while conspiracies like the "debt trap" are groundless and unhelpful for Ethiopia and Africa in general. On April 19, 2022, in the dialogue between Dr. Henry Huiyao Wang and Ambassador of Ethiopia to China, Teshome Toga Chanaka highlights real experiences and the successes of cooperation between Africa and China as well as China-Ethiopian relations and recent developments in Ethiopia.

Henry Huiyao Wang: Welcome to CCG's Ambassador Dialogue. I'm very pleased today to present Ambassador Teshome Chanaka, His Excellency the Ambassador from Ethiopia. Ambassador Chanaka, welcome to CCG.

Teshome Toga Chanaka: Thank you very much Dr. Wang for having me for episode of Ambassador Dialogue.

Henry Huiyao Wang: As we all know, China and Africa are really strong partners, and we just had a FOCAC last year, a very successful China–African Cooperation Forum. Ethiopia is one of China's largest trading partners in Africa, so what is your impression in general about your experience in China and your overview of China–African and China–Ethiopian cooperation?

Teshome Toga Chanaka: Thank you Dr. Wang again, and yes I have been in Beijing for the last three years, and I have been asked about my impression about this country. I think there are areas of civilization, culture, history, diversities this and that, but the most singular impression I carry with me always about China is its transformation in the last 45 years. In the history of human development, I think this country has made a phenomenal transformation in just four decades. But Africa has more again to offer, because the continent has huge untapped natural resources. Apart from the scale of our population, we actually have the youngest population in the world. So I say that it is quite natural for China and Africa to partner, to cooperate, and to work together. No serious country can avoid China, and no serious country can avoid the continent of Africa. China has taken on a major infrastructure project in Ethiopia and that project, because of the way we define it, has actually been contributing not only in creating infrastructure, but also in alleviating poverty. Then of course we have investment from China, we have trade with China, we have technology transfers, we have financing cooperation with China. So this is a partnership benefiting both sides.

When Chinese companies invest in Ethiopia and in Africa, the first thing they do is they create jobs for our young people. They boost our capacity and productivity. They increase our exports, which means earning foreign currency that we need. It is also about technology transfer and building capacity. If you look at Ethiopia, cooperation with China is not only limited to industrialization, to trade; we also cooperate in the digital economy and technology transfers. The first satellite for Ethiopia was launched here in China with the support from the government of China. I think the beauty of our partnership is that this is a partnership based on what we truly call on equality, on mutual respect and allowing countries to choose policies and strategies that suit their own situation. Outside Africa and outside China many perceive this as a partnership benefiting China. This is not correct because I always argue that a partnership that does not benefit both will not last long.

Henry Huiyao Wang: Africa is a fascinating place, absolutely, I remember when I was a child my father went to Africa and worked on the Tanzania–Zambia railway. That was in the 1970s. I remember he came back from Africa and told me how vast, how rich and abundant in natural resources, and how big the continent is. What do you think about the cooperation under the Belt and Road, for example? How we can really work together to strengthen such cooperation?

Teshome Toga Chanaka: We have defined the Addis Ababa–Djibouti railway, which is part of the Belt and Road Initiative, as our number one priority. Why? Because 90% of Ethiopian imports and exports go through Djibouti. So you can see how critical that project is. China financed the project, and they also helped us in the construction of the railway. At the same time they are managing and training Ethiopians to actually take over the management of the railway. This is a two-nations-owned infrastructure project that benefits both Djibouti and Ethiopia, but China and Chinese companies also benefit from it.

Secondly let me also take another important Belt and Road project—industrial parks. These are the basis for industrialization and have made us competitive in terms of attracting investment because they serve as one center with all infrastructure necessary in one place. You can see how this makes Ethiopia competitive and attractive for foreign direct investment. Now, we know how much the digital economy is contributing to the Chinese economy, and we are just starting. Not many, actually very few, African countries have been integrated into the digital economy, but it is at a very young stage. But we have a Chinese company that is willing to work with us in this regard, so this is sort of what we call win–win situation for both the Chinese enterprise and for African countries like Rwanda. Countries like Ethiopia and I think a few other countries like Tanzania all are joining the digital economy. For your information, I promoted an Ethiopian coffee trading brand in Shanghai online, and in five seconds, we sold 11,000 bags of Ethiopian coffee. In five seconds, I mean this was totally unthinkable in the past. So we can see the miracle of e-commerce and the digital economy. We understand the importance and significance of this infrastructure. I think the opportunity is there and we have challenges here and there, but

Appendix

again my thinking is that you have challenges and in every cooperation the best way is to continue and to do more cooperation, not less.

Henry Huiyao Wang: You have many good stories about the private sector. We actually know of a company called Hua Jian and you know President Zhang. He actually invested in Africa through industrial parks and is one of the biggest shoe manufacturers there, which helps Ethiopian exports. There are several private sector areas there—textiles, shoes, and pharmaceuticals—working in Ethiopia. Job creation is a huge contribution as I said. One company has created jobs for 8000 Ethiopians. But it is not only creating jobs, if you take an average family in Ethiopia with five members, that is about 40,000 people being supported in one single project. We need to bring in the private sector when it comes to investment, when it comes to even the digital economy, when it comes to pharmaceuticals. We look forward to really enhanced, strengthened, and revitalized work with the Chinese public and private sectors.

Teshome Toga Chanaka: I see a lot of similarity between Africa and China, so I think China's experience and China's path of development can be transferred to Africa to some extent. But of course you know there is some criticism on that. Some say China is creating a "debt trap" there, which I think it is not true. A loan is not something that is imposed on any country. Let me say that very clearly. I can talk for my own country. A loan is not imposed or debt is not imposed on us, but there is a structural problem when debt is accumulated. We come and ask for loans ourselves. We borrowed $4 billion for the railway project between Djibouti and Ethiopia and we needed it. We came and asked China for the loan, because no other country was willing to finance that project. I think this is the case with most of the countries that borrow money and of course the problem is the "debt trap" concept. I do not know why when it comes to loans from China that it becomes a "debt trap", but not when it comes from other sources.

The problem is that with some infrastructure projects, because of capacity, technological, and management problems, most projects are not completed in time and then the debt matures. In order to pay off the debt you get another loan and the result is what we call debt accumulation. I think the best way again is to sit down and address the critical structural bottleneck that is facing debtor countries. That is exactly what we are trying to do, but to create this perception that getting a loan from China puts African countries into a "debt trap", and to say that African countries should not borrow money from China is not a fair approach. It is not even helpful for Africa. I think the best way for China and Africa think of a way forward is to recognize that we are already in it. We need to sit down and discuss and find a solution.

Henry Huiyao Wang: Now I understand that in Ethiopia there are some civil conflicts in some northern parts. And so what has been going on probably is of concern for Ethiopia and the people there. Perhaps you could give a bit of explanation of what is going on there?

Teshome Toga Chanaka: The conflict actually started in the northern part of Ethiopia and of course there is political background to it. We had political differences with the party that is ruling the northern part of Ethiopia and the region with the federal government, and we have opted for dialogue to resolve political problems, to find a political solution. Unfortunately, the forces in the northern part of Ethiopia opted to use military means, and they attacked one of our command forces. We introduced law enforcement operations in that part of the country. We actually succeeded in that, but when we moved our military out of that region, they regrouped themselves and they came, attacked, and extended the war to two other regions, but now they have been pushed back to that region again.

We have a number of issues actually. One is that the government of Ethiopia again declared humanitarian truce so that humanitarian assistance can go to the needy in the northern part of country unfettered and impeded. Currently there is no ongoing sort of conflict, but the problem is that forces there are two armed groups that are trying to undermine the ongoing process. But as a government, we are trying our best so that the national dialogue can succeed. Any issue under the sun can be brought to the table so that we can discuss, then we have to set a priority whether it is a change of constitution or a change of governance. Everything should be done through dialogue. We have an ongoing AU effort to which Ethiopia has given its support. That is where we are in terms of the political process in the country.

Of course the economy has been hit hard by both the pandemic as well as the conflict in the northern part of the country. Yes, we currently have a challenge, but we hope that we will overcome it soon. We need wisdom and a unity of purpose. We really need to join hands with the leadership of Prime Minister Abiy Ahmed so that we can enhance the efforts that we have already launched. In particular, we need to make sure that we are positively contributing and getting involved in the national dialogue process. If we have limitations here and there, we should try to make our own contribution in a very constructive way, in a very forward looking way and we should not get stuck in our past.

Henry Huiyao Wang: I think we need to move forward and that is what we are trying to do. We really hope that there will be more dialogue and more consensus as we try to minimize the conflict as much as possible. We can really see peaceful development and continued prosperous development for Ethiopia. I think we have all come to the conclusion that there will be enormous opportunities, potential, and cooperation between China and African countries like Ethiopia. Let me once again thank you, Ambassador for your insights. And thank you for coming to CCG. We hope to see you again.

Teshome Toga Chanaka: Thank you for having me.

"Ba tie"—The Time Tested Ironclad Brotherhood Between China and Pakistan

H. E. Moin Ul Haque
Ambassador of Pakistan to China

Dr. Henry Huiyao Wang
Founder and President of the Center for China and Globalization (CCG)

The turbulent times in which we find the world today require unity and cooperation to weather the many storms of conflict, climate change, and uneven recovery in a post-pandemic world. China and Pakistan have always had a unique relationship, and for Chinese people, the term "Ba Tie" represents the ironclad brotherhood that the two nations share. This has helped them through a number of difficult times and proves to be a constant reminder of what cooperation can achieve. On April 12, 2022, in this dialogue between Dr. Henry Huiyao Wang and Pakistani Ambassador to China Moin Ul Haque, we will see how this relationship was formed and maintained, and how it has laid a foundation for development and progress.

Henry Huiyao Wang: Welcome to CCG's Ambassador Dialogue. I'm very pleased today to welcome the Ambassador from Pakistan, His Excellency Moin Haque. Welcome to CCG. China and Pakistan have really enjoyed a good friendship that's been really called an "iron brotherhood"—"Ba Tie". It really means a friendship that is as good as iron, as strong as iron, as solid as iron, so that is really a great compliment. So you have been in China for a year and half now. What is your general impression of China? Particularly China–Pakistan relations?

Moin Ul Haque: Thank you, Dr. Wang. It is a great pleasure and honor to be at the Center for China and Globalization (CCG). This is my first time here, and I'm very pleased to be on this episode of the Ambassadors Dialogue series. You are right to mention the expression "Ba Tie" to describe the friendship between China and Pakistan. In my last 18 months in China, wherever I have gone, to different cities to small towns, to villages, when I tell them that I'm from Pakistan, they say "Ba Tie". It is so touching that everybody in China knows about China–Pakistan friendship. This iron brotherhood, Mr. Wang, is time-tested. It is timeless! This relationship between our two countries is very unique and very special. And it has been nurtured over the years by successive generations of our leadership and our people. No matter which government is in power either in Pakistan or in China, our relationship remains constant. It has not been affected by any upheavals or vicissitudes in international and regional politics or development. That is the strength of our relationship. It has remained rock solid over all those years; a very solid relationship between two governments and between two peoples.

We, last year, celebrated our 70 years of diplomatic relation. In the last seven decades of our journey, we have come a long way in terms of putting a very strong framework and foundation for political and high-level exchanges between our leadership. In recent years, we have also realized the importance of a relationship in the areas of trade, in the areas of investment, economic, and financial cooperation. The

China–Pakistan Economic Corridor is one of the manifestations of that. China has become Pakistan's largest trading partner. And despite the COVID-19 pandemic, our trade volume last year increased by more than 17%, which is remarkable. We are now trying to find various ways and means to expand access to each other's market. We have a free trade agreement with China, phase two of which was launched in January 2020. This has also contributed to this growing trade relationship.

Henry Huiyao Wang: I know of there has been a recent change in Prime Minister, but as we said at the beginning, historically no matter how many changes there are in the government, the strong ties between the two countries has always been there and been sustained. So we certainly can hope that our strong iron relationship will continue even with the new Prime Minister that is coming up.

Moin Ul Haque: Surely, you know Mr. Shehbaz Sharif who was elected as the new Prime Minister of Pakistan last night. After his election in the National Assembly in the Parliament of Pakistan when he was making a speech and talking about foreign policy, the first country that he mentioned was China. He passionately spoke about this relationship for quite a long time because he has been coming to China quite often with his elder brother Mr. Nawaz Sharif, a three-time Prime Minister of Pakistan, and had very close relationship with China's leadership. Mr. Shehbaz Sharif was the Chief Minister of Punjab at that time, and many important projects, including under CPEC, were executed in Punjab, the largest province of Pakistan. Especially the Orange Metro Train, which is the first mass-transit project in Pakistan and was constructed by China under the CPEC and many other energy projects. So he is very passionate. I'm sure that he would be looking forward to visiting China very soon and welcoming President Xi in Pakistan for his next visit.

Henry Huiyao Wang: So we know that actually China and Pakistan have enjoyed such a great relationship and in China's Belt and Road Initiative one of the main routes was in Pakistan, the China–Pakistan Economic Corridor. That is really a very important project. Perhaps you can shed some light on the progress and what has been achieved and how we can cooperate further.

Moin Ul Haque: CPEC, as I mentioned, is a very important project. In fact, it is one of the most important projects under the BRI. For Pakistan, it has been a transformational project and a game changer. The first phase of CPEC focused on infrastructure development, energy, and the development of Gwadar Port. It helped in improving highways and upgrading our railway lines, which are all part of CPEC. Pakistan had faced for last many years an acute shortage of energy, but under CPEC major energy projects, be it hydro or thermal, coal or solar were built. It helped to add thousands of megawatts of energy into our system and helped to address the acute energy shortages.

Most importantly, Dr. Wang, the second phase of CPEC is extremely important because it aligns with the socio-economic development agenda of our country and our government. It focuses on industrialization, a very important area because we think that CPEC has to go into the next phase of building a chain of industries in different sectors in the country for which we have established special economic zones. Attractive incentives are being offered for Chinese investors as well as other foreign investors who would like to take part in CPEC projects like Gwadar Port, which we call the "crown jewel of CPEC". Located in the south of Pakistan about 300 km from Karachi, it is a deep water port and already functional and facilitating trade. A new international airport is being built. So this was just a fishing village, and we hope that following the developmental model of Shenzhen, which some years ago also used to be a fishing village, Gwadar can become a world-class port city. We are now also inviting third countries to take part in CPEC projects. We have also discussed with China to extend CPEC projects to neighboring countries, first being Afghanistan.

Henry Huiyao Wang: That is actually a very good approach I think. If Gwadar Port becomes another special economic zone like Shenzhen that would really make a lot of progress for the region. I'm also glad to hear that now you are welcoming third parties to come into CPEC, which is great. I think it reflects the Belt and Road principle, which is to consult, build, and benefit jointly. This is a good approach. So, you mentioned the region and neighboring countries. I know that China and Pakistan recently, as well as Afghanistan and Russia, six countries including the United States had a meeting in Anhui in Tunxi recently. I remember last year even before the United States pulled out of Afghanistan, China, and Pakistan had a meeting of foreign ministers in China. So how do you assess the stability and future development of Afghanistan?

Many places in the world are in crisis. I think we now China and Pakistan and other countries can work together to really calm Afghanistan, which used to be in crisis. Now if the reconstruction of Afghanistan works well, that could serve as a good example for future crises and reconstruction of other troubled areas. So what is your take on cooperation between China, Pakistan, and other countries in rebuilding Afghanistan and how we can ensure a new, prosperous Afghanistan in the future?

Moin Ul Haque: Afghanistan is a neighbor of both China and Pakistan, and the instability in Afghanistan and the war in Afghanistan for the last two decades has been a great concern of both other countries. I think end of war in Afghanistan, the withdrawal of the US forces and the fall of Kabul in August last year brought a new hope for the region and for the people of Afghanistan. Pakistan and China have been very closely cooperating and coordinating their position to assist the people of Afghanistan as they move forward and establish their own government and in their rebuilding efforts. We have also coordinated in bringing together the neighboring countries of Afghanistan, to discuss this very important issue among themselves in a way to have a regional approach to this problem, which is common to all of us instead of someone from outside dictating or interfering.

I think in that respect, this regional approach has worked so far. We have had three meetings and synergized many of our thoughts and many of our actions. Most importantly, I think, the new Afghan leadership also understands the concerns of not only the neighboring countries, but the international community. The most important part of the six neighboring countries meeting held in Tunxi, Anhui recently was to see how we can help the Afghan people in terms of their immediate humanitarian needs, rebuilding of their infrastructure, education, hospitals, roads, and their financial institutions. We have called on the international community, especially the

United States and European countries, to release their frozen assets, which are needed by the Afghan people at this very critical stage.

Of course, there is a new government, which has just been there only for seven or eight months. We need to give them time to settle down. We need to strengthen their capacity so that they are able to help their people. In that respect, I think the neighboring countries in the region can play a very important role. As I mentioned, Pakistan and China have helped not only in terms of sending humanitarian aid but also in terms of training Afghan nationals and capacity building. Now with the extension of CPEC to Afghanistan and other projects that China is also assisting in, the people of Afghanistan will be able to stand on their own feet.

Henry Huiyao Wang: Stability in Afghanistan will certainly make our world a little safer. We hope that the Ukraine situation can be calmed down. China probably can also try to work with the international community to do some mediation and things like that. So I think the process in Afghanistan is very important to the world.

Moin Ul Haque: I agree with you because I think the Ukrainian crisis has brought a new dimension to an already tense regional environment that we had due to Afghanistan. On the Ukrainian crisis we have a very similar position to China that we should respect the UN Charter, respect the sovereignty of the countries and do not interfere in their internal affairs. We are also calling on all the parties concerned to resolve the crisis through dialogue and diplomacy. We in Pakistan know that military action is not a solution. Afghanistan is a case in point. It has suffered for the last four decades because of military conflict. This is a lesson for others to see that military action is not a solution. We need to resolve our differences through dialogue.

Henry Huiyao Wang: What we can do to further enhance and promote bilateral relations? They are already good, but how can we make China–Pakistan relations even better?

Moin Ul Haque: The level of our relationship at this moment is excellent. I would say it is the best time between our two countries. It was very much manifested by last year's celebrations of 70 years of diplomatic ties with more than 140 events that were organized to celebrate this milestone, which is unprecedented and saw high level of participation by our leadership both in Pakistan and China in these events. This was not only reflection on what we achieved in the 70 years past, but was also very important to chart a new roadmap for the next 70 years. What is also very important, Mr. Wang, is that the new generations now know about the importance of this relationship. The investments that have been made in the past by our elders and our leadership should not go waste, rather, we should build on that. As I was mentioning earlier, the areas which are very important for us to take forward are trade, investment, agriculture, and tourism. Tourism is a very important area. I'm very passionate about that. Both our countries are beautiful countries, historical countries, rich in history and heritage. We need to work more to have more exchanges of people, travelers and tourists, scholars, and artists between our countries so we can make this relationship even stronger. COVID is of course a factor that has impacted our physical exchanges, but it will soon go away. We are working on that. Just to give you an example, we have prepared a Web site on tourism in Chinese. We are going to launch it formally soon. We are now working with Chinese tour operators and tour agencies to see as soon as COVID is over how we can bring Chinese tourists to Pakistan and how we can bring Pakistanis to come and see China. I think it will be a good means to promote our friendship.

Henry Huiyao Wang: Once again thank you very much for coming today and really appreciate your insights.

Moin Ul Haque: Thank you very much for having me.

A Collection of Speeches by Ambassadors at CCG Events

Shaping Global Governance Together Amid Severe Challenges

H.E. Rahamtalla M. Osman
Ambassador of Africa Union to the People's Republic of China

Although the issue is focusing on the service sector, I would like to handle the matter from a different angle, because the issues of concern for the developing and poor countries are not the same as the issues of consent to the developed ones.

So it is apparent that global economic governance is facing a lot of daunting challenges, which are a result of, among other things, of the inability of the existing global economic institutions to cope with a perpetual economic crisis, which was recently compounded by the eruption of COVID-19 and the war in Ukraine.

This has led to derailing the implementation of the SDGs. The institutions which were created 60 years ago in Bretton Woods need a call for restructuring in order to cope with the new complicated realities.

Not only that, we seriously believe that it is imperative to augment the role of United Nations institutions and regional economic mechanisms like ours, and to have greater engagement to lead in the formulation of the economic order that we have been asking for a long time. Because this will, in turn, strengthen transparency, engagement, and ownership of the poor countries who are currently excluded from the shaping of global economic governance.

This speech was delivered on September 2, 2022, during an Ambassador Roundtable at the 9th China Inbound-Outbound Forum organized by CCG in conjunction with CIFTIS 2022.

Services Sector in Post-pandemic Era: Governance and Cooperation

H.E. Luis Quesada
Ambassador of Peru to the People's Republic of China

Thank you once again to CCG for inviting me to participate in this Ambassador's Roundtable, focusing on the services sector at this year's CIFTIS. Colleagues, ladies, and gentlemen.

The China International Fair for Trade Services is among the most important trade fairs in the People's Republic of China, along with the China International Import Expo (CIIE) in Shanghai and the China Import and Export Fair (Canton Fair) in Guangzhou, which provides a well-established framework for the promotion of trade, not only of goods but also of services.

The COVID-19 pandemic has been the biggest trial we had to face in a generation, and we should acknowledge the fact that the deceleration of global economic growth can only be overcome with open markets that allow goods, services, capital, and mainly people, to move seamlessly between countries. Among those four aspects, promoting trade in services is the best way to enhance the value of service supply chains.

The confluence of many issues such as the general disruption of international trade, interrupted services supply chains, decoupling that hinders technological and digital advances, travel restrictions within and between countries, inflation, economic recession, and the effects of global food scarcity and climate change are the most important factors leading to a the slowed growth in trade in services.

Governments and international organizations around the world should seek solutions to these urgent issues, providing an optimal foundation to promote trade in services such as education, tourism, health, and financial services to eventually overcome the gloomy and uncertain economic outlook we are facing today.

The best strategies to tackle these problems are promoting inclusive policies for services, rebuilding resilient supply chains, and easing travel restrictions. Countries should stay committed to globalization and openness and the challenges for emerging markets must be taken into consideration. We need more inclusive and sustainable policies that benefit of all the entire world, which requires improved market access and the continued promoting of economic integration.

To demonstrate that we are working toward worldwide recovery and strong global economic integration, trade and investment must flow without barriers, people should travel freely again, and our health systems and networks of cooperation must be strengthened and better coordinated to cope with existing and future issues.

China, since it entered the World Trade Organization in 2001, has compromised to pursue an open, productive, and participatory development strategy. Moreover, China will have to show that, apart from its engagement with its circular economy, it is at the same time even more engaged with the world economy as a whole and that it is ready to play its part in the strengthening of global trade.

China's active participation in APEC—as a mechanism of cooperation—and the RCEP—as a regional trade agreement—and its interest to adhere to other regional economic treaties such as the CPTPP, of which Peru is a member, and DEPA are encouraging signals. However, structural internal reforms will be needed.

The Memorandum of Understanding between China and the Republic of Korea to foster resilient supply chains is another good example. Let us get together as partners to seek new ways to promote overall trade and specifically trade in services.

The key meetings of APEC in Thailand and G-20 in Indonesia next November should be opportunities to find and propose new strategies as equals.

Peru is now promoting the recovery of its economy, as many other emerging markets in the world, by strengthening our supply chains and attracting new and better investments, especially in digital transformation, and tourism. Peru is eager to continue its efforts to attract more capital and businesses, which are essential for our post-pandemic recovery, especially since an important segment of our society slipped back into poverty in between 2020 and 2021.

Our Presidency of APEC in 2024 would be an amazing opportunity to make great leaps toward our goals of inclusive economic development. The same could be said of our Presidency in the Andean Community and the Pacific Alliance next year. It is important that partners work hand in hand to develop comprehensive solutions to trade issues.

Some regions have an unfaltering commitment to open markets while others have pursued different points of view, reflecting their mix of risk tolerance, needs, resources, capacity, and past pandemic experiences. Only through an open economy we can obtain inclusive and sustainable economic development.

Without a doubt, the next decade will be even more challenging. The creation of jobs and the reduction of poverty through flexible and innovative policies, the renewal of academic exchanges, as well as the intensive use of technology, should be our common approach. Underlying all of this should also be an unwavering commitment to open markets and more open borders.

This speech was delivered on September 2, 2022, during an Ambassador Roundtable at the 9th China Inbound-Outbound Forum organized by CCG in conjunction with CIFTIS 2022.

Social Progress and Ecological Preservation Keys to Sustainable Growth

H.E. Wim Geerts
Ambassador of the Netherlands to the People's Republic of China

Dear colleagues, distinguished guests, ladies and gentlemen, as the only representative on this session of an EU member state, I would like to make a couple of points. China's speed and scale development continue to be impressive even during this pandemic. The OECD estimates that 1/3 of post-Covid growth worldwide in the next ten years will come from China. So the world needs China to recover from the pandemic in an economic sense.

The other way around, China needs to ensure that its growth is both high quality and sustainable. The first economic indicators are promising, but we cannot take economic recovery for granted with huge challenges worldwide due to the pandemic, reducing trade tensions and maintaining economic openness are more important than they ever were.

Let me offer a few lessons from history that could be instructive for today's world. You may have heard of a Dutch Nobel Prize winner Jan Tinbergen. He was a founding father of economic policy making and development economics. He was preoccupied with restoring the economy of a war ravaged Netherlands and had witnessed, first hand, the Great Depression and policy responses in which major economies turned inwards and led to social and political upheaval.

His fundamental principle was that the economy is fundamentally unstable. So to create the conditions for social progress and ecological preservation, one needs independent institutions with checks and balances, not only at the national level, but also internationally. A framework had to be put into place to ensure that stability and long-term prosperity. It would be there, which would allow all economies both developed and developing to make full use of their comparative advantages. Therefore, he was a firm proponent of free trade in a rules-based order. The most durable international trading systems are the ones that are underpinned by a set of enforceable rules, which generate equitable outcomes. And these principles have been the foundation for Dutch, European, and indeed Chinese prosperity over the past decades. The current rules-based system is under pressure relating to both enforceability and the fact that the current set of rules does not create equitable outcomes.

So it is more important than ever that all big trading blocks in the world assume the responsibility to ensure the system functions properly and do not feel compelled to resort to protectionism, because they feel they are losing out from the current order. This requires more dialogue and cooperation rather than division and confrontation.

We, the Dutch, remain firmly committed to a rules-based multilateral trading system, where conflicts can be solved in a fair and transparent manner within the framework of the WTO as my Australian colleague mentioned earlier. Because it's only through a rules based system that we can ensure a balanced global economic recovery. This requires a genuine effort from all trading blocks to ensure that trade is not politicized and unpredictability for businesses is reduced.

Last, but not least I want to stress that economic recovery will have to be conducted in a sustainable manner with the limited natural resources we have, and the increasingly visible effects of human-induced climate change around the globe.

It is crucial that all of us strive toward a sustainable and durable economic growth trajectory. Mister Jan Tinbergen, whom I mentioned earlier, saw social progress and ecological preservation as two sides of the same coin, which required a global institutional checks and balances.

This underlines the importance of standardizing sustainability in all aspects of trade and investment. Trade and investment agreements, both regional and international, should provide a framework in which sustainability is part and parcel of the way in which cross border economic activity is conducted.

The EU has a long history when it comes to pursuing sustainability and trade and investment agreements. Public interest for sustainability is growing in the Netherlands and elsewhere, also given recent extreme weather events around the world. Not only does this influence the way in which governments view trade agreements, multinational corporations also feel compelled to ensure that they make a contribution toward sustainability and not just aim for short-term profits.

One can only encourage this development. The private sector has a crucial role to play in achieving the UN Sustainable Development Goals and the goals of the Paris Agreement to which China has also signed up. We very much welcome China's commitment to achieve carbon neutrality by 2060. Let us ensure together that trade is harnessed in such a way that we can achieve both a balanced and a sustainable economic recovery from this pandemic. Thank you.

This speech was made on the 7th China and Globalization Forum (July 30, 2021).

African Recovery is Part of Collective Global Recovery

H.E. Siyabonga Cwele
Ambassador of the Republic of South Africa to the People's Republic of China

My input will focus on South African and African efforts to improve mobility and rate of advancement within the open and fair, multilateral rules order. The effect of the COVID 19 pandemic in developing countries, such as those in Africa, are devastating and threatening to reverse the hard won developmental gains, particularly for the poor and vulnerable. The mutation of the virus and the lack of access to lifesaving vaccines, continue to affect lives and livelihoods of many as it disrupts health services and mobility, resulting in a huge, negative impact on socioeconomic development. In addition to this, our economic recovery remains slow because of reactive global shifts of funds and production to us.

Our efforts to improve mobility and livelihoods include first implementing national economic recovery plans and aligning them to regional and continental efforts. We have kept our borders relatively open while implementing scientific LED epidemic control measures and adapting new technologies to improve trade, communication, and sustainability.

This year we have begun the implementation of the African Continental Free Trade Agreement, AFCTFA, to boost intra-Africa trade and links with the outside world through mechanisms, such as the Belt and Road Initiative, promoting South-South cooperation and continuing to push trade and development.

We have also joined in mobilizing resources to fight the pandemic under the African Center for Disease Control and African Development Bank. In this aspect, we are working with friendly countries such as China and developed nations to build our capacity to deal with global disaster and future pandemic as well as expanding the current vaccine production sites in Africa. We welcome production facilities in countries such as South Africa and Egypt and many more to come.

Furthermore, we continue to improve our investment, trade, climate, and make greater efforts to support the vulnerable sectors, such as tourism, agriculture, and mineral resources. In an effort to cushion the impact of rising unemployment, what needs to be done going forward?

The pandemic is not an epidemic. It is not a national problem, but a global challenge that will be won or lost at a global level. This virus does not respect political boundaries. It needs faster global response and vaccination to defeat it. We are in it together, and no one or country should be left behind in the fight against the pandemic.

As a global community, we must increase our vaccination, protection, and vaccine production and decentralize it in order to have speedy access to vaccines in order to build global immunity to protect us against its devastating impact.

This is why we have been pushing for a temporary waive on tariffs or intellectual property rights as a measure to boost vaccine production and access. It may be early to talk about vaccine passport requirements until significant numbers of global populations have fully been vaccinated. Otherwise, we may worsen unfair discrimination among the poor.

Two, we must follow the signs in measures to fight the control and spread of the virus and avoid political protectionism, artificial barriers, conspiracies, fake news, and the spread of undue fear.

Thirdly, we must continue the global solidarity in times of need and build and improve on open, fair, and rule-based international trade order. As President Ramaphosa put it earlier this year, the events of the last year have demonstrated that no country, no people, and no continent can stand alone in the face of challenges that confront humanity, from pandemics to climate change, from war to poverty. We need to overcome shared problems through collective actions.

This speech was made on the 7th China and Globalization Forum (July 30, 2022).

About the Center for China and Globalization

The Center for China and Globalization (CCG) is a Chinese non-governmental think tank based in Beijing. CCG has been granted the official special consultative status by the Economic and Social Council of the United Nations (ECOSOC) as a non-governmental organization. In the "2020 Global Go To Think Tank Index" by the University of Pennsylvania Think Tank and Civil Society Program (TTCSP), CCG ranked 64th of the top think tanks worldwide and among the top 50 global independent think tanks. CCG has also been recognized as a "4A non-governmental organization" by Beijing Municipal government civil affairs department.

Founded in 2008 and headquartered in Beijing, the Center for China and Globalization (CCG) is China's leading global non-governmental think tank. It has more than ten branches and overseas representatives with over 100 full-time researchers and staff engaged in research on globalization, global governance, international economy and trade, international relations, and global migration. CCG is also a national Postdoctoral Programme Research Center certified by the Chinese Ministry of Human Resources and Social Security.

While cultivating its own research teams, CCG has also built an international research network of leading experts in China and overseas. CCG engages in ongoing research on China and globalization from an international perspective. CCG publishes more than 10 books every year in English and Chinese and a series of research reports. It shares its research findings with the public and has published hundreds of thousands of related books and reports, which receives hundreds of thousands of website visits annually.

CCG has been involved in promoting many national development and global governance policies. It regularly submits policy recommendations to Chinese state agencies and ministries, many of which have been commented on by the central leadership and have served as reference for major decisions made by relevant departments, continually promoting government policymaking and institutional innovation.

About the China and Globalization Series

The Ebb and Flow of Globalization: Chinese Perspectives on China's Development and Role in the World

Author: Huiyao Wang

Publisher: Springer (August 2, 2022)

Globalization is an irresistible force. Given the high stakes at hand—for stability, continued growth, and the future of our planet—it is more important than ever that China gain a deeper understanding of the rest of the world, and that the rest of the world also comes to a clearer understanding of China.

This book focuses on globalization and China's evolving role in the world, offering unique perspectives on a remarkable period, which saw the global landscape reshaped by China's continued rise, intensifying great power competition, and a deadly pandemic.

These essays center on three interconnected themes—China's remarkable development under its policy of Reform and Opening-up, China's deepening integration into the global economy and rise in an increasingly multipolar world, and the quest to reinvigorate global governance and multilateralism to address the pressing global challenges of the twenty-first century.

These insights are useful for academics, policymakers, students, and anyone trying to deepen their understanding of China's development and role in making globalization work for our multipolar world.

Soft Power and Great-Power Competition: Shifting Sands in the Balance of Power Between the United States and China

Author: Joseph S. Nye, Jr.

Publisher: Springer (April 26, 2023)

This open access book consists of essays selected from Joseph S. Nye, Jr.'s last three decades of writing and illustrates a variety of perspectives on the nature of power, the role of the United States in the world, and United States–China relations. Through this collection, it is hoped that readers will gain a better understanding of today's global environment and find that while great power competition may be inevitable as centers of power shift, cooperating to address transnational challenges can be a positive sum game.

The contents of this book are divided into four main parts. Part I discusses the origins and political progress of the concept of "Soft Power". Part II explores soft power in the American experience, its sources and interaction with US foreign policy, as well as its ebb and flow in the age of Obama, Trump, and Biden. Part III examines the rise of and the opportunities and difficulties for Chinese soft power, focusing on

China's investment in soft power and how this demonstrates its commitment to a peaceful rise. However, it also addresses the question of how can China get "smart" on how it uses soft power. Part IV provides a bird's eye view of power shifts in the twenty-first century and the interactions between the United States as an established power and China as a rising power, while also reassuring readers that Thucydidean fears are unnecessary and a Cold War is avoidable. Both countries have to realize that some forms of power must be exercised with others, not over others, and that the development of soft power need not be a zero-sum game. Ultimately, the US–China relationship will most likely to be a "cooperative rivalry" where a successful strategy of "smart competition" is necessary and cooperation on transnational challenges like climate change, pandemics, cyberterrorism, and nuclear proliferation will serve to benefit not only China and the United States, but the world as a whole.

China and the World in a Changing Context: Perspectives from Ambassadors to China

Editors: Huiyao Wang and Lu Miao
 Publisher: Springer (March 5, 2022)
 This book is open access under a CC BY-NC-ND license.

Ambassadors are diplomatic envoys serving as pivotal contact points between nations across a wide range of fields, from economics and culture to health and the environment. The special group of ambassadors in this book—those based in Beijing—are at the forefront of what for many countries is one of their most important bilateral relationships, as well one of the most striking and consequential aspects of global affairs in the twenty-first century: the rise of China on the world stage.

This book aims to present an overview of China and the world from diverse angles. It brings together essays by ambassadors to China on a range of bilateral and multilateral issues, including trade and investment, regional economic cooperation, sustainable development, technology and innovation, and entrepreneurship. Given their familiarity with China and extensive international experience, the insights of these ambassadors are useful for policymakers, academics, entrepreneurs, students, and anyone trying to make sense of our rapidly changing world.

Transition and Opportunity: Strategies from Business Leaders on Making the Most of China's Future

Editors: Huiyao Wang and Lu Miao
 Publisher: Springer (February 17, 2022)
 This book is open access under a CC BY-NC-ND 4.0 license.

Multinational corporations (MNCs) have long played a crucial role in the Chinese economy. This role is one that is set to continue in the post-pandemic era as China works to transition to a high-quality growth model that is more sustainable and innovation-driven. With global experience and front-line involvement in some of the most pressing economic, technological, and environmental issues of our day, leading figures in MNCs and chambers of commerce are well placed to share insights that could potentially contribute to policymaking and development strategies so that everyone can "make the most" of China's future.

This collection of essay aims to share these invaluable insights with a wider audience, offering balanced and diverse perspectives from companies and advocacy groups working on a range of issues related to China's domestic development, international economic cooperation, and China–US competition. These insights are useful not only for the wider business community, but also for academics, policymakers, students, and anyone trying to deepen their understanding of this exciting period of "transition and opportunity" and make the most of China's bright future.

The Asian 21st Century

Author: Kishore Mahbubani

Publisher: Springer (January 1, 2022)

This open access book consists of essays written by Kishore Mahbubani to explore the challenges and dilemmas faced by the West and Asia in an increasingly interdependent world village and intensifying geopolitical competition.

The contents cover four parts. Part I discusses the end of the era of Western domination. The major strategic error that the West is now making is to refuse to accept this reality. Mahbubani simply states that the West needs to learn how to act strategically in a world where they are no longer number one. Part II discusses the return of Asia. From the years 1 to 1820, the largest economies in the world were Asian. After the spectacular rise of the West in the nineteenth and twentieth centuries, even great Asian civilizations like China and India were dominated and humiliated, but the twenty-first century will see the return of Asia to the center of the world stage. Part III discusses the peaceful rise of China. The shift in the balance of power to the East has been most pronounced in the rise of China. While this rise has been peaceful, many in the West have responded with considerable concern over the influence China will have on the world order. Part IV discusses the challenges of globalization, multilateralism, and global cooperation. Many of the world's pressing issues, such as COVID-19 and climate change, are global issues and will require global cooperation to deal with. In short, human beings now live in a global village. States must work with each other, and we need a world order that enables and facilitates cooperation in our global village.

Consensus or Conflict? China and Globalization in the 21st Century

Editors: Huiyao Wang and Alistair Michie

Publisher: Springer (September 28, 2021)

This open access book brings together leading international scholars and policymakers to explore the challenges and dilemmas of globalization and governance in an era increasingly defined by economic crises, widespread populism, retreating internationalism, and a looming cold war between the United States and China. It provides the diversity of views on those widely concerned topics such as global governance, climate change, global health, migration, S&T revolution, financial market, and sustainable development.

Index

A
ABB, 23
ABC, 41
Abhayagiriya dagoba (pagoda), The, 28
Abhayagiriya Monastery, 28
Action for Peacekeeping (A4P), The, 126
Afghanistan, 120, 121, 123, 128, 129, 179, 199, 200
African Continental Free Trade Agreement, The, 207
Akanda National Park, 110
Alakeshwara, 30
Albiñana, Jorge Toledo, 50
Algeria, 159–161
Al Husseini, Hussam A. G., 78
All-Weather Strategic Cooperative Partnership, 5
Ambassadors Roundtable, vi
Amoghavajra, 28
Ankara, 9, 18
Anti-Foreign Sanctions Law, The, 87
Arabic Civilization, The, 77
Artificial Intelligence (AI), 6, 7, 33, 91
ASEM, 121
A Shared Community of Mankind, 4
Asia, 12, 21, 28, 30, 32, 50, 66, 67, 77, 106, 121, 147, 149, 150, 153, 166, 167, 172, 191
Asian Century, 150
Asia-Pacific Economic Cooperation (APEC), 95, 150–153, 204
Asia-Pacific region, The, 95
Association for Sri Lanka-China Social and Cultural Cooperation, The, 33
Association of Southeast Asian Nations (ASEAN), 150, 151, 154, 158, 172
Athens, 82

AU, 196
Australia, 18, 31, 48, 87, 95–98, 147
Ayeyawady-Chao Phraya-Mekong Economic Cooperation Strategy (ACMECS), The, 156
Azerbaijan, 165–169

B
Bandaranaike Memorial International Conference Hall, The, 31
Bandaranayaka Memorial Conference Centre, The, 31
Bandaranayaka, Sirimao, 31
Batie, 3
Beijing, 7, 9, 13, 14, 16, 20, 25, 31–33, 35, 44, 49, 56, 82, 96, 97, 103, 107, 137, 153, 161, 165, 167, 175, 189, 192, 193
Beijing Normal University, xvi
Beijing Research Institute of Uranium Geology (BRIUG), The, 106
Beijing Sports University, The, 16
Belfast, 130
Belgian, viii
Belgium, 78, 83, 93, 108, 169
Belt and Road Initiative (BRI), 4, 11, 14, 16, 29, 32, 33, 35, 36, 87, 89, 91, 142, 144, 156, 157, 160, 164, 165, 167, 168, 194, 198, 207
Belt and Road Initiative, The, 4, 11, 14, 16, 29, 32, 33, 35, 36, 142, 157, 160, 164, 165, 168, 194, 198, 207
Bio-Circular-Green (BCG), 152
Biological Diversity Beyond National Jurisdiction, 36
Bosnia, 116, 120

Brazil, 137, 138, 189–192
Bretton Woods Institutions, 84
BRICS, 84, 150, 160, 189, 191
Brookings Institute, xv
Brudeset, Signe, 63
Brussels, 9, 25, 44, 82, 93
Budapest, 38, 82
Buddha, 27, 29, 31, 35
Buddhism, 27, 29
Build-Operate-Transfer (BOT), 144
Burri, Jürg, 25

C
C919, 68
Cabo Delgado, 142
CACF, 90
Canberra, 82, 151
CanSino, 71
Carbon capture, utilisation and storage (CCUS), 98, 103, 104, 107
Carbon dioxide (CO_2, 95, 101–105, 109, 111, 113
Carbon Recycling International (CRI), 104
CEEC, 90
CEEC-China Cooperation, 16
Center for China and Globalization (CCG), 137, 177, 182, 184, 189, 193, 196, 197, 203, 204
Central African Forest Initiative - CAFI, The, 111
Central Bank of Mexico (Banxico), The, 66
CEO, 151
Ceylon, 31
Cheena–Adi, 29
Chengdu, 16, 20, 34
Chengdu Institute of Biology of the Chinese Academy of Science, The, 16
Chief of State Protocol, 5
China, 3–9, 11–24, 27–40, 43–50, 56, 62, 63, 65–72, 75–77, 79–81, 83, 86–92, 95–98, 101–104, 106, 107, 109, 113, 121, 125, 127, 130, 135, 137, 139–146, 150, 153–157, 159–161, 163–168, 171–175, 177, 178, 180, 182, 183, 185–187, 189–195, 197–207
China and Globalization Forum, 206, 208
China Association for International Exchanges (CEAIE), The, 70
China-CELAC, 90
China Center for International Economic Exchanges (CCIEE), The, 71

China Compulsory Certification (CCC), 38
China International Import Expo (CIIE), The, 203
China Miracle, 4
China-Pakistan Digital Corridor, 7
China-Pakistan Economic Corridor (CPEC), 4–8, 198–200
China-Pakistan Economic Corridor, The, 4, 6, 8, 198
China Petrochemical Corporation (Sinopec), The, 103
China Road and Bridge Corporation (CRBC), The, 12
Chinese Civilization, The, 77
Chinese Cultural Center, The, 31, 32
Chinese Culture Translation and Studies Support Network (CCTSS), The, 34
Chinese People's Institute of Foreign Affairs, xv
CHIPS, 86
CNOOC, 182
Cobro Digital (CoDi), 67
Columbia, 36
Colombo, 9, 31–34
Colombo Lotus Tower, 33
Communist Party, The, 5
Community of Latin American and Caribbean States (CELAC), The, 70
Comprehensive Strategic Association, The, 66
Confucius Institute, The, 34, 69, 143, 154
Congo Basin, The, 110, 111
Consulate General of Switzerland, The, 19
Cooperation in Technical and Vocational Education and Training (TVET), 7
COP15, 81, 102
COREPER, 93
Covid-19 pandemic, 22, 34, 71, 86, 140, 141, 143, 149, 171, 172, 198, 203, 207
CPTPP, 204
Croatia, 11–18
Czech Republic, The, 108

D
Dalian, 16
Decarbonization, 95–97
Mazarredo, Rafael Dezcalla de, 41
Deng, Xiaoping, 5, 32, 89
Denmark, 101, 116, 119, 177, 185
DEPA, 204
Department of Foreign Affairs and Trade (DFAT), The, 98

Index 217

Derwin, Ann, 130
Devundara, 30
Diamond Era, 11
Direct Air Capture (DAC), 104
Djibouti, 194, 195
DNA, 27
DOK-ING, 12, 13
Duke Kunshan University, xv

E

Eastern Europe Cooperation, 11
Edrisi, 29
Egypt, 28, 207
El País, 41
Emperor Xiaowu, 29
Equinor energy company, The, 59
Eritrea, 180
Ethiopia, 41, 123, 193–196
EU Emissions Trading System (EU ETS), The, 102
EU Member States, The, 50, 85, 90
EUR, 14, 46
Eurasian Northern Corridor, The, 166
Europe, vi, viii, 11, 12, 14, 15, 32, 39, 43, 46, 49, 73, 77, 86, 95, 106, 116–119, 146, 149, 165–168, 173, 174, 179, 180, 187
European Bank for Reconstruction and Development (EBRD), The, 166
European Economic Area (EEA), 102, 108
European Economic Area (EEA), The, 102, 108
European Geothermal Energy Council (EGEC), The, 106
European Great Wall, 11
European Union (EU), 11–18, 24, 25, 37, 39, 43–50, 81, 83, 86–93, 102, 108, 116, 117, 121, 129, 138, 151, 173, 174, 206
EV, 33

F

FAO, 90
Fa Xian, 28
Federal Institute of Technology in Lausanne (EPFL), The, 22
Federal Republic of Germany, The, 41
Finland, 39, 79–82, 101, 116, 118–121, 177, 179–182
Fletcher, Graham, 98
Fordham, 36

Foreign Direct Investment (FDI), 14, 21, 32, 46, 47, 66, 76, 154, 173, 194
Foreign Service, The, 41, 147, 189
Forum for China-Africa Cooperation (FOCAC), 90, 142, 193
Forum for Cooperation between China and Portuguese Speaking countries (Macau Forum), The, 142
Four Modernizations, 6
14th Five-Year Plan, The, 88
France, 9, 21, 38, 108, 113, 120
Free Trade Agreement of the Asia-Pacific (FTAAP), The, 153
Free Trade Agreement, The, 21, 25, 108, 153
FSC, 110

G

4G, 76
5G, 76
G20, 70, 84, 150, 190
G-20 Summit, The, 31
G7, 48, 190
Gabon, 109–113
Galle, 30
Galvão, Marcos, 138, 189–192
GATT, 84
GDP, 8, 33, 67, 68, 72, 79, 102, 111, 120, 150
Generation Equality Forum (GEF), The, 125
Geneva, 24, 78, 113, 129, 169
Germany, 21, 120, 172, 173
Global Civilization Initiative (GCI), 4
Global Development Initiative (GDI), 4, 8, 89, 91, 152
Global Geothermal Alliance (GGA), The, 106
Global Geothermal Development Plan (GGDP), The, 106
Global Security Initiative (GSI), 4, 89, 91
Global South, 172
Global Strategic Cooperation Partnership (GSCP), 139, 140, 143, 146
Global Trade, 149, 164, 171, 203
Global Young Leader Dialogue (GYLD), xvi
Godawaya, 30
Google, 167
Government Pension Fund Global, The, 57, 184
Greater Bay Area (GBA), The, 155

Great Nabatean kingdom of Petra, The, 77
Great Rejuvenation of the Chinese Nation, 5
Greece, 28
GRÓ Geothermal Training Programme (GRO GTP), The, 103, 106
Guangzhou, 7, 19, 20, 203
Guangzhou Institute of Software Application Technology (GZIS), The, 7
Gustava, Maria, 147

H
Hainan, 16
Halliday, Fred, 136
Hambanthota Port, 35
Hambantota Harbour, 33
Han Dynasty, 27
Hangzhou, 13, 16
Haque, Moin Ul, 9, 197–201
Harbin, 16
Harvard, 36
Harvard Kennedy School, xv
Hebei, 16, 103
Henan, 16, 29, 32, 104
Hong Kong, 15, 20, 50, 73
Hoogmartens, Jan, 93
Huanglong, 16
Huawei, 167
Huazhong University of Science and Technology (HUST), The, 22
Hu, Jintao, 5, 89
Hungary, 78, 108, 168

I
IACA, 78
IAEA, 78
Ibsen, Thórir, 108
ICAO, 90
Iceland, 101–108, 177, 186, 187
Iceland Renewable Energy Cluster and the Geothermal Research Cluster (GEORG), The, 106
ILO, xv
Independence Day, 139
India, 28, 50, 95, 108, 150, 191
Infobip, 13
International Cooperation Office, The, 22
International Data Corporation (IDC), 67
International Monetary Fund (IMF), 84, 88, 151

International Renewable Energy Agency (IRENA), The, 103, 106
International Security Assistance Force (ISAF), The, 120
Internet of Things (IoT), 69, 91
IOM, xv
Iraq, 63, 120, 179
Ireland, 123–130
Irish Defence Forces, The, 127
Islamic Republic of Pakistan, The, 9
IT, 5, 7, 38, 144, 171
Italy, 21, 108, 121
ITU, 90

J
Japan, 50, 63, 87, 93, 138, 172, 190
Jethavanaramaya, 28
Jiang, Zemin, 5, 89
Jiuzhaigou, 16

K
Kabul, 128, 199
Kandy, 34, 35
Karandamudra Sutra, 28
Khmer, 28
King Abdullah II Ibn Al Hussein, 77
King Mahanama, 29
King Parakramabahu VI, 29
Kohona, Palitha, 36
Končar Mjerni transformatori d.d. (KMT), 13
Korčula, 12, 17
Korean War, The, 31
Krka, 16
Kublai Khan, 29

L
Lancang River, The, 156
Laos, 155, 156
Liaoning, 16, 103
Li, Yan, xi
Libreville, 110–112
Libya and Kosovo (KFOR), 120
Li, Keqiang, 11, 12
Lingguang Temple, 31, 35
Lithuania, 48, 87, 119
Liu, Hong, xi
LLB, 36
Lope Park, The, 110
LTTE, 32

Index 219

M
Macao, 15
Madrid, 130
Mali, 116
Manilla Galeon, 72
Mao, Zedong, 5
Maritime Silk Road, The, 27, 32
Massaha Ancestral Forest, The, 110
Maurer, Ueli, 20
Mekong-Lancang Cooperation (MLC), The, 156
Mekong River, 156
Mexico, 65–73, 125, 126, 128
Mexico-China High-Level Business Group (GANE), The, 69
MFA, 138
Micro, Small and Medium-sized Enterprises (MSMEs), 67
Middle East, 63, 77, 82, 146
Middle Kingdom, The, 30
Miguel Hidalgo Order, The, 73
Mihelin, Dario, 18
Mikkola, Leena-Kaisa, 82, 180
MINUSMA, 116
Mobility, 37, 38, 173, 207
Modrić, Luka, 16
Monash University, 147
Mongolia, 18, 25, 63, 108, 121, 166
Mozambique, 139–147
Mrvica, Maksim, 16
Multilateral Development Banks (MDBs), 107
Munich SecurityMunich Security Conference Young Leader, xvi
Myanmar, 156

N
Nanjing, 29
Nansha Seaside Park, The, 13
National Action Plan (NAP), 102, 125
National Administration of Press and Publication of China, The, 34
National Autonomous University of Mexico (UNAM), 66, 69
National University of Science and Technology (NUST), The, 7
NATO, 13, 39, 63, 108, 115–121, 187
Ndong Ella, Baudelaire, 113
Neutral Nations Supervisory Commission (NNSC), The, 116
Nevera, 13
New International Land-Sea Trade Corridor (NILSTC), The, 155

New York, 9, 25, 32, 36, 113, 125, 159, 185
New York University, xvi
NGOs, 107
Ningbo, 16
Niushou Mountain, 29
Non-governmental organization of the Economic and Social Council (ECOSOC), 209
Non-Proliferation Treaty for nuclear weapons (NPT), The, 119
Nordic Defence Cooperation (NORDEFCO), 115, 120
Nordic Development Fund (NDF), The, 106
Norges Bank Investment Management (NBIM), 57, 58
Norinco International, 12
North Africa, 63
Norway, 55–57, 59–63, 101, 102, 116, 119, 177, 182–184
Norwegian Gender Equality Act, The, 61
Norwegian School of Economics (NHH), The, 63
Norwegian State Educational Loan Fund, The, 61

O
Obrador, López, 73
Observatory of Economic Complexity (OEC), The, 66
Oceania, 18, 121, 147
Ogooué–Ivindo, 110
Old North American Free Trade Act (NAFTA), The, 67
One China Policy, The, 31
One-China principle, The, 65
ONUC, 116
Operation Unified Protector (OUP), 120
Organization for Security and Co-operation in Europe (OSCE), The, 78, 116, 117, 129
Organization of Economic and Cooperation Development (OECD), The, 13, 58, 66, 85, 108, 205
Osijek, 14, 16
Oslo, 63

P
Pacific Alliance (PA), The, 70, 204
Paris, 9, 102, 110, 116
Paris Agreement, The, 49, 102, 109, 110, 112, 113, 206
Pearl River, The, 13, 19

Pelješac Bridge, The, 12
People's Democratic Republic of Algeria, The, 161
People's Republic of China (PRC), 5, 19, 20, 24, 25, 40, 41, 65, 73, 82, 113, 138, 147, 154, 158, 161, 169, 203
Perovskite, 22
Persia, 28
Plitvice Lakes, 16
Ploče, 14
Política Exterior, 41
Poland, 25, 166, 171–175
Polo, Marco, 12, 17, 29
Polonnaruwa, 33
Post-Pandemic Times, vi
Post World War II era, The, 56, 59
Pretoria, 78
Private Seán Rooney, 127
Prostoria, 13
Provisions for an Unreliable Entity List, 87
Ptolemy, Claudius, 28
Public-Private Partnerships (PPP), 144
Pula, 14
Purchasing Power Parity (PPP), 72

Q
Qingdao, 16, 34, 103
Qing Dynasty, The, 19
Qinghai, 16, 156
QR, 67
Queen's University, 130

R
R&D, 6, 13, 68, 69, 106
Rabehi, Hassane, 161
Reform and Opening Up, 5, 48
Ren, Yueyuan, xi
Republic of Finland, The, 82
Republic of Gabon, The, 110, 113
Rijeka, 14, 16
Rimac Automobili, 13
Rimac, Mate, 13
Robinson, Mary, 124, 130
Rome, 28, 116
Rubber-Rice Agreement, 31
Rules on Counteracting Unjustified Extra-Territorial Application of Foreign Legislation, 87
Russia, 24, 38, 39, 44–46, 116–120, 150, 166, 175, 187, 191, 199
Russian Federation, The, 38

S
Sångeland, Helena, 121, 178
Sacred Tooth Relic, The, 29, 31, 35
Sahel Region, The, 111
São Paulo, 191
SAR, 73
Science and Technology (S&T), 6, 7, 19, 22, 68, 72, 102, 134, 154
Science and Technology Subcommittee of the Permanent Committee, The, 69
Scientific Outlook on Development, 5
Seade, Jesús, vii, 73
Second World War, The, 83
Security Council, 17, 24, 39, 70, 117, 123–130, 142, 160
Senj, 12, 16
Seventh China and Globalization Forum, vi
Shanghai, 13, 14, 16, 20, 21, 171, 194, 203
Shanghai Cooperation Organization (SCO), The, 166
Shanxi, 28, 103, 105
Shaolin Temple, 29, 32
Shared Community of Mankind, 5
Sharif, Shehbaz, 8, 198
Shi Yongxin, 29
Šibenik, 14
Sichuan, 16
Sigiriya, 28, 35
Silk Road, The, 4, 28, 77, 154
Singapore, 147
Sinhala, 28, 29, 34, 35
Sinopharm, 34, 71
Sinovac, 71
Sisak, 14
Slavonski Brod, 14
Slovakia, 78, 108
SMEs, 67, 68
South Asia, 4, 32, 33, 167
South China Sea, The, 45, 87
Southern Gas Corridor, The, 168
Sovereign Wealth Fund, 57, 58, 184
Soviet Union, The, 39, 118, 181
Spain, 37, 38, 41, 50, 108, 119, 130
Special Administrative Measures for Access of Foreign Investments, 37
Special Economic Zone, 6, 32, 198, 199
Special Technology Zones Authority (STZA), The, 7
Split, 14, 16
Sri Lanka, 27–36
Sri Pada Mountain, 28
Srisamoot, Arthayudh, 158
Statement of Intent, 116

Ston, 11
Strategic Innovation Dialogue, 20
Sukhothai Era, The, 154
Sumatra, 28
Sustainable Developmental Goals (SDGs), 4, 71, 76, 129, 202
Sweden, 39, 101, 115–121, 173, 177–180
Sweden's University, 121
Swiss Federal Council, The, 19
Switzerland, 19–25
Syria, 63, 180

T
Taipei, 63, 87
Taiwan, 15, 87
Taliban, 128, 129
TANAP, 168
Tang, Beijie, xi
TAP, 168
Taprobane, 28
TBEA (Shenyang) Transformer Group Co., Ltd., 13
Tesla, 33
THAAD, 87
Thailand, 108, 147, 149–158, 204
Thoughts on Governance, 5
Tiānxià, 4
Timor Leste, 147
Tokyo, 78, 93
Trans-Caspian International Transport Route (Middle Corridor or TITR), The, 165
2022 Asia-Pacific Economic Cooperation (APEC), 95
2022 Global Innovation Index, The, 68
20th Congress of the Communist Party of China, The, 113
29th APEC Economic Leaders' Meeting (AELM), The, 151
Two-step Dispute Settlement Body, 84

U
Ukraine, 14, 17, 24, 38, 39, 44–46, 80, 88, 116, 118, 119, 123, 166, 171, 174, 175, 180, 187, 200, 202
UNESCO, 8, 9, 35, 108, 110
UNIDO, 78, 90
UNIFIL, 127
United Kingdom (UK), 36, 38, 108, 120
United Nations' 2030 Agenda, The, 21, 152, 157
United Nations Charter, The, 159

United Nations General Assembly, The, 39
United Nation (UN), 4, 17, 24, 25, 32, 36, 38, 39, 44, 45, 65, 70, 71, 81, 86, 90, 109, 113, 116–119, 123–129, 142, 158–160, 169, 174, 200, 202, 206
United States, The, 21, 33, 38, 66, 67, 83, 85–92, 95, 116, 119, 120, 150, 152, 158, 172, 199, 200
Universal Declaration of Human Rights, The, 39
Universidad Veracruzana, The, 69
University of Barcelona, 63
University of Chicago, The, 158
University of Colombo, The, 34
University of Helsinki, The, 82
University of Manchester, xv
University of Nantes, 113
University of Western Ontario, xv
University of Zagreb, The, 16, 18
UNOV, 78
UNPROFOR, 116
UN University Geothermal Programme (UNU GTP), The, 103
Upulwan Shrine, 30
Uruguay Round, The, 80
US, 91
US–Mexico–Canada Agreement (USMCA), 67, 73
USA, 18, 73
US Inflation Reduction Act (IRA),The, 86
Usnisa Palace, 29
USSR, 89, 90
Utah Valley University, 36

V
Value-Added Tax (VAT), 57
Vancouver, 9
VDO screens, 153
Venetian Republic, 12
Vocational and Professional Education and Training (VPET), 23
Vukovar, 14, 16

W
Wang, Yi, 125
Washington, D.C, 18, 41, 98
Washington Quarterly, The, 41
Wassenaar Agreement, The, 86
Western Hemisphere, The, 72
White Horse Temple, The, 30, 32
White, Lee, 112

Women, Peace and Security (WPS)
    Agenda, The, 123, 125
World Bank's Energy Sector Management
    Assistance Program (ESMAP), The,
    106
World Bank, The, 79, 88, 106, 191
World Economic Forum, the, 23
World Geothermal Congress (WGC), The,
    107
World Health Organization, The, 70
World Trade Organization (WTO), 38, 46,
    49, 80, 84, 86, 88, 92, 138, 151, 203,
    205
World Trade Organization (WTO), The, 38,
    49, 80, 84, 88, 92, 138, 203, 205
World War II, 38, 39, 44, 56, 59, 79
WPS-Humanitarian Action (WPS-HA),
    The, 125

X
XCMG, 13
Xi, Jinping, 4, 5, 20, 31, 32, 77, 95, 141,
    153, 157, 164, 165, 172

Y
Yale, 36
Yangtze River Delta (YRD), The, 155
Yapauwa, 29
Yarmouk University, 78
Year of Culture and Tourism of Spain in
    China, 37
Yuan Dynasty, 154

Z
Zadar, 14, 16
Zajączkowski, Wojciech, 175
Zeynalli, Akram, 169
Zhang, Yingying, xi
Zheng, He, 30
Zhongguancun, 7
Zhongguancun Belt and Road Industrial
    Promotion Association (ZBRA),
    The, 7
Zhou, Enlai, 5, 31
Zurich Stock Exchange, The, 21